Microprocessor
Sourcebook
for Engineers

Microprocessor Sourcebook for Engineers

George Loveday

CEng, MIERE
Senior Lecturer/Bromley College of Technology

Pitman, London

John Wiley & Sons, Inc., New York, Toronto

PITMAN PUBLISHING LIMITED
128 Long Acre, London WC2E 9AN

A Longman Group Company

© G. C. Loveday 1986

First published 1986

Available in the Western Hemisphere from
John Wiley & Sons, Inc.
605 Third Avenue, New York, NY 10158

ISBN 0 273 02154 0 (Pitman)
ISBN 0 470 20341 2 (Wiley)

Contents

Preface

This book, arranged as a series of interrelated topics in A to Z order, is intended to be used as a basic reference manual for anyone wishing to understand the complexities of microprocessors and microprocessor-based systems. My aim has been to put in the sort of information, in as concise a form as possible, that is required particularly by personnel and students working in the service and test areas of the microelectronic and allied industries. More advanced data—what might be called "state of the art" material—has been deliberately left out. Thus the central core of the book is the section giving operating details on the industry-standard 8-bit processors. For students, whether technician or undergraduate, the book can variously provide easily-accessible learning material and a ready reference with design and project work.

G. L. 1986

Absolute Address

An address that is permanently assigned to a particular storage location. This assigning will be done at the design stage of the machine. Also called specific address, machine address, actual address, and real address.

Another way of looking at this is to say that an absolute address is a pattern of bits on the address bus (in machine code) that identifies, without any further modification, a unique storage Location.

● ADDRESS ● ADDRESS DECODING ● MEMORY MAP

Absolute Addressing Mode

An addressing mode where the op-code is followed by a 2-byte address (for 8-bit micros); in other words, the operand of the instruction will be an absolute address.

Example

STX $31AØ   Store content of X reg. at address $31AØ

This mode of addressing is usually called **direct** or **extended** in most processors. An exception is the 6502 which does have an *absolute addressing mode*. Note that with this processor the second byte of the operand in machine code provides the most significant half of the address. In the example given above, using the 6502, the instruction would read:

STX $31AØ   (Machine code = 8E   AØ31)

In machine code, the low byte of the address is specified first.

● ADDRESSING MODE ● MICROPROCESSOR [6502]

Access Time

The word "access" is used as a verb in microelectronics to describe the operation of obtaining data from any memory location, either RAM or ROM, or from a peripheral; a typical statement is

"The data at memory address XXXX was accessed"

The *access time* refers to the speed with which the content of any location within a memory can be made available. It is the time interval between the instant that an address is sent to the memory and the instant that the data stored at that memory address is presented at the output.

Random access, where any location in the store can be reached in the same time as any other, is the fastest method. Both RAM and ROM chips are random access devices. Backing stores, such as magnetic disk, drum and tape, use accessing methods which are cyclic (disk, drum) or serial (tape). The access time, then, varies for different store locations, and an average time for access is then quoted; this would be the time for one half revolution in a cyclic system

Access times for semiconductor i.c. memory chips are typically:

NMOS ROM   450 nsec
NMOS static RAM   300 nsec
CMOS static RAM   200 nsec

● MACHINE CYCLE ● MEMORIES

Accumulator

There will be at least one, but usually two or more accumulators within a microprocessor unit. An *accumulator*, often referred to as simply a **register**, acts as a temporary storage location inside the processor and is very important for arithmetic, logic and data manipulation operations. The accumulator will hold the result of arithmetic and logic operations carried out by the ALU.

Example

ADD A $1ØØØ   Add the content of address $1ØØØ to Accumulator A

The result of the addition will then be held in accumulator A.

The movement of data within a microcomputer system to or from memory locations and the microprocessor will probably use an accumulator.

1

Example

LDA $3200   Load Accumulator from memory location $3200

or

STA $0F20   Store content of Acc at address $0F20

Apart from these examples, other instructions that will operate on the accumulator include:

INCREMENT   DECREMENT   AND   OR   EXCLUSIVE-OR
TRANSFER (between accumulators)   ROTATE   SHIFT
COMPLEMENT

● MICROPROCESSOR   ● REGISTER

ACIA

Abbreviation for ● Asynchronous Communications Interface Adaptor.

Active State

This refers to the logic level or a logic change of state (called *transition*) on an input pin to a microprocessor or other microelectronic chip, which activates, or triggers on, a required function.

There are four possible conditions:

ACTIVE LOW   A logic Ø state initiates action. This is usually indicated by a bar over the function, i.e. $\overline{\text{RESET}}$.

ACTIVE HIGH   A logic 1 state initiates action.

ACTIVE TRANSITION   Low to High: the positive-going edge triggers the required function.

ACTIVE TRANSITION High to Low: the negative-going edge triggers the required function.

● ENABLE   ● INTERRUPT

Adder

A microprocessor has to have circuits to perform the arithmetic operations of addition, subtraction, multiplication and division. An adder, a circuit that adds digital signals, is therefore an essential part of the ALU (*fig. A1*).

In computing, the basic arithmetic operation is addition, since subtraction can be performed by taking the twos-complement of the number to be subtracted and then adding it to the other number. Similarly, multiplication and division are carried out by shifting and adding.

The *half-adder* is the basic circuit. It adds two bits together and produces a sum and carry. A *full adder* is an extension of this circuit so that a carry bit from a previous addition can also be considered.

For an adder, the inputs are

Addend   An
Augend   Bn
Carry   Cn-1   (from next lower bit)

and the outputs are

Sum   Sn
Output carry   Cn

Full adders are linked together as shown to make a parallel adder (4 bits in diagram). Note that addition can be carried out serially but this is obviously a much slower process.

● ARITHMETIC AND LOGIC UNIT (ALU)

Fig. A1 Adders

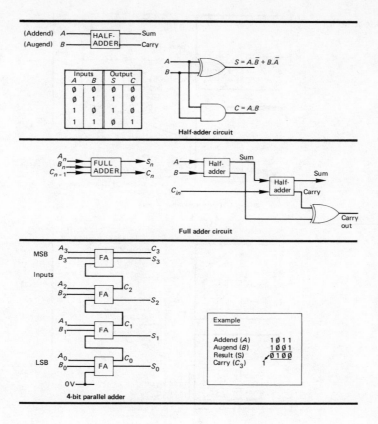

Half-adder circuit

Full adder circuit

4-bit parallel adder

Example

Addend (A)	1 0 1 1
Augend (B)	1 0 0 1
Result (S)	0 1 0 0
Carry (C_3)	1

ADD Instruction

These form part of the arithmetic instruction set for a microprocessor. They are

ADD	Add without carry (memory to accumulator)
ADC	Add with carry (memory to accumulator)
ABA	Add accumulators.

The carry bit will be a flag within the status (condition code) register. The C flag will normally be set if there is a carry from the most significant bit of the result; it will be cleared otherwise. (See *fig. A2*.)

For most arithmetic operations, ADD WITH CARRY is the instruction that should be used.

Typical add instructions for some microprocessors are:

| OPERATION | SYMBOLIC NOTATION | MNEMONIC | | |
		6800	6502	Z80
ADD	$A + M \rightarrow A,C$	ADD A		ADD (A)
		ADD B		ADD (HL)
ADD WITH CARRY	$A + M + C \rightarrow A,C$	ADC A	ADC	ADC (A)
		ADC B		ADC (HL)
ADD ACCUMULATORS	$A + B \rightarrow A$	ABA		

The full range of addressing modes can usually be used with these instructions.
● CARRY AND CARRY BIT ● INSTRUCTION

Fig. A2 ADD instructions

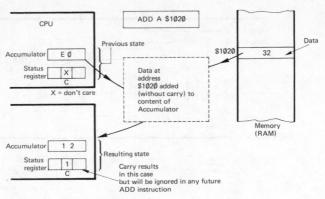

(a) ADD without carry from previous result

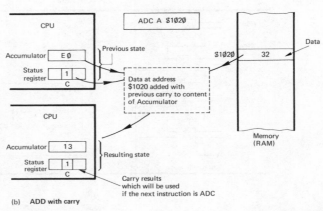

(b) ADD with carry

Address

A binary coded number or word that is used to specify a location within memory or input/output ports.

A unique location has to be provided for all the data and each of the instructions used in a program. These memory locations, which are in ROM, RAM and I/O, are each identified by an *address* which is simply the pattern of binary bits sent out by the microprocessor over the address bus. An 8-bit microprocessor will have 16 address lines (A_0 to A_{15}) so that it can address 2^{16} possible locations, with each location containing one byte of information.

$2^{16} = 65\,536$, which is normally referred to as 64 K.

As an example, consider the simple arrangement of a 256×4-bit semiconductor RAM chip. The 256 store has 16×16 locations arranged as 16 rows and 16 columns; this is shown in block form in *fig. A3*. To access any location within this RAM chip, an 8-bit binary coded address can be used, 4 lines for X and 4 for Y. For example if the address is

$$X = 0110 \quad (= 6_{10})$$

$$Y = 1010 \quad (= 10_{10})$$

then only the memory location (holding 4 bits of data in this case) at X_5 and Y_9 will be addressed. Note that $X = 0000$ and $Y = 0000$ is the first location at row zero and column zero.

In a practical system, the memory i.c.s have chip select or chip enable signals which are decoded from the upper address line signals. In this way, memory i.c.s can be allocated certain memory areas without overwrite.

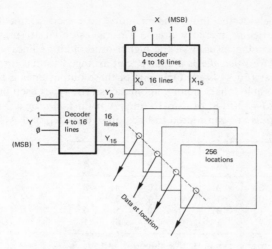

Fig. A3 Principle of addressing

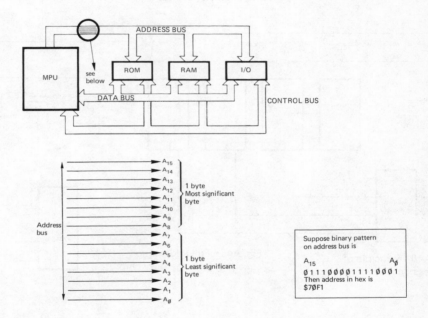

Fig. A4a Address bus

Suppose binary pattern on address bus is

A_{15} A_{0}
0 1 1 1 0 0 0 0 1 1 1 1 0 0 0 1
Then address in hex is
$70F1

As stated, an address is a binary number and this is what is required by the machine. In machine code and mnemonic (assembly) language, addresses will be specified in hex. For a 16-bit address the range in hex. is from $0000 up to $FFFF.

● ABSOLUTE ADDRESS   ● ADDRESS DECODING   ● MEMORY MAP

Address Bus

A bus is a major set of parallel conductors used within a microelectronic system to minimise the amount of interconnecting. The address bus in a microcomputer is unidirectional and typically 16 or more bits wide. It conveys address information from the microprocessor unit to memory as a binary pattern. (*Fig. A4a.*)

● ADDRESS   ● ADDRESS DECODING   ● BUS SYSTEMS

Address Decoding

Each of the individual memory i.c.s used within a system must be allocated particular memory areas. This is essential to prevent any overlap. Address decoding, usually of the higher-order address lines, is used for this purpose. An *address decoder* is a logic circuit arranged so that for n inputs there are 2^n output lines (*fig. A4b,c*). Only one of these output lines is high (or low) for each of the possible binary input combinations. The types used in microprocessor systems are 2-to-4, 3-to-8, or 4-to-16 line. A truth table for a 2-to-4 line decoder where the inputs are considered to be address lines A_{14} and A_{15} illustrates the principle:

INPUTS		OUTPUTS			
A_{15}	A_{14}	1	2	3	4
Ø	Ø	1	Ø	Ø	Ø
Ø	1	Ø	1	Ø	Ø
1	Ø	Ø	Ø	1	Ø
1	1	Ø	Ø	Ø	1

In many systems the decoder output is the complement of this table.

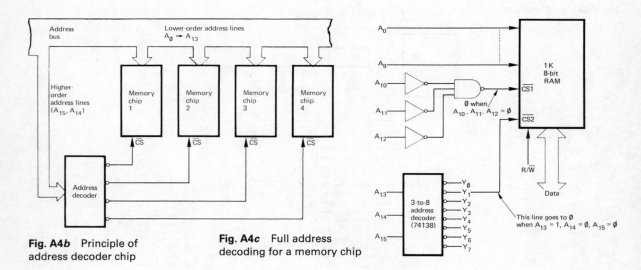

Fig. A4b Principle of address decoder chip

Fig. A4c Full address decoding for a memory chip

The memory i.c.s used within the system are provided with one or more chip select or chip enable lines (CS, CE) and the outputs of the address decoder are connected to these enable pins on the various i.c.s as shown.

In some systems where the memory required is small, for example a dedicated controller, not all the address lines need be decoded, but this will result in overwrite (one memory i.c. occupying a larger area of memory than it actually requires). In other cases, all address lines must be fully decoded. Take the example of a $1\,K \times 8$-bit RAM i.c. with two chip select lines. The lower-order address lines $A_{\emptyset}$ to A_9 ($2^{10} = 1024$) are used to select a particular location within the RAM. The binary pattern on these lines is decoded by circuits inside the chip. The higher-order address lines are decoded fully using a logic circuit for A_{10}, A_{11} and A_{12}, while A_{13}, A_{14} and A_{15} give a signal to $\overline{CS2}$ via the address decoder. The address is then from $\$2\emptyset\emptyset\emptyset$ to $\$23FF$, and there will be no overwrite.

● ADDRESS ● MEMORY MAP ● PAGE

6

Addressing Mode

Consider the process of loading a register within a microprocessor with data from a memory location. There are several ways of specifying the location of this data: it could be at an absolute address, or held in the memory location immediately following the load instruction, or within an area of memory pointed to by an index register. The method of specifying the exact location is termed the *addressing mode*. In the above example we have, in order: Absolute (or Extended), Immediate, and Indexed addressing (*fig. A5*).

The variety or richness of the addressing modes employed by a microprocessor enhances its processing capability. Microprocessors do not all possess identical addressing modes and some manufacturers have different names for a particular mode. The most common are the following:

Addressing modes
Implied (or Inherent)
Immediate
Direct (or Zero Page)
Extended (or Absolute)
Indexed
Relative

Each of these is covered in a separate section and further examples are given under the section on microprocessors.
● ABSOLUTE ADDRESS   ● ABSOLUTE ADDRESSING MODE   ● IMMEDIATE ADDRESSING   ● INDEX REGISTER AND INDEXED ADDRESSING
● MICROPROCESSOR

Fig. A5   Addressing modes

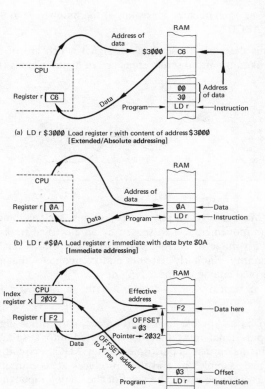

(a) LD r $3000 Load register r with content of address $3000
[Extended/Absolute addressing]

(b) LD r #$0A Load register r immediate with data byte $0A
[Immediate addressing]

(c) LD r 03, X Load register r with contents of address given by Xreg. + offset
[Indexed addressing]

7

Address Register

Sometimes known as Memory Address Register (MAR), this is a register, usually in the central processor, that stores an address.
● ADDRESS

Algorithm

A complex task can usually be divided up into several small, easily followed steps. The set of well-defined steps or processes for the solution of the task is called an *algorithm*. In other words, an algorithm describes a way in which a rather complicated task can be solved, or demonstrates that it cannot be solved.

Take the example of clearing a block of memory that consists of *n* addresses. The algorithm for this could be:

1) Load a counter with a number equal to *n*.
2) Set the index register to point to the first address of the block of memory to be cleared.
3) Clear the address pointed to by the index register.
4) Increment (add 1) to the index register.
5) Decrement (subtract 1) from the counter.
6) Check to see if the counter has reached zero. If it has not, then return to repeat 3); otherwise end.

The structure of the program is now defined, which should make the writing of the program easier.

The word "algorithm" or "algorism" is derived from the surname of the Arab mathematician 'Abu Ja'far Muhammed ibn Musa al-Kuwarizmi (the man of Kuwarizm).
● FLOWCHART

Alphanumeric Code

A set of characters consisting of the numbers 0 to 9 and the letters A to Z.
● ASCII

Analog

This describes those types of signal which are of a continuous nature, and not broken up into discrete steps as are digital signals (*fig. A6*).

Fig. A6 Analog signal

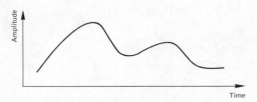

Most changes in physical conditions, such as temperature, light level, pressure, and movement, when sensed by an electrical transducer result in analog signals. The voltage or current varies in a way that is analogous to the change in input quantity. Similarly, circuits and components that process these signals are also termed analog or linear type devices.
● ANALOG-TO-DIGITAL CONVERTOR   ● DIGITAL-TO-ANALOG CONVERTOR
● SENSOR

Analog-to-Digital Convertor (ADC)

To be acceptable to a microprocessor or other digital logic system, any varying input signal must first be converted into a suitably coded digital word. This conversion task is performed by an ADC: a circuit which accepts an analog input signal, samples it, and then produces at its output a digital word with a weight that corresponds to the level of the analog input (*fig. A7*).

Take the example of a 3-bit ADC where the digital output can have a coded value from ∅∅∅ up to 111. This means that the analog input is split up or

8

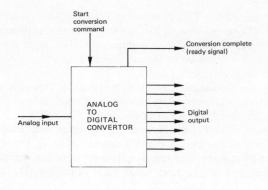

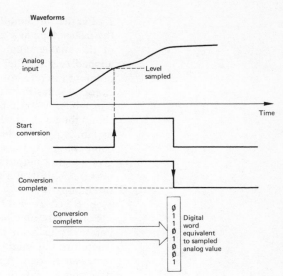

Fig. A7 Principle of analog-to-digital conversion

"*quantised*" into 8 levels. Suppose that each quantum level is 350 mV. A table showing the values of analog input voltage with corresponding digital codes will be:

ANALOG INPUT	DIGITAL CODE
0 V	000
0.35 V	001
0.70 V	010
1.05 V	011
1.4 V	100
1.75 V	101
2.1 V	110
2.45 V	111

Since the analog input is a continuous signal, there will be some uncertainty over the conversion. This uncertainty is called **quantising error** and will be $\pm\frac{1}{2}$ LSB.

The **useful resolution** of an ADC indicates that no missing codes will be present at the digital output. The table above has no missing codes and therefore the 3-bit ADC can be said to have a useful resolution of 3 bits.

Because of the uncertainty in the conversion, some information detail in the analog input signal will always be lost in the conversion process. This loss can be minimised by increasing the number of bits used. For example, with an 8-bit ADC the analog input will be quantised into 256 levels, and a 12-bit ADC will have 4096 levels.

An important parameter of an ADC is the **conversion time**: the time interval between the command being given to start the conversion and the appearance at the output of the complete digital equivalent of the analog input. The speed of conversion varies with the type of ADC and ranges from the relatively slow (milliseconds) and cheap, to the ultra fast (50 nsec) and relatively expensive. In many applications speed may not be the main consideration and an ADC that is relatively slow can be used.

There are many ways of performing analog-to-digital conversions. The commonly used methods in microelectronic systems are:

Parallel or simultaneous conversion (flash convertor)

Single ramp and counter   Tracking convertor   Successive approximation.

9

1 Parallel or Simultaneous ADC This type, often called a *flash convertor*, is the fastest type available. This is because all the bits for the digital representation of the analog input level are determined simultaneously. The analog input is applied to a parallel bank of voltage comparators, each of which responds to a different discrete level of input voltage.

Fig. A8 illustrates the principle for just 3 bits but the available types are usually 6 or 8 bits. A constant current source supplies a chain of resistors R_1 to R_7. These set up the levels at which the seven comparators switch, i.e. 0.5 V, 1 V, 1.5 V, 2 V up to 3.5 V. If the analog input just exceeds 1.5 V, then the outputs of comparators A, B and C will be the logic Ø, while comparators D, E, F and G will give a logic 1 output. The logic gates then convert the outputs of the comparators into the 3-bit digital output, Ø11 in this case. To give Ø11 at the output, the logic has inputs

$$\bar{A} \cdot \bar{B} \cdot \bar{C} \cdot D \cdot E \cdot F \cdot G$$

For *n* bits of binary in the conversion, the method requires $(2^n - 1)$ comparators plus a lot of logic. An 8-bit flash convertor requires 255 comparators. Therefore this method is not cheap, but now that LSI circuits are available it is increasingly used. An example of the type is the 3300 which is a 6-bit CMOS logic flash convertor with a conversion speed of 15 MHz ($V_{DD} = 8$ V).

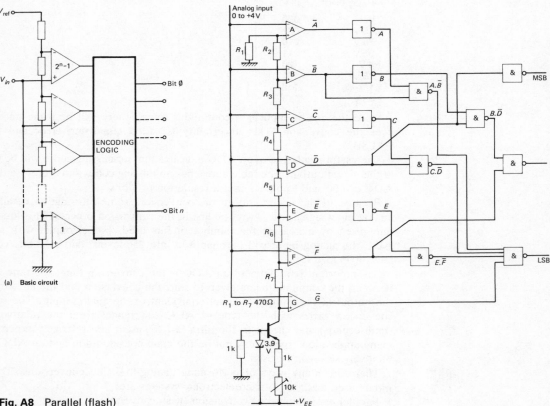

(a) **Basic circuit**

Fig. A8 Parallel (flash) convertor

(b) **Example of 3-bit flash ADC**

10

2. Ramp and Counter ADC (*fig. A9*) The analog input voltage is compared with a linear ramp, this ramp being generated by a DAC circuit. While the input is greater than the ramp from time t_1 the counter accumulates clock pulses; but as soon as the ramp just exceeds the input level at time t_2 the control bistable is reset and the counter is stopped. The content of the counter is a digital word proportional to the analog input.

The method is useful for medium accuracy where speed is not important. The conversion time, which may be several milliseconds, is set by the clock frequency and the comparator's slew rate. When a clock of 10 kHz is used, a full 8-bit conversion takes 25.5 msec.

Accuracy is limited by the linearity of the ramp, i.e. by the linearity of the DAC. The comparator must also have low offset drift.

The ZN425E 8-bit dual mode ADC/DAC i.c. is typical of this type. To use the i.c. as an ADC, an external comparator and one logic i.c. are required (*fig. A10*). The operation is as follows:

A negative pulse is applied to the Convert Command input. While this input is low,

a) The control bistable is set. Gate B output goes high.

b) Status rises high.

c) The internal counter in the ZN425E is reset.

At the end of the convert pulse, clock pulses pass through gate C to the ZN425E. The 8-bit counter accumulates counts and inside the i.c. the state of the counter is converted by an R-2R network [● DAC] into a ramp output (pin 14). The ramp, which can have a maximum of 255 steps and a voltage level of 2.5 V, is then compared with the analog input. When the ramp exceeds this analog input, the

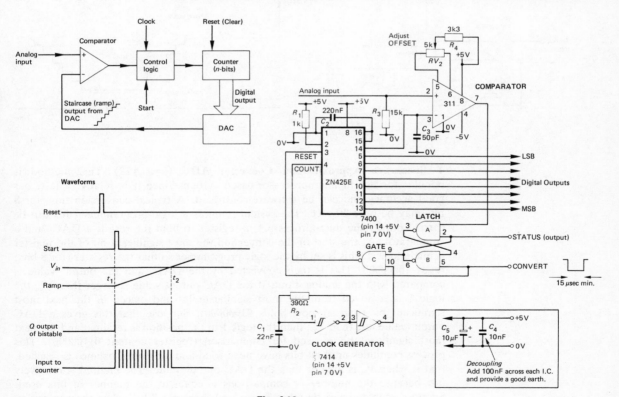

Fig. A10

11

comparator switches low and resets the bistable. No further clock pulses are allowed through to the counter and the state of the counter will be a digital word with a weight proportional to the analog input. The status level goes low to signal that the conversion is complete.

3 Tracking ADC (*fig. A11*) This is a variation of the ramp and counter method that enables changes in the analog input signal to be followed, or tracked, more rapidly. A window comparator is used which give changes of state if the input is outside defined levels. The comparator drives the control of an up/down counter, which is in turn connected to an R-2R network. In this way the digital state of the counter, which is the output word, is continuously converted into analog. When the analog input is above the level from the R-2R ladder, the comparator output forces the counter to count up, thereby causing the DAC output tracking signal to follow the analog. If the digital value is greater than the analog input, the comparator switches in the opposite direction and causes the counter to count down. The counter is stopped when the DAC output is equal to the analog input $\pm\frac{1}{2}$ LSB; the input is then within the "window" of the comparator.

A tracking convertor is thus inherently faster than a simple ramp and counter because, once the first conversion, starting from zero, has been carried out, all further conversions require only that number of clock pulses necessary to track any rise or fall in the analog input.

Fig. A11 Tracking ADC

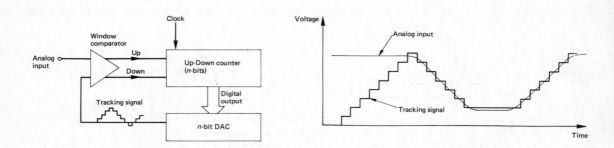

4 Successive Approximation Convertor ADC (*fig. A12*) This method is popular for use in microprocessor-based systems since it is relatively fast, has good accuracy and can be software-controlled. A typical conversion time for 8 bits may be only 20 μsec. The system requires a logic programmer (this can be carried out by the microprocessor); a register to hold the result; a DAC; and a comparator. At the start of the conversion the most significant bit of the register is made logic 1; this is set by the logic programmer so that the register (for 8 bits) reads 1ØØØØØØØ. This is then converted by the DAC, and the output value is compared with the analog input. If the DAC output value is larger than V_{in}, the logic 1 is removed from the most significant bit and placed in the next most significant bit (register now holds Ø1ØØØØØØ). Suppose that this gives a DAC output value less than V_{in}; then the logic 1 in the position is retained and the next most significant bit is used for comparison (register content Ø11ØØØØØ). This process continues until all bits have been tried and a point of balance is reached, that is when V_{in} is greater than the DAC output value. The method is relatively fast because the number of comparisons is equal to the number of bits used. Suppose each comparison takes 5 μsec and there are 8 bits; then the conversion

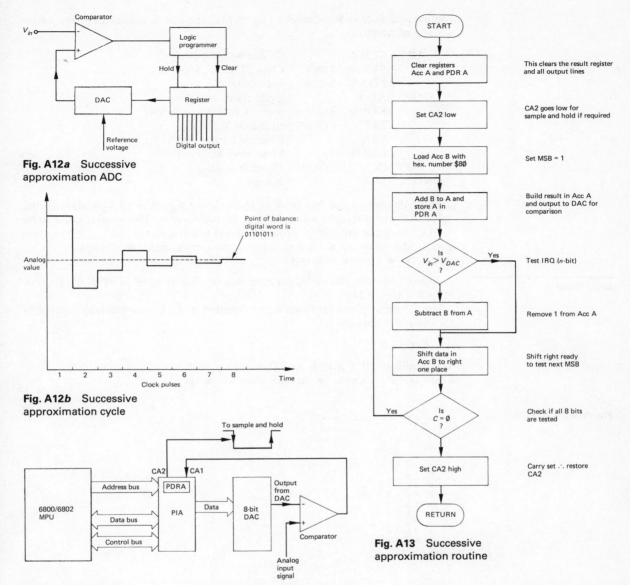

Fig. A12a Successive approximation ADC

Fig. A12b Successive approximation cycle

Fig. A12c Successive approximation using a micro

Fig. A13 Successive approximation routine

Flowchart annotations (Fig. A13):

- Clear registers Acc A and PDR A — This clears the result register and all output lines
- Set CA2 low — CA2 goes low for sample and hold if required
- Load Acc B with hex. number $80 — Set MSB = 1
- Add B to A and store A in PDR A — Build result in Acc A and output to DAC for comparison
- Is $V_{in} > V_{DAC}$? — Test IRQ (n-bit)
- Subtract B from A — Remove 1 from Acc A
- Shift data in Acc B to right one place — Shift right ready to test next MSB
- Is $C = \emptyset$? — Check if all 8 bits are tested
- Set CA2 high — Carry set ∴ restore CA2

Point of balance: digital word is 01101011

time is $5 \times 8 = 40\,\mu$sec. A successive approximation cycle, sometimes called a "put and take", is illustrated in *fig. A12b*.

It will be useful at this stage to look at how a microprocessor system can be connected and programmed to give a successive approximation ADC, taking the M6800 processor with its PIA, the 6821, as an example.

The block diagram *fig. A12c* shows that only a DAC and comparator are required as extras to create the convertor. The 6800 microprocessor carries out the function of the logic programmer under software control and one of the data registers in the PIA is used as the successive approximation register (SAR). The operation will be exactly as described previously, that is the analog input will be compared with the DAC output successively as each bit from the MSB to the LSB is tried and then retained or discarded. Assuming that the PIA is correctly initialised, the assembly language program for the successive approximation

13

routine is as follows (see flowchart *fig. A13*). The PIA is assumed to have a base address of $4000.

```
START   CLR A                Clear result register
        STA A   $4000        Clear PDR A (SAR)
        LDA B   $8000        Set MSB = 1
LOOP1   ABA                  Build result in AccA
        STA A   $4000        Store A in PDR A (SAR)
        TST     LOOP2        Branch if V_IN > V_DAC
        SBA                  Remove 1 from AccA
        LSR B                Make next MSB = 1
        BCC     LOOP1        Check if finished
END     RTS                  Return
```

After this subroutine has been completed, the digital word equivalent to the value of the analog input will be held in Accumulator A. This word could then be used by the main program or stored in RAM until required.

● CONTROL SYSTEM   ● DIGITAL-TO-ANALOG CONVERTOR   ● INTERFACE CIRCUITS   ● SAMPLE AND HOLD

AND Gate

A logic circuit that gives a logic 1 at its output only when all of its inputs are also at logic 1 (*fig. A14*).

For a 3-input AND gate with inputs labelled A, B, C, the Boolean expression for the AND function is

$$F = A \cdot B \cdot C$$

The output is 1 if A AND B AND C are 1.

● BOOLEAN ALGEBRA   ● DIGITAL CIRCUIT   ● GATE

Fig. A14   AND gate

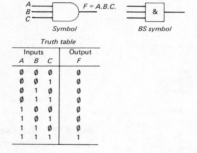

Symbol   BS symbol

Truth table

Inputs			Output
A	B	C	F
0	0	0	0
0	0	1	0
0	1	0	0
0	1	1	0
1	0	0	0
1	0	1	0
1	1	0	0
1	1	1	1

AND Instruction

This instruction carries out the logical AND function between each bit of data word A and the corresponding bits in data word B.

For 2 bits, the AND function is as follows (note that in Boolean Algebra the AND is represented by the symbol ·):

$$0 \cdot 0 = 0$$

$$0 \cdot 1 = 0$$

$$1 \cdot 0 = 0$$

$$1 \cdot 1 = 1$$

Only when both bits of the two words are at logic 1 will the result for that bit position also be 1. For example, consider the binary word 1011 ANDed with the binary word 1000. The result is

```
1011   Word A
1000   Word B
1000   Result
```

The AND instruction can be useful in masking, whenever it is necessary to test the state of one bit in a word or to separate out, say, the lower 4 bits from the upper 4 bits and so on.

Example   *a*) Testing the state of bit 3.

```
Assume the Accumulator holds $39      00111001
  AND (A)   #$08                       00001000
  Result left in Accumulator           00001000
Bit 3 = 1 (in this case)
```

b) Masking upper 4 bits
```
Assume the Accumulator holds $A7      10100111
  AND (A)   #$0F                       00001111
  Result left in Accumulator           00000111
Lower 4 bits only
```

● INSTRUCTION   ● LOGICAL INSTRUCTIONS AND OPERATION   ● MASKING

Architecture

In computing, this term is used to describe the structure and arrangement of the hardware of a system. The word is also used in microelectronics to describe the internal organisation of a microprocessor chip.

● MICROPROCESSOR

Arithmetic and Logic Unit (ALU)

An arrangement of logic circuits within the central processing unit (microprocessor) which is used to perform the arithmetic and logical operations (*fig. A15*). The circuit consists of a group of eight (or sixteen) full adders each with a complementor so that subtraction can also be performed. Operations available on the ALU will include:

ADD   SUBTRACT   AND   OR   EXCLUSIVE-OR

Suppose the instruction SUBA $30F0 is performed [subtract the contents of address $30F0 from the Accumulator and place the result in Accumulator]. The instruction is decoded and the control lines to the ALU are set for subtraction. The content of address $30F0 is applied to the data input of the ALU and then complemented. The ALU then adds this data to the data from the Accumulator and the result is stored back into the Accumulator.

Fig. A15   ALU operation

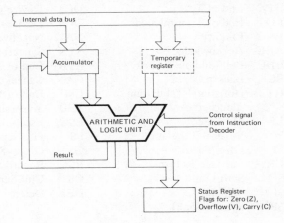

15

An acronym for American Standard Code for Information Interchange, a 7-bit code used extensively for transfer of information between computers and peripheral devices such as typewriters and printers. The full set of ASCII codes is given in *fig. A16*. The table is used as follows:

Character E   Most significant bits = 1ØØ
               Least significant bits = Ø1Ø1
∴   Code for E is 1ØØØ1Ø1 or 45 in hex.

Fig. A16   ASCII character set (7-bit code)

M.S. CHAR / L.S. CHAR	0 000	1 001	2 010	3 011	4 100	5 101	6 110	7 111
0 0000	NUL	DLE	SP	0	@	P		p
1 0001	SOH	DC1	!	1	A	Q	a	q
2 0010	STX	DC2	"	2	B	R	b	r
3 0011	ETX	DC3	#	3	C	S	c	s
4 0100	EOT	DC4	$	4	D	T	d	t
5 0101	ENQ	NAK	%	5	E	U	e	u
6 0110	ACK	SYN	&	6	F	V	f	v
7 0111	BEL	ETB	'	7	G	W	g	w
8 1000	BS	CAN	(	8	H	X	h	x
9 1001	HT	EM	)	9	I	Y	i	y
A 1010	LF	SUB	*	:	J	Z	j	z
B 1011	VT	ESC	+	;	K	[	k	{
C 1100	FF	FS	,	<	L	\	l	:
D 1101	CR	GS	−	=	M	]	m	}
E 1110	SO	RS	°	>	N	↑	n	~
F 1111	SI	VS	/	?	O	↓	o	DEL

The explanation of the special control functions in columns 0, 1, 2 and 7 is:

NUL	Null	DLE	Data Link Escape
SOH	Start of Heading	DC1	Device Control 1
STX	Start of Text	DC2	Device Control 2
ETX	End of Text	DC3	Device Control 3
EOT	End of Transmission	DC4	Device Control 4
ENQ	Enquiry	NAK	Negative Acknowledge
ACK	Acknowledge	SYN	Synchronous Idle
BEL	Bell (audible signal)	ETB	End of Transmission Block
BS	Backspace	CAN	Cancel
HT	Horizontal Tabulation (punched card skip)	EM	End of Medium
		SUB	Substitute
LF	Line Feed	ESC	Escape
VT	Vertical Tabulation	FS	File Separator
FF	Form Feed	GS	Group Separator
CR	Carriage Return	RS	Record Separator
SO	Shift Out	US	Unit Separator
SI	Shift In	DEL	Delete
SP	Space (blank)		

ASCII codes are stored as 8 bits, usually by prefixing a Ø to each code.

Character	7-bit ASCII	8-bit ASCII
Y	1Ø11ØØ1	Ø1Ø11ØØ1

The eighth bit can therefore be used for parity checking to detect errors during transmission.

● SERIAL DATA FORMAT ● SERIAL INTERFACE ADAPTOR

Assembler

This is software designed to convert assembly language statements on a one-to-one basis into machine code.

Assembly language, which uses mnemonic code for instructions, is a means of writing programs for a microprocessor that can be regarded as a half-way step between machine language (binary code) and high-level languages such as Basic, Pascal, and Fortran. Assembly programming with its symbolic code, ST for store, LD for load, EOR for exclusive-OR, and so on, is most useful when the fastest program run-time is necessary, for example when the microprocessor is being used in closed loop control. It does however require a good understanding of the internal architecture of the particular processor, its instruction set, and its addressing modes.

Having written an Assembly Language program, the programmer can then assemble it by looking up the various codes on the processor's instruction code sheet and matching the mnemonic with its hex. equivalent. This basic approach is quite efficient for short programs but becomes time-consuming and error-prone for programs with lengths above 100 lines. The Assembler (software held on disc) automatically carries out the required conversion, producing machine code ready to be directly loaded into the machine. It also calculates offset for destination addresses within the program, allows the user to introduce symbols for operands (for example OUTPUT instead of writing an address in hex.), and provides error checking on the syntax and structure of the mnemonic program.

The program written in assembly language is called a **source program** and, when this has been converted into binary code for the machine, the resulting program is referred to as the **object program**.

In addition to assembly language instructions there are certain pseudo-instructions called **directives** (instructions to the assembler itself) which are used to control the assembly process. Commonly used directives are:

NAM	Name
ORG	Origin
EQU	Equate
END	End
FCB (FB)	Form constant byte
FDB	Form constant double byte
FCC	Form constant character

The use of these is best illustrated by an example (*fig. A17*).

Fig. A17 Typical field format for source statements in an assembler

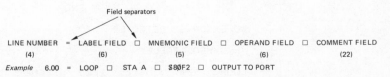

The figures in brackets refer to the usual number of characters allowed per field.

Note that the source program format is arranged so that there are five distinct sections called **fields**. Each of these fields has a specific purpose as will be made clear in the program example (*fig. A18*). This assembly language program using the T.S.C. DISC Editor/Assembler [M6800] performs the task of finding the largest number in a block of 64 numbers. The block is held in memory beginning at address $1050; the result (the largest value) is to be stored at address $3500; and the program origin is at address $2000.

The assembler directives NAM, ORG, and EQU are placed at the beginning of the source program in the mnemonic field. Note that a label must be used with the EQU directive, in this case it has been called RESULT. At Line 13, RESULT has been typed in the operand field as a symbol, and by this the Assembler knows that the largest number in the block is to be placed in address $3500. In the same way, LOOP has been used as a label in line 7 so that, on the conditional branch instruction BNE (in line 12), the symbol LOOP will cause the assembler to calculate the appropriate offset to branch back to line 7. The directive END terminates the source program.

Fig. A18   Source program

```
+++ASN W=1
+++EDIT, MAXNUM
NEW FILE:
    1.00= NAM MAXNUM
    2.00= ORG $2000
    3.00=RESULT EQU $3500
    4.00=START LDAB £$40 BLOCK LENGTH
    5.00= LDX £$1050 SET POINTER
    6.00= LDAA $3F,X LOAD LAST
    7.00=LOOP CMPA $00,X COMPARE
    8.00= BHI NEXT
    9.00= LDAA $00,X RELOAD
   10.00=NEXT INX POINTER +1
   11.00= DECB COUNTER -1
   12.00= BNE LOOP
   13.00= STAA RESULT
   14.00= SWI
   15.00= END
   16.00=£
   15.00= END
£S
+++ASMB MAXNUM

                      NAM      MAXNUM
   2000               ORG      $2000
   3500        RESULT EQU      $3500
   2000 C6 40  START  LDA B    £$40       BLOCK LENGTH
   2002 CE 10 50       LDX     £$1050     SET POINTER
   2005 A6 3F          LDA A   $3F,X      LOAD LAST
   2007 A1 00  LOOP    CMP A   $00,X      COMPARE
   2009 22 02          BHI     NEXT
   200B A6 00          LDA A   $00,X      RELOAD
   200D 08     NEXT    INX                POINTER +1
   200E 5A             DEC B              COUNTER -1
   200F 26 F6          BNE     LOOP
   2011 B7 35 00       STA A   RESULT
   2014 3F             SWI
                       END


NO ERROR(S) DETECTED

    SYMBOL TABLE:

LOOP  2007   NEXT   200D   RESULT 3500   START  2000
```

Having typed in the source program and edited it if necessary (most assemblers are usually provided with a text editor which can be used to delete lines, correct mistakes within a line, and introduce new lines), the source program is saved on the disc and then assembled using the ASMB utility. The machine code is produced on a one-to-one basis for each instruction, the program is checked for errors, and if required a symbol table is produced. The directives FCB, FDB and FCC can be used as follows:

1 FCB (Form Constant Byte) A directive that assigns values (of one byte) which can be used to load blocks of data, written into the program, into memory. The directive can be used with a label.

Example

```
25.00 =  ORG   $4000
26.00 =  FCB   $2F,$00,$FD,$82,$0C
```

After assembly, the memory locations starting at $4000 would be assigned these values:

ADDRESS	CONTENTS (hex.)
$4000	2F
$4001	00
$4002	FD
$4003	82
$4004	0C

2 FDB (Form Constant Double Byte) This directive is similar to FCB. It is used for constants that require two bytes of memory.

3 FCC (Form Constant Character) A directive used for storing ASCII characters (in binary form) in a block of memory.

Example

```
30.00 =  ORG   $2080
31.00 = TABLE   FCC   /WHAT?/
```

The assembler would assign the ASCII codes as follows:

ADDRESS	CONTENTS (hex.)	CHARACTER
2080	57	W
2081	48	H
2082	41	A
2083	54	T
2084	3F	?

Note the use of the delimiter / in this example.

● ASSEMBLY LANGUAGE   ● CROSS-ASSEMBLER   ● HIGH-LEVEL LANGUAGE
● MACHINE CODE   ● MACHINE LANGUAGE

Assembly Language

Assembly language is a way of writing programs for a microcomputer using mnemonics of the instructions. This shorthand way of stating each step is a useful aid for both writing and understanding programs. For example CLR is the Assembly Language statement for clear address, ST is used for store, MOV for move, and so on. Each type of processor has its own Assembly Language but these various codes naturally have many similarities.

The actual instructions for any microprocessor (or computer) must be in binary. This binary code is called **machine language**. Writing programs in machine language is very tiresome, so normally a hexadecimal number is used in place of the binary; this gives what is called **machine code** or **op-code**. An example using the 6800/6802 microprocessor instruction set illustrates the three codes. The program is a time delay routine:

	ASSEMBLY LANGUAGE (Mnemonics)		MACHINE CODE (Op-code in hex.)	MACHINE LANGUAGE (Binary)
	LDX #$3FAØ	LOAD X REG. IMMEDIATE WITH #$3FAØ	CE 3F AØ	11001110 00111111 10100000
LOOP	NOP	NO OPERATION	Ø1	00000001
	DEX	DECREMENT X REG.	Ø9	00001001
	BNE LOOP	BRANCH IF NOT Ø	26 FC	00100110 11111100
	RTS	RETURN FROM SUBROUTINE	39	00111001

● ASSEMBLER ● INSTRUCTION ● MICROPROCESSOR

Asynchronous Communications Interface Adaptor (ACIA)

This type of interface integrated circuit is designed to provide controlled connection between a microprocessor and peripheral devices that receive and transmit data in serial form. The parallel data from the micro is stored in a data register within the ACIA, it is formatted (i.e. provided with start, stop and parity bits), and then outputted one bit at a time at a rate acceptable to the peripheral. Communication is naturally possible the other way, with serial data from the peripheral being accepted and stored by the ACIA and then converted into a parallel byte suitable for the microprocessor. Thus the main uses of an ACIA are in interfacing between a microprocessor and equipment such as teletypes and cassette tape and in transmitting and receiving data over a telephone line or radio link. In the latter case, a modulator/demodulator (modem) is required.

The format used for asynchronous serial data transmission is shown in *fig. A18*. The signal line is normally high, so the beginning of a character is indicated by a start bit going low. The data bits, seven for ASCII characters, are then sent and a parity bit (D7) can be used for error detection. The end of character is indicated by two stop bits, both high states.

The two commonly used ACIA chips are the 6850 and the 6551. Both can be used in 6800 or 6502 based systems. The 6551 has most of the features of the 6850 but includes an on-chip baud rate generator. The operation of the 6850 chip will be described here.

The simplified view of the ACIA in *fig. A19* shows that it contains four main registers:
1) Transmit Data Register TDR (Write only)
2) Status Register SR (Read only)
3) Control Register CR (Write only)
4) Receive Data Register RDR (Read only)

Since a register is either a write only or read only type, the read/write line is used as part of the addressing. The ACIA is memory-mapped using CSØ, CS1, $\overline{CS2}$ and RSØ and it appears as only two addressable memory locations. The register select pin together with R/$\overline{W}$ is used to select each register as shown in the table.

ADDRESS LINE AØ CONNECTED TO RSØ	READ/WRITE R/$\overline{W}$	REGISTER SELECTED IN ACIA
Ø	Ø	CR
Ø	1	SR
1	Ø	TDR
1	1	RDR

Fig. A19 Simplified view of an ACIA

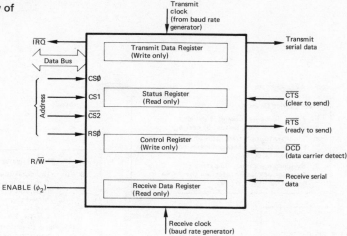

The device requires an external transmit and receive clock circuit but the clock can be divided down by 1, 16 or 64 by setting the first two bits in the control register:

BIT 1	BIT 0	RESULT
0	0	÷1 clock
0	1	÷16 clock
1	0	÷64 clock
1	1	Master reset

For interfacing with modems, three signals are provided, which provide handshake facility:

CLEAR TO SEND $\overline{\text{CTS}}$

DATA CARRIER DETECT $\overline{\text{DCD}}$

REQUEST TO SEND $\overline{\text{RTS}}$

When a modem is not used, $\overline{\text{CTS}}$ and $\overline{\text{DCD}}$ are connected to 0 V and $\overline{\text{RTS}}$ can be left unconnected.

The **initialisation** of the ACIA is shown in flowchart form in *fig. A20*. A typical assembly language initialisation for an ACIA at base address D000 could be

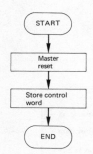

Fig. A20 Initialising an ACIA

```
LDA    #$03  ⎱  Master reset
STA    $D000 ⎰  Clears all ACIA registers

LDA    #$05  ⎱      Control word gives
STA    $D000 ⎰  7 data bits, odd parity, 2 stop bits
                    and a ÷16 clock
```

The formats for the control and status registers are shown in *fig. A21*.

When in use as a receiver, the Receive Data Register fills with data one bit at a time at a rate supplied by the peripheral. When it is full and therefore contains a valid character that can be read by the micro, bit 0 in the status register goes high. An input routine (*fig. A22*) is therefore

```
Loop   LDA    $D000    Load ACIA status
       BIT A  #$01     Check bit 0
       BEQ    LOOP     Bit 0 not set ∴ Loop
       LDA    $D001    Load data
```

An output routine in flowchart form is also given.

● PARITY ● SERIAL INTERFACE ADAPTOR ● UART

21

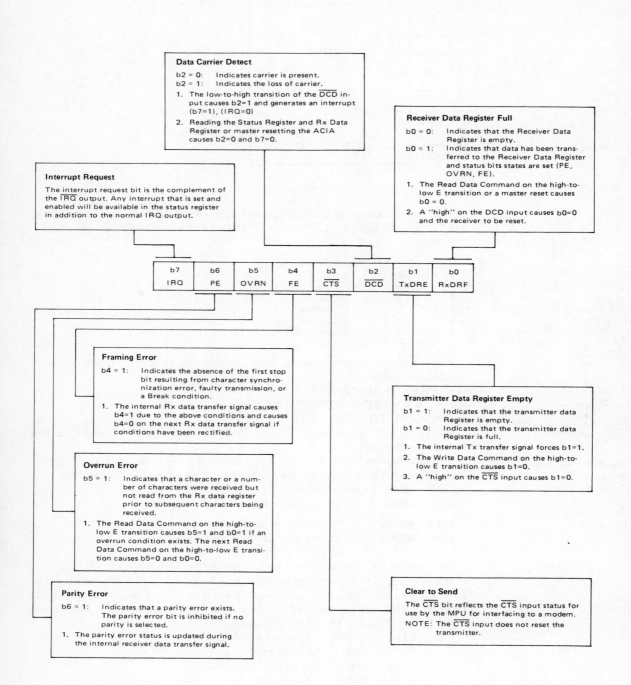

Data Carrier Detect

b2 = 0:   Indicates carrier is present.
b2 = 1:   Indicates the loss of carrier.

1. The low-to-high transition of the $\overline{DCD}$ input causes b2=1 and generates an interrupt (b7=1), (IRQ=0)
2. Reading the Status Register and Rx Data Register or master resetting the ACIA causes b2=0 and b7=0.

Receiver Data Register Full

b0 = 0:   Indicates that the Receiver Data Register is empty.
b0 = 1:   Indicates that data has been transferred to the Receiver Data Register and status bits states are set (PE, OVRN, FE).

1. The Read Data Command on the high-to-low E transition or a master reset causes b0 = 0.
2. A "high" on the DCD input causes b0=0 and the receiver to be reset.

Interrupt Request

The interrupt request bit is the complement of the $\overline{IRQ}$ output. Any interrupt that is set and enabled will be available in the status register in addition to the normal IRQ output.

b7	b6	b5	b4	b3	b2	b1	b0
IRQ	PE	OVRN	FE	$\overline{CTS}$	$\overline{DCD}$	TxDRE	RxDRF

Framing Error

b4 = 1:   Indicates the absence of the first stop bit resulting from character synchronization error, faulty transmission, or a Break condition.

1. The internal Rx data transfer signal causes b4=1 due to the above conditions and causes b4=0 on the next Rx data transfer signal if conditions have been rectified.

Transmitter Data Register Empty

b1 = 1:   Indicates that the transmitter data Register is empty.
b1 = 0:   Indicates that the transmitter data Register is full.

1. The internal Tx transfer signal forces b1=1.
2. The Write Data Command on the high-to-low E transition causes b1=0.
3. A "high" on the $\overline{CTS}$ input causes b1=0.

Overrun Error

b5 = 1:   Indicates that a character or a number of characters were received but not read from the Rx data register prior to subsequent characters being received.

1. The Read Data Command on the high-to-low E transition causes b5=1 and b0=1 if an overrun condition exists. The next Read Data Command on the high-to-low E transition causes b5=0 and b0=0.

Parity Error

b6 = 1:   Indicates that a parity error exists. The parity error bit is inhibited if no parity is selected.

1. The parity error status is updated during the internal receiver data transfer signal.

Clear to Send

The $\overline{CTS}$ bit reflects the $\overline{CTS}$ input status for use by the MPU for interfacing to a modem.
NOTE: The $\overline{CTS}$ input does not reset the transmitter.

Fig. A21*a* ACIA status register format

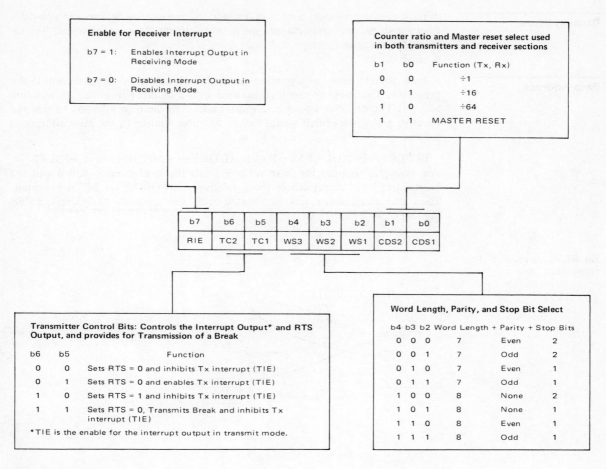

Enable for Receiver Interrupt

b7 = 1: Enables Interrupt Output in Receiving Mode

b7 = 0: Disables Interrupt Output in Receiving Mode

Counter ratio and Master reset select used in both transmitters and receiver sections

b1	b0	Function (Tx, Rx)
0	0	÷1
0	1	÷16
1	0	÷64
1	1	MASTER RESET

b7	b6	b5	b4	b3	b2	b1	b0
RIE	TC2	TC1	WS3	WS2	WS1	CDS2	CDS1

Transmitter Control Bits: Controls the Interrupt Output* and RTS Output, and provides for Transmission of a Break

b6	b5	Function
0	0	Sets RTS = 0 and inhibits Tx interrupt (TIE)
0	1	Sets RTS = 0 and enables Tx interrupt (TIE)
1	0	Sets RTS = 1 and inhibits Tx interrupt (TIE)
1	1	Sets RTS = 0, Transmits Break and inhibits Tx interrupt (TIE)

*TIE is the enable for the interrupt output in transmit mode.

Word Length, Parity, and Stop Bit Select

b4	b3	b2	Word Length	+ Parity	+ Stop Bits
0	0	0	7	Even	2
0	0	1	7	Odd	2
0	1	0	7	Even	1
0	1	1	7	Odd	1
1	0	0	8	None	2
1	0	1	8	None	1
1	1	0	8	Even	1
1	1	1	8	Odd	1

Fig. A21b ACIA control register format

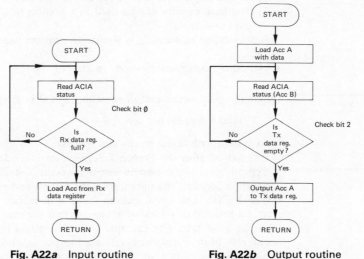

Fig. A22a Input routine from ACIA

Fig. A22b Output routine to ACIA

Backing Store

A large-capacity memory unit used for bulk storage of records, programs or data. Backing stores are non-volatile and have relatively slow access times. Typical examples are magnetic tape and disc.

● MEMORIES

Base Address

A base address refers to a number that is usually stored in a register within the processor. This number can then be used with a modifier to obtain an absolute address. The modifier would be an offset added to the base address, so that the effective address specified would have a location relative to the base address as follows:

EFFECTIVE ADDRESS = BASE ADDRESS + MODIFIER (OFFSET)

For example: suppose the base register holds the hex. number $3080 and the instruction: Load Accumulator (base relative) with OFFSET = $0F is executed. Then the accumulator will be loaded with the contents of address $308F (fig. B1).

Fig. B1 Base relative addressing

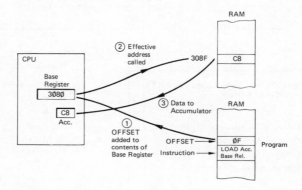

The advantage of using addressing in this way is that:
1) Only a single byte is required in the operand, this being the required offset.
2) The base register can be used as a pointer to a block of memory containing data or a table.

Base relative addressing is similar to register indirect and indexed addressing modes.

● INDEXED ADDRESSING MODE   ● OFFSET

Baud Rate

Originally used as the unit of signalling speed in telegraphy.

1 Baud = 1 pulse per sec

(in a system with equal marks and spaces).

It is named after the French Telegraph engineer J. M. Baudot (1845–1903).

Typical baud rates used in microprocessor systems for sending and receiving serial data between the microprocessor system and peripherals are 110, 150, 300, 600 and 1200. The value quoted for a system *may* include transmission of the start, parity, and stop bits, which means that the rate of data transmission is lower than the baud rate. For example with eleven bits transmitted per character, the actual rate of data transfer is 80 data bits per second for a baud rate of 110.

● ASYNCHRONOUS COMMUNICATION INTERFACE ADAPTOR   ● SERIAL DATA FORMAT

Benchmark Program (Benchmark Test)

One way of comparing the performance of microprocessors as an aid in selecting the best one for a particular application is to test each candidate with a specially designed program. This benchmark program, not overlong (say 100 to 200 statements of assembly language), would be written with the specific application in mind. It would probably test I/O addressing, subroutine calls, and the execution times of key instructions.

● MICROPROCESSOR

Binary and Binary Coded Decimal

Binary numbers, i.e. numbers with a base of 2, are very important in computing and microelectronics. The reason for this is that only two symbols, Ø and 1, are necessary to give the value of one binary digit; these two states can be easily represented by electronic switching devices.

One binary digit is called a **bit**.

Any combination of bits arranged to make a binary number is called a **word** and an 8-bit word is usually called a **byte**.

Within a microelectronic system, the maximum size of the binary number used is normally limited to a fixed number of bits, hence we have 8, 16 and 32 bit microprocessors.

In the binary system, a large number of digits are required to represent numbers. If n is the number of bits in the binary word, then the number of distinct combinations is 2^n. Thus one byte (8 bits) can be used to represent decimal numbers in the range 0 to 255 ($2^8 = 256$). Other commonly used abbreviations are as follows:

BINARY WORD	COMBINATION	ABBREVIATION
10 bit	1024	1 K
11 bit	2048	2 K
12 bit	4096	4 K
13 bit	8192	8 K
14 bit	16 384	16 K
14 bit	32 768	32 K
16 bit	65 536	64 K

Unsigned binary is the basic form of number representation for machine language. In this all numbers are assumed positive. Therefore an 8-bit word has values as follows:

ØØØØØØØØ to 11111111		Binary
Ø to 255		Decimal
$00 to $FF		Hexadecimal

In unsigned binary arithmetic, the length of the result from an operation can be extended to 9 bits (IFF in hex.) by using the carry bit in the status or flag register.

Signed binary is used when it is necessary to represent positive and negative numbers. The twos complement form is the one most commonly used. For an 8-bit word the most significant bit (bit 7) is used as the **sign bit** and the remaining seven bits (bit Ø to bit 6) are used for magnitude.

The sign bit is Ø for POSITIVE numbers
and 1 for NEGATIVE numbers.

It follows that the range of numbers in twos complement signed binary is:

Positive numbers

ØØØØØØØØ to Ø1111111		
0_{10} to $+127_{10}$		
$00 to $7F		

Negative numbers

11111111 to 10000000

-1_{10} to -128_{10}

$FF   to $80

Note that negative numbers are formed by counting backwards from zero.

Binary coded decimal (BCD) is often used in place of pure binary since with BCD it is very easy to convert to and from decimal. Each decimal digit is represented by a 4-bit binary code:

$8_{10} = 1000$ in BCD

$5_{10} = 0101$ in BCD

In this way the decimal digits 0 to 9 can be represented and their BCD value will be the same as pure binary. This form is referred to as **unpacked BCD**.

When decimal numbers greater than 9 are converted into BCD, each separate digit is assigned its appropriate 4-bit code. This gives what is called **packed BCD**. For example,

$83_{10} = 1000\ 0011$ in BCD

$692_{10} = 0110\ 1001\ 0010$ in BCD

When BCD numbers are added together, which is the same process as pure binary addition, then provided the result does not exceed 9_{10} it will be correct. If 9_{10} is exceeded, invalid codes will be generated. For example,

$7_{10} + 6_{10}$

BCD   0111+
          0110
          1101   Result not valid in BCD.

The answer should be 00010011 (13_{10}).

The correct result can be obtained by adding a correction factor of 6_{10} (0110):

          0111
          0110
          1101   Invalid code in BCD
          0110   Correction factor (6_{10})
    00010011   Correct BCD result.

This correction process, called *decimal adjusting*, can be made on packed as well as unpacked BCD. Processors such as the 6502 can operate in the decimal mode and automatically carry out this adjustment process. Other processors [6800, Z80] require an instruction called DECIMAL ADJUST ACCUMULATOR (DAA) written into the program. This tests both the accumulator contents and the half carry flag and provides the correct adjustment to the BCD number if required.

● HEXADECIMAL NUMBERS   ● OCTAL NUMBERS   ● SIGN BIT

Bipolar

Used in two senses:

1 As in **bipolar transistor** to describe a device that requires both negative (electrons) and positive (holes) charge carriers for its operation. This distinguishes the ordinary transistor from the Field Effect Transistor (FET). The latter is a unipolar device.

2 A signal that swings both positively and negatively about zero (*fig. B2*). Bipolar signals are often used in digital transmission systems since there is no d.c.

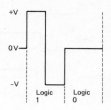

component present in the waveform and therefore less power loss than if unipolar pulses are transmitted.

● ANALOG-TO-DIGITAL CONVERTOR

Fig. B2   Bipolar digital signals

Bistable

One of the basic requirements within digital systems is for some kind of memory, in other words a circuit that can be set to logic 1 by a pulse or edge and which will hold this level until the circuit gets a reset pulse. The *bistable* is the name given to this type of circuit and it forms the basis for all other types of sequential logic; that is registers, shift registers, counters, dividers, and memories.

Fig. B3   Bistable circuits

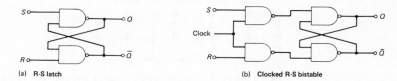

(a)   R-S latch   (b)   Clocked R-S bistable

1   As the name implies, the bistable is a circuit which has two possible stable states and the simplest arrangement uses two cross-coupled NAND gates (see *fig. B3*). This gives what is called an **R-S latch**. To SET the circuit, the S input is taken momentarily to logic Ø. This forces the Q output to be logic 1 and the $\bar{Q}$ output logic Ø. Because of the cross-coupling, the logic Ø from the $\bar{Q}$ output will force the Q output to remain high at logic 1 even when the S input returns high.

Only by applying a logic Ø momentarily to the R input will the bistable again change its state. The action is usually described by a truth table, but the previous state of the bistable must be included along with the input conditions.

Truth table for the R-S bistable

INPUTS		PREVIOUS STATE OF Q	RESULTING STATE OF Q	
R	S	Q_n	Q_{n+1}	
Ø	Ø	Ø	X ⎫	Indeterminate state
Ø	Ø	1	X ⎭	
Ø	1	Ø	Ø ⎫	Ø on the R forces
Ø	1	1	Ø ⎭	the Q to Ø
1	Ø	Ø	1 ⎫	Ø on the S forces
1	Ø	1	1 ⎭	the Q to 1
1	1	Ø	Ø ⎫	
1	1	1	1 ⎭	No change

You will notice from this that the R-S has a basic limitation: for if two Øs are applied simultaneously and then removed, the output state will be either a Ø or a 1. This restricts the use of the R-S to a few basic applications.

2   To overcome the limitation of the R-S, two other bistables are widely used: the D type (Data latch) and the J-K (usually a master-slave arrangement). Both of these are extensions of a clocked R-S (*fig. B3b*). Adding a **clock line** greatly extends the capability of a bistable because it can then be operated synchronously with other circuits.

27

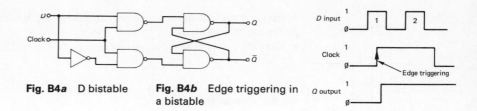

Fig. B4a   D bistable   **Fig. B4b**   Edge triggering in
                             a bistable

The **D type bistable** is used for storage of data and has, apart from the clock, one input D for data entry (*fig. B4a*). When the clock is high, the state of the D input will be transferred to the Q output, but when the clock is low no change of state can take place. This is called *level clocking*.

Truth table for the D bistable

Clock	D	Q_n	Q_{n+1}
H (high)	0	0	0
H	0	1	0
H	1	0	1
H	1	1	1

With many IC bistables (TTL and CMOS), the Q output can only change state on *one* edge of the clock waveform. This is called **edge triggering** and has the advantage that data is "locked out" at all times except for the brief instant when the clock changes state (*fig. B4b*).

3   The other very useful bistable is called the **J-K bistable** (*fig. B5a*). It is a clocked bistable but, unlike the D, has two inputs. The J-K is therefore similar to the R-S except that it does not have any indeterminate output conditions. This is achieved because of the internal feedback from the Q output which gates the K input and from the $\bar{Q}$ output which gates the J input. When the J and K inputs are both 0, there is no change of state, and if they are both logic 1 the output complements.

Truth table for the J-K bistable (with all states it is assumed that a clock signal is applied)

J	K	Q_n	Q_{n+1}	
0	0	0	0 ⎫	$J = K = 0$
0	0	1	1 ⎭	no change
0	1	0	0 ⎫	$J = 0, K = 1$
0	1	1	0 ⎭	Q forced to 0
1	0	0	1 ⎫	$J = 1, K = 0$
1	0	1	1 ⎭	Q forced to 1
1	1	0	1 ⎫	$J = K = 1$
1	1	1	0 ⎭	Q complements

Many IC forms of the J-K are **master-slave** types. These have the distinct advantage of being free from timing problems—the sort that might cause false changes of state at the output. The master-slave is really two bistables in one, but it is the "slave", to which the Q and $\bar{Q}$ outputs are connected, which changes state on the trailing edge of the clock pulse (see *fig. B5b*).

Bistables are usually provided with PRESET and CLEAR inputs. These inputs are asynchronous and will therefore operate without a clock signal being present (*fig. B6*).

Fig. B5a Basic J-K bistable

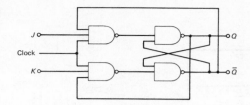

Fig. B5b J-K master-slave bistable

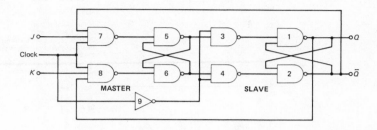

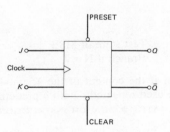

Fig. B6 Symbol for J-K bistable with Preset and Clear inputs; active low

A signal to the Preset will force the Q output to logic 1 and a signal to the Clear will force the Q output to logic Ø. If these inputs are not to be used, connect them to a fixed voltage level, usually $+5\,V$ for TTL and $0\,V$ for CMOS.

● COUNTER ● MEMORIES ● REGISTER

Bit

This is the basic binary data unit used in digital systems and computers. One bit can have a value of either 1 or Ø and several bits grouped together comprise a binary word. The name BIT is taken from the first letter and last two letters of BINARY DIGIT.

● BINARY ● WORD ● SIGN BIT

Bit Test

An instruction that carries out the logical AND function between each bit of a register and the corresponding bits in a memory location but which does not place the result of the test in the register. The register and the memory location contents are unchanged and only the appropriate flags (N and Z usually) in the condition code or status register are affected. A bit test is similar to a COMPARE instruction and can be used to examine the state of one or more bits of a register contents (or memory location). A branch usually follows a bit test.

Fig. B7 Bit test

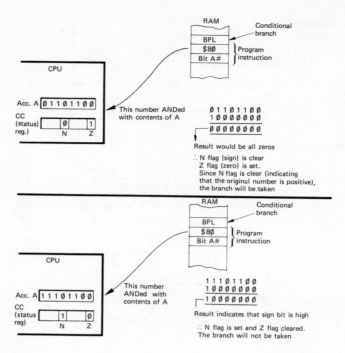

RAM

Conditional branch

BPL
$8∅
Bit A#
} Program instruction

CPU

Acc. A | 0 1 1 0 1 1 0 0

CC (status reg.) | ∅ | 1
N Z

This number ANDed with contents of A

```
0 1 1 0 1 1 0 0
1 0 0 0 0 0 0 0
0 0 0 0 0 0 0 0
```

Result would be all zeros

∴ N flag (sign) is clear
Z flag (zero) is set.
Since N flag is clear (indicating
that the original number is positive),
the branch will be taken

RAM

Conditional branch

BPL
$8∅
Bit A#
} Program instruction

CPU

Acc. A | 1 1 1 0 1 1 0 0

CC (status reg) | 1 | ∅
N Z

This number ANDed with contents of A

```
1 1 1 0 1 1 0 0
1 0 0 0 0 0 0 0
1 0 0 0 0 0 0 0
```

Result indicates that sign bit is high

∴ N flag is set and Z flag cleared.
The branch will not be taken

Example (fig. B7)

BIT	A #$8∅	Test state of MSB
BPL	(LABEL)	Branch if N = ∅

A branch will occur if the content of the accumulator is positive (MSB = ∅). A test like this can be used repeatedly until a predetermined condition is achieved.
● ACIA ● AND GATE ● BRANCH INSTRUCTION ● COMPARE INSTRUCTION

Boolean Algebra

A type of algebra, invented in the 19th century by George Boole, for the mathematical analysis of logic. It is based on logical statements which are either true or false and it is therefore a powerful tool in the design and analysis of digital circuits and systems.

In Boolean algebra, instead of writing "both inputs A *and* B must be present to give output F", we write

$$F = A \cdot B$$

The AND function is represented by the symbol ·
Similarly the statement, "either input C *or* input D will give a logical output" is written

$$F = C + D$$

The OR function is represented by the symbol +
The NOT function is represented by a bar:

$$F = \bar{A} \quad \text{means input A must be a ∅ to give a 1 at } F.$$

From this we have:

NOR FUNCTION $F = \overline{A + B}$ (NOT-OR)
NAND FUNCTION $F = \overline{A \cdot B}$ (NOT-AND)

Fig. B8 Identities and rules
of Boolean Algebra

IDENTITIES

$$A + 0 = A \qquad A.0 = 0$$
$$A + A = A \qquad A.1 = A$$
$$A + 1 = 1 \qquad A.A = A$$
$$A + \bar{A} = 1 \qquad A.\bar{A} = 0$$

RULES

$$A + B = B + A \qquad (A+B) + C = A + (B+C)$$
$$A.B = B.A \qquad (A.B).C = A.(B.C)$$

$$A + A.B = A \qquad \text{since } A.(1+B) = A.1$$
$$A.(A+B) = A \qquad \text{since } A.A + A.B = A + A.B$$
$$A + \bar{A}.B = A + B$$

$$\overline{A+B} = \bar{A}.\bar{B} \qquad \text{de Morgan's rules}$$

$$\overline{A.B} = \bar{A} + \bar{B}$$

The identities and rules of Boolean Algebra together with symbols for the common gates are shown in *fig. B8*.

Logical operations that can be performed by a microprocessor (using the ALU) are carried out using the following instructions:

AND   Logical AND between a register and contents of a memory location.

OR   Logical OR (inclusive-OR) between a register and contents of a memory location.

EOR   Exclusive-OR between a register and contents of a memory location.

COM   Complement (NOT function) on each bit of a register or memory location.

The NAND and NOR functions can be simulated by following AND or OR (as required) with the COM instruction.

● DIGITAL CIRCUIT   ● KARNAUGH MAP   ● LOGICAL INSTRUCTIONS AND OPERATIONS

Bootstrap

A technique used to load in a main program using a short introductory program which contains call instructions enabling the loading process to be set into action. Often used to start up a disk-based system or to load, for example, an assembler/editor from disk into the main memory. Hence the use of the words "Booting the system".

BRANCH Instruction (Jump Instruction)

Quite often in a program it is necessary to move away from the main program path, to break the normal sequential flow of instructions, and to jump to another location which contains a new (or repeat) instruction. This movement away from the set sequence is called a **branch** and the operation is initiated by a **branch instruction**. This type of instruction can be **conditional** (dependent on the result of the previous instruction or operation) or **unconditional** (carried out regardless of any previous conditions). The terms "branch" and "jump" are often used by manufacturers of microprocessors to describe the same operation. For example the following are both branch instructions:

JPZ   Jump if equal to zero   [Z80]
BEQ   Branch if equal to zero   [6800]

These instructions are conditional and the branch would only take place if the result of the previous operation were zero (*fig. B9*).

Fig. B9 Branching in a program

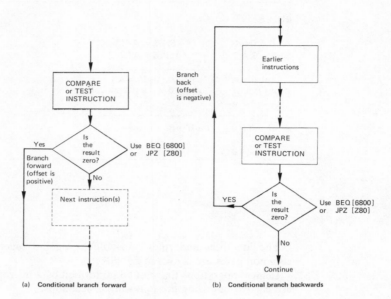

(a) **Conditional branch forward**   (b) **Conditional branch backwards**

Since the object of a branch instruction is to cause a change in the sequence, a branch instruction of any kind must be followed immediately in the program by either a destination address or an offset value to be added or subtracted from the content of the program counter. In the latter case, for conditional branch instructions, the RELATIVE ADDRESSING MODE is normally used.

Typical examples of branch instructions are:

Unconditional
BRA   Branch always
BSR   Branch to subroutine

Conditional
BNE   Branch if the result does not equal zero
BCC   Branch if the carry bit is clear
BCS   Branch if the carry bit is set
         and so on

An illustration of the use of branch instructions is shown in the next program segment [M6800 code] to output a ramp signal to an output port. The ramp consists of 15 steps (see flowchart *fig. B10*). The following addresses are assumed:

Program start $1000
Port $C004
Monitor $24F0
Subroutine (WAIT) $1550

Fig. B10 Flowchart for ramp output

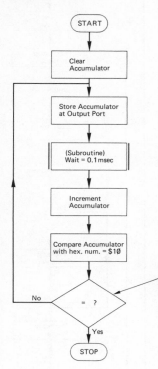

LABEL	MNEMONIC	OPERAND	COMMENT	ADDRESS	HEX.	CODES
	CLR A		CLEAR ACC.	1000	4F	
LOOP	STA A	$C004	OUTPUT TO PORT	1001	B7	C004
	JSR	WAIT	JUMP TO SUB.*	1004	BD	1550
	INC A		INCREMENT ACC.	1007	4C	
	CMP A	#$10	COMPARE ACC.	1008	81	10
	BNE	LOOP	BRANCH IF NOT ZERO	100A	26	F5
	JMP	MON.	RETURN	100C	7E	24F0

* The subroutine WAIT is not shown.

The BNE code ($26) is followed by an offset of $F5. This is required by the processor to enable calculation of the destination address, which in this case is $1001. The program has to branch back 11_{10} places and the offset for the relative addressing mode is found by converting 11_{10} into its twos complement hexadecimal equivalent ($F5).

Note that both jump instructions are unconditional and that extended (absolute) addressing is used.

● LOOP ● MICROPROCESSOR ● RELATIVE ADDRESSING

Conditional branch
BNE Instruction tests the state of the zero flag (Z) and causes a branch until the Z flag is set

Breakpoint

This is one of the useful features of a development system, as an aid in locating and correcting software errors (debugging). It allows the programmer to insert temporary halts, or breaks, at suitable points in the program, these halts being inserted by a breakpoint editor. A *breakpoint* stops the program and allows the user to examine register and memory contents and usually to execute the program in single step mode. Most development systems allow a number of breakpoints to be inserted which gives the programmer the added advantage of being able to separate a program into well-defined blocks. Each block can then be tested and debugged separately.

● DEBUG

Bubble Sort

This is the name commonly given to a program that sorts the data within a block of memory into ascending order, so that the end result is the highest number at the top of the block and the lowest at the bottom.

One method for doing this task is shown in the flowchart (*fig. B11*) and in the program shown using 6800/6802 code. Basically the program, using the index register as a pointer, compares the magnitude of each number with the next in the block and causes an exchange if the first is smaller than the second. If an exchange occurs, a flag is set. In this way the highest number rises or "bubbles" to the top. The procedure is repeated until no further exchanges are necessary.

In the program the block is considered to consist of 10 numbers held at consecutive locations from $1200 onwards. Address $1050 is used to hold the flag and the program start is at $1000.

● BRANCH INSTRUCTION ● INDEX REGISTER AND INDEXED ADDRESSING

Fig. B11   Bubble sort

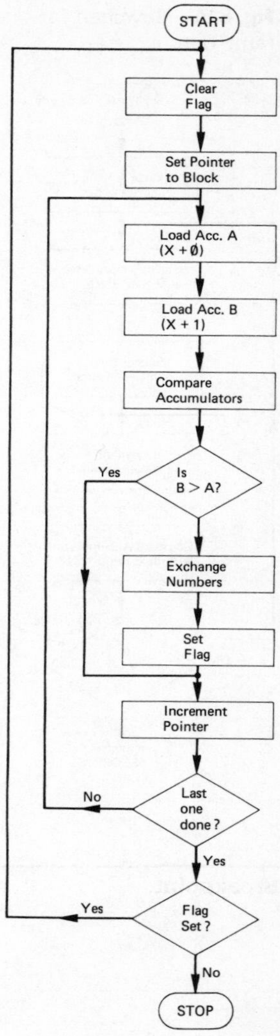

```
 1.00= NAM BUSORT
 2.00=MON EQU $E0E3
 3.00=BLOCK EQU $1200
 4.00=FLAG EQU $1050
 5.00= ORG $1000
 6.00=SORT CLR FLAG
 7.00= LDX £BLOCK
 8.00=NEXT LDAA 0,X
 9.00= LDAB 1,X
10.00= CBA
11.00= BLS NOSWOP
12.00= STAB 0,X
13.00= STAA 1,X
14.00= INC FLAG
15.00=NOSWOP INX
16.00= CPX £BLOCK+$9
17.00= BNE NEXT
18.00= LDAA $FLAG
19.00= BNE SORT
20.00= JMP MON
21.00= END
£18= LDAA FLAG
£S
+++ASMB BUSORT+NY
```

```
    1                     NAM    BUSORT
    2  E0E3        MON     EQU    $E0E3
    3  1200        BLOCK   EQU    $1200
    4  1050        FLAG    EQU    $1050
    5  1000                ORG    $1000
    6  1000 7F 10 50  SORT  CLR   FLAG         Clear flag
    7  1003 CE 12 00        LDX   £BLOCK       Set pointer to start
    8  1006 A6 00    NEXT  LDA A  0,X          First number
    9  1008 E6 01           LDA B  1,X         Next number
   10  100A 11              CBA                Compare
   11  100B 23 07           BLS   NOSWOP       If first lower, branch
   12  100D E7 00           STA B  0,X       ⎫
   13  100F A7 01           STA A  1,X       ⎬ Exchange numbers
   14  1011 7C 10 50        INC   FLAG         Set flag
   15  1014 08      NOSWOP  INX                Increment pointer
   16  1015 8C 12 09        CPX   £BLOCK+$9    Compare pointer with end
   17  1018 26 EC           BNE   NEXT         Repeat
   18  101A B6 10 50        LDA A  FLAG      ⎫
   19  101D 26 E1           BNE   SORT       ⎬ Check flag and branch if set
   20  101F 7E E0 E3        JMP   MON          Return to monitor
   21                       END
```

NO ERROR(S) DETECTED

SYMBOL TABLE:

```
BLOCK  1200    FLAG   1050    MON    E0E3    NEXT    1006    NOSWOP 1014
SORT   1000
```

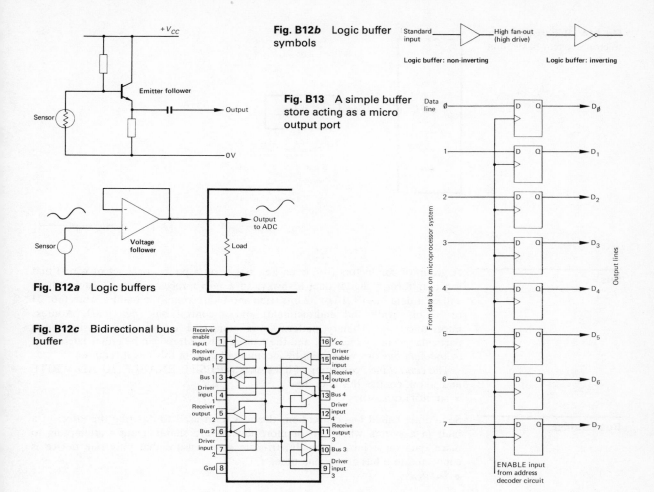

Fig. B12b Logic buffer symbols

Standard input — High fan-out (high drive)

Logic buffer: non-inverting

Logic buffer: inverting

Fig. B13 A simple buffer store acting as a micro output port

Emitter follower

$+V_{CC}$

Sensor

Output

0V

Sensor

Voltage follower

Output to ADC

Load

Fig. B12a Logic buffers

Fig. B12c Bidirectional bus buffer

Receiver enable input — 1 — 16 V_{CC}
Receiver output 1 — 2 — 15 Driver enable input
Bus 1 — 3 — 14 Receive output 4
Driver input 1 — 4 — 13 Bus 4
Receiver output 2 — 5 — 12 Driver input 4
Bus 2 — 6 — 11 Receive output 3
Driver input 2 — 7 — 10 Bus 3
Gnd — 8 — 9 Driver input 3

Data line

Ø — D Q — $D_\emptyset$
1 — D Q — D_1
2 — D Q — D_2
3 — D Q — D_3
4 — D Q — D_4
5 — D Q — D_5
6 — D Q — D_6
7 — D Q — D_7

From data bus on microprocessor system

Output lines

ENABLE input from address decoder circuit

Buffer

1 An *amplifier* used to prevent loading, and hence degradation of the signal, on the output of a circuit. The buffer has a high input resistance and presents a light load to the signal from the circuit, but has a low output resistance and is therefore capable of driving a much heavier load.

Typical examples of buffers in analog circuits are the emitter follower and voltage follower. These can be used to match the signals from sensors to the input of an ADC or other circuit (*fig. B12a*).

Logic buffers, which can be inverting or non-inverting, are used for the same purpose in digital circuits (*fig. B12b*).

In microprocessor systems, bus buffers (bus extenders) are used to prevent serious loading of bus signals, and are essential in systems that have several RAM, ROM and I/O chips. Bidirectional bus buffers are used for the data bus, with tri-state control inputs allowing buffers not being used to be effectively removed from the bus (*fig. B12c*).

2 Used to describe any unit that forms a *temporary store of data* between two devices. A *buffer store*, usually a register or RAM, allows for differences in data transfer speeds between the devices, typically between a micro system and peripherals (*fig. B13*).

● BUS ● SENSOR ● TRI-STATE

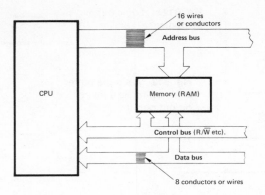

Fig. B14 Bus system in a microprocessor-based unit

CPU

16 wires
or conductors

Address bus

Memory (RAM)

Control bus (R/W̄ etc).

Data bus

8 conductors or wires

Bus

A group of conductors (inside an i.c., tracks on a p.c.b., or a set of wires) that together form a digital data highway. In a microprocessor-based system, there will be a data bus (8, 16 or 32 bits wide and bidirectional), an address bus (16, 24 or 32 bits wide and undirectional) and a control bus (*fig. B14*). Address information as a binary pattern flows along the *address bus* to select one particular memory location, and the data at this address can be either latched on to the *data bus* or overwritten by incoming data from this bus if required.

The *control bus*, consisting of lines such as RESET, ENABLE, READ/WRITE and so on, control this data flow.

● MICROPROCESSOR

Bus Conflict

Sometimes called **bus contention**, this is a term used to describe the effect of a fault in a system when two or more devices are simultaneously attempting to place data on a bus. Normally, tri-state gates ensure that only one device is connected to a bus at any one time.

● TRI-STATE

Bus Systems
(standards)

The various connections within a microcomputer and the links between it and peripherals can be made by dedicated wiring; but this may result in a rather inflexible arrangement, not capable of expansion and unable to accommodate all types of peripheral. Many of these problems can be overcome by using a standard interconnection method. These standard bus systems can be divided into *internal* (linking circuit boards together to make a working microcomputer) and *external* (connections between the micro and peripherals).

Some of these industry standards are:

Internal	*External*
S-1ØØ bus	RS-232-C
Motorola EXORcist bus	RS-422/3
Intel MULTIBUS	IEEE-488 (GPIB)

The external bus systems are clearly of more importance and will be dealt with here.

1 RS-232-C This is a serial bus system which can operate up to 20 kilobits per second at a range of up to 15.3 m. Connection to the bus is via a standard 25-pin connector (but not all manufacturers use the same pin connections) (see *fig. B15*).

Fig. B15 Common configuration for RS-232-C pins

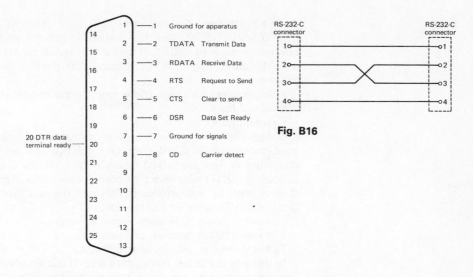

1 — 1	Ground for apparatus
2 — 2	TDATA Transmit Data
3 — 3	RDATA Receive Data
4 — 4	RTS Request to Send
5 — 5	CTS Clear to send
6 — 6	DSR Data Set Ready
7 — 7	Ground for signals
8 — 8	CD Carrier detect

20 DTR data terminal ready — 20

Fig. B16

Logic levels are typically

$$\text{Transmitter}\begin{cases}\text{Logic } \emptyset & +5\text{ V to } +12\text{ V} \\ \text{Logic } 1 & -5\text{ V to } -12\text{ V}\end{cases}$$

$$\begin{cases}\text{Logic } \emptyset & +3\text{ V to } +8\text{ V} \\ \text{Logic } 1 & -3\text{ V to } -8\text{ V}\end{cases}$$

NEGATIVE LOGIC is used, and a 2 V noise immunity is provided.

RS-232 will ensure that signal and other voltages are compatible and also will set up handshaking between connected devices. A separate RS-232 cable is required for each peripheral linked to the microcomputer. The bus is widely used for connection between microcomputers and modems, VDUs and Teletypes. The majority of systems do not require the full standard set of connections and this has meant that various subsets have been defined; these are called Levels I, II and III.

LEVEL I   used where equipment is tied directly (*fig. B16*)
Pin 1   Protective ground
Pin 2   Transmitted Data ⎫
Pin 3   Received Data ⎭ channel 1
Pin 7   Logical ground

LEVEL II   includes handshaking
Level I plus
Pin 6   Data Set Ready
Pin 8   Data Carrier Detect
Pin 20   Data Terminal Ready

LEVEL III   for more precise control of data flow
Level II plus
Pin 4   Request to Send
Pin 5   Clear to Send
Pin 22   Ring Indicator

2 IEEE-488 Bus Developed by Hewlett Packard for linking their own equipment (called HPIB), this bus system is general purpose (hence the further alternative name of GPIB). It uses a byte-serial, bit parallel transmission method with the data being in ASCII format. The parallel bus has 24 lines divided as follows:

8 bidirectional data lines (these can operate at 1 Mbytes/sec)

8 control lines

8 ground lines

Connection to the bus is usually provided by a special 24-pin socket/plug combination which enables up to 15 devices to be "piggy-backed". The 15 maximum devices are linked to each other via the bus system in a daisy-chain fashion (*fig. B17*) with each connection being up to 20 m long. At least one of the devices must be a controller (CPU) and the rest can be a mixture of devices described as listeners and/or talkers:

Listeners—printers, plotters, signal generators.

Talkers—DMMs, sensors, counters.

Talker/Listener—programmable DMM.

In this way the IEEE bus enables several instruments to be linked up to form a test system which can be automatically controlled via the program in the controller.

The transfer and control of data flow (in ASCII code) is achieved using the control lines. These are three handshake lines and five management lines.

Handshake lines are:

DAV   Data Valid
NRFD   Not Ready for Data
NDAC   Not Data Accepted

and a typical transfer would be arranged as follows:

1) The Listener sets NFRD line low as soon as it is ready to accept a data byte.
2) If the Talker has valid data and it sees the NRFD line go low, it sets DAV high.
3) The Listener on seeing the DAV line go high responds by resetting the NRFD line.
4) Listener now accepts the data byte.
5) On seeing the NDAC line go low the Talker resets DAV low.
6) The Listener resets NDAC high when DAV goes low.

Following this sequence (*fig. B18*) the cycle can then recommence.

Management lines are:

ATN	(Attention)	Indicates that data on the bus is either an address or command.
IFC	(Interface Clear)	Initializes the interface command. Used by the controller to clear the interface.
SRQ	(Service Request)	Requests asynchronous service (from a device).
REN	(Remote)	Specifies remote or local.
EOI	(End of Identify)	Indicates last byte of data used by a device to indicate the end of a multi-byte transfer.

Each device on the bus is allocated a unique 5-bit address which is set up using 5 address switches on the rear of the instrument. In this way the controller can specify which device it wishes to communicate with by placing the appropriate device address on the bus.

● ASYNCHRONOUS COMMUNICATIONS INTERFACE ADAPTOR   ● INTERFACE CIRCUITS

Fig. B17 Interface bus structure: the controller (device A, not shown) is able to talk, listen and control

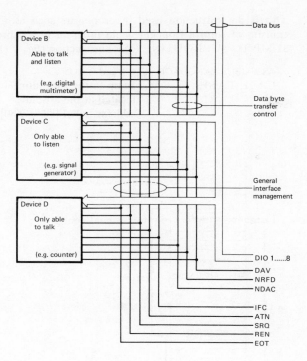

Device B

Able to talk and listen

(e.g. digital multimeter)

Device C

Only able to listen

(e.g. signal generator)

Device D

Only able to talk

(e.g. counter)

Data bus

Data byte transfer control

General interface management

DIO 1......8
DAV
NRFD
NDAC

IFC
ATN
SRQ
REN
EOT

Fig. B18

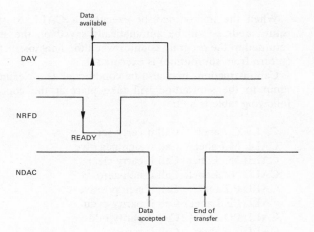

Data available

DAV

NRFD

READY

NDAC

Data accepted   End of transfer

CALL Instruction

This is an instruction used in processors such as the 8080/8085 and Z80 for transfer of control from the main program to a subroutine. It is the same as a JUMP TO SUBROUTINE (JSR) instruction (*fig. C1*).

ASSEMBLY LANGUAGE
CALL LABEL

EXPLANATION
Jump to the subroutine
located at the absolute
address Label [8080, Z80]

Fig. C1 Call to subroutine

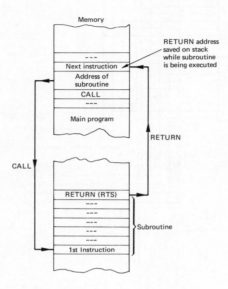

When the microprocessor executes a CALL to subroutine instruction, the return address will be automatically saved on the stack. This address will be returned to the program counter when the final instruction in the subroutine RET (return from subroutine) is executed.

Call instructions may also be conditional as for example in the Z80, where the jump to the subroutine will take place if the condition as described in the following table is met:

CALL C,Label	Call if carry set
CALL M,Label	Call if sign negative
CALL NC,Label	Call if carry clear
CALL NZ,Label	Call if non-zero
CALL P,Label	Call if sign positive
CALL PE,Label	Call if parity even
CALL PO,Label	Call if parity odd
CALL Z,Label	Call if zero.

Suppose a subroutine with label OUT is located at address $3F24, then the instruction and hex. code for CALL NZ, would be

ASSEMBLY LANGUAGE
CALL NZ,OUT

HEX. CODE
D4 3F 24

● CONDITIONAL TEST   ● JUMP   ● STACK   ● SUBROUTINE

Carry and Carry Bit

A carry occurs during arithmetic operations such as the addition of two numbers when the result of the addition of two lower-order digits exceeds or equals the base of the number system.

Examples

$8_{10} + 3_{10} = 8+$

$$\begin{array}{r} 3 \\ \hline \text{carry } 1 \leftarrow 1 \end{array} \quad \text{answer} = 11_{10}$$

$\emptyset 1_2 + \emptyset 1_2 = \emptyset 1+$

$$\begin{array}{r} \emptyset 1 \\ \hline \text{carry } 1 \leftarrow \emptyset \end{array} \quad \text{answer} = 1\emptyset_2$$

All microprocessors are provided with a carry flag (C) located in the status (or condition code) register. This flag is used to indicate when a carry out from the MSB of a register occurs. For example, the C bit will be set after an ADD instruction if the result of the addition gives an answer that is greater than the length of the register. For 8-bit processors this effectively gives the accumulator a length of 9 bits.

Example

Accumulator content	1$\emptyset\emptyset\emptyset$1$\emptyset$11	($8B)
ADD (immediate)	$\emptyset$1111$\emptyset\emptyset\emptyset$	($78)
Result	1 ← $\emptyset\emptyset\emptyset\emptyset\emptyset\emptyset$11	$103
	carry	

The use of the carry is essential in multiple precision arithmetic where the carry bit would be used, for example, in the addition of *n* bytes of data as shown in *fig. C2*.

Fig. C2 Addition of two
24-bit numbers
Assembly language program [6800/6802]

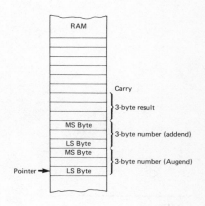

```
        LDX    #TABLE
        CLC                    Clear Carry Flag
LOOP    LDA A  $0,X            Load byte of augend
        ADC    $3,X            ADD with Carry
        STA A  $6,X            Store result
        INX                    Increment pointer
        CPX    #TABLE+3
        BNE    LOOP            Repeat if last byte not added
        BCC    END
        LDA A  #$01
        STA A  $7,X            Store Carry
END     RTS
```

As this example shows there are other instructions concerned with the carry bit:
CLEAR CARRY FLAG
SET CARRY FLAG
BRANCH IF CARRY SET
BRANCH IF CARRY CLEAR

Fig. C3 Here the Accumulator is loaded with $80 and then shifted to the right until a 1 appears in the carry bit

Assembly language

```
        LDA A   #$80
LOOP         } other instructions as required
        LSR A
        BCC   LOOP
        RTS
```

Suppose a bit is being shifted through a register for, say, a successive approximation routine; then a check for "all bits done" would be BBC (Branch if Carry Clear) (see *fig. C3*).

● ADD INSTRUCTION ● ANALOG-TO-DIGITAL CONVERTOR ● FLAG

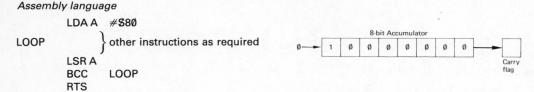

8-bit Accumulator

Carry flag

Central Processor Unit (CPU)

The part of a microcomputer which carries out the important tasks of instruction decoding and execution (*fig. C4*). It also includes the ALU (arithmetic and logic unit), a set of registers (program counter, stack pointer, accumulator, and status register), and control and timing circuits.

● MICROPROCESSOR

Fig. C4 General form of CPU

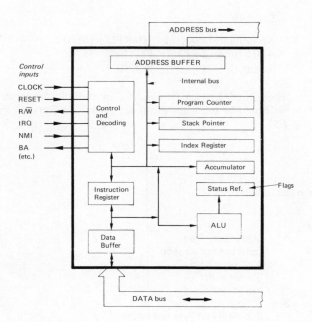

Chain

Used to describe a method for connecting a number of peripherals to a computer in which the peripherals are linked in series as opposed to a star connection (*fig. C5*).

Also used in programming to explain a method of linking program segments where the last instruction of the first segment causes a jump to the start of the second and so on.

● BUS SYSTEMS

Character

Any letter (A, B, C, . . . , Z), numeral (1, 2, 3) or symbol (! * ?) which can be read, stored or printed out by a computer.

● ASCII

Fig. C5 Chain connection

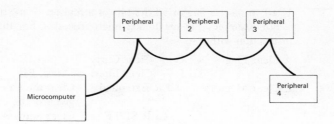

Chip

Originally this referred to the piece of silicon (or other semiconductor material) in which the various transistors and other components were diffused to create a working microcircuit. This chip is then provided with connecting pins and encapsulated to make the complete integrated circuit (i.c., IC). In practice, however, the word "chip" is now used to describe the completed integrated circuit.

● CHIP SELECT

Chip Select (Chip Enable)

The i.c.s used within a microsystem, i.e. the RAM, ROM and Interface Adaptor chips, must be provided with the capability of being activated by a unique address or range of addresses. In this way the devices are memory mapped and only one device is enabled and connected to the data bus at any one time. The operation of the $\overline{\text{CS}}$ pin on the memory device is illustrated in *fig. C6*. The lower-order address lines are decoded inside the i.c. to pick out the particular location required and at the same time the higher-order address lines are decoded by an external logic circuit to give a logic signal to the chip select input. This signal enables the input/output select logic which will then switch the tri-state buffers to connect the memory cell to the data bus. Data can then be written into (R/$\overline{\text{W}}$ line = $\emptyset$) or read from (R/$\overline{\text{W}}$ line = 1) the selected memory location. Some memory i.c.s are provided with several chip select inputs to make the task of address decoding within a system an easier task for the designer. As shown, the $\overline{\text{CS}}$ is usually active low.

● ADDRESS DECODING   ● MEMORIES   ● TRI-STATE

Fig. C6 Use of Chip Select CS on a memory chip

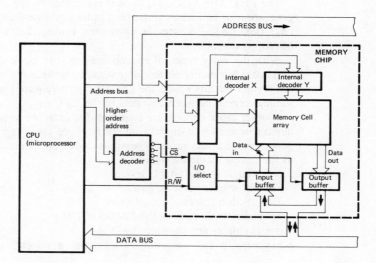

CLEAR Instruction

Used to reset a flag or all the bits of a register or memory location to logic Ø.

For example, the 6800/6802 microprocessor has the following types of clear instruction within its set:

Clear Flag	CLC	Clear Carry	
	CLI	Clear Interrupt Mask Bit	
Clear Memory	CLR Extended	Clear the absolute address given in the operand	
	CLR $17FF	Clear address 17FF	
	CLR Indexed	Clear the address pointed by the index register plus offset	
	CLR $Ø9,X	Clear m = X + 9	
Clear Register	CLR A	Clear Accumulator A	

Not all processors contain the CLEAR instruction. In these devices the register is cleared by Loading immediate with $ØØ, i.e.

LDA #$ØØ   Clear Accumulator   [6502]

● BISTABLE ● COUNTER ● REGISTER

Clock Signal and Clock Pulse Generator

Apart from a small minority of circuits, most digital systems are synchronous types and therefore must be provided with a clock circuit of some kind. The *clock generator* outputs a train of well-defined pulses which is transmitted round the system to control the timing of all operations. Data transfers within the system are then synchronised and occur at specific points on the clock waveform. A typical clock waveform with definitions of important features is shown in *fig. C7*. The main requirements of a clock circuit are:

1) Good frequency stability.

2) Low output impedance to give high drive capability. (Usually a buffer amplifier is necessary.)

3) A clean and undistorted waveshape.

4) Well-defined logic levels.

The pulses produced must be compatible with the type of logic being driven; for example TTL would require the clock to switch from less than 0.4 V (logic Ø) to greater than +2.4 V (logic 1) with rise and fall times of better than 100 nsec.

In microprocessor systems, when the requirement may be to produce accurate time delays, the clock circuit must be crystal-controlled. Such a circuit gives the highest frequency stability.

The FETCH/EXECUTE cycle is controlled by the clock circuit, usually by the generation of two non-overlapping pulse signals called phase 1 (ϕ_1) and phase 2 (ϕ_2) (*fig. C8*). For specific clock and timing diagrams, see the section on ● Microprocessors.

With the early types of microprocessor, the clock circuit was external to the CPU chip but nearly all the later versions include the master clock generator and the divider circuits inside the i.c. All that is required is for the user to connect a suitable crystal between two pins of the CPU i.c.

If other clock circuits are required, for example to provide timing for external devices or analog-to-digital convertors, there are several square circuits and pulse generators that can usefully serve as clock generators. These using *RC* networks as the timing elements include

555 Timers in the astable mode

Schmitt trigger invertor gates

Unijunction relaxation oscillators

Specialised ICs such as the CMOS 4047B

Some examples are shown in *fig. C9*.

● MACHINE CYCLE ● MICROPROCESSOR ● TIMER

Fig. C7 Clock waveform

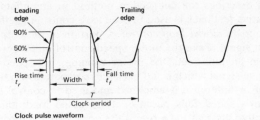

Clock pulse waveform

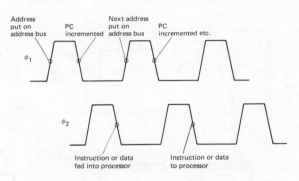

Possible distortions to clock signals

Degraded rise and fall times

Fig. C8 Two-phase clock signal

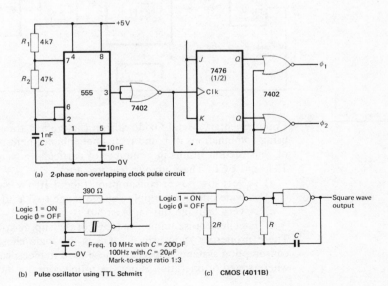

Fig. C9 Clock pulse generators

(a) 2-phase non-overlapping clock pulse circuit

Logic 1 = ON
Logic Ø = OFF

390 Ω

Freq. 10 MHz with *C* = 200 pF
100Hz with *C* = 20μF
Mark-to-sapce ratio 1:3

(b) Pulse oscillator using TTL Schmitt

Logic 1 = ON
Logic Ø = OFF

Square wave output

2R

R

C

(c) CMOS (4011B)

Closed Loop

This describes the connection method in amplifiers and control systems where negative feedback is used to produce a controlling effect on the overall gain of the system. In *closed loop control*, a portion of the output is fed back to oppose the input signal. Take the motor speed control unit shown in block form in *fig. C10a*. When an input sets the motor running, the speed transducer gives an output voltage signal which is fed back and compared with the input reference level. The error or difference is amplified and used to control the output. Imagine that the motor's speed falls because of increased load; then the feedback signal also initially falls, causing a rise in the error signal and consequently more drive to the motor. This brings its speed back to nearly the desired value. Without feedback the system would be **open loop** and no compensation for changes in output conditions could be made. Closed loop systems, whether analog or digital, can be made to be highly accurate and to have rapid response but they do have inherent problems of instability.

A digital version of a closed loop motor speed control system is also shown (*fig. C10b*). This is more complex and has the additional problem that the feedback signal has to be sampled. This means that the digital controller, under software control, switches, between samples of the feedback signal, from closed loop to open loop conditions. Care has to be taken in the design to ensure that the sampling rate is sufficiently high to avoid additional instability in response.

● CONTROL SYSTEM ● DEDICATED CONTROLLER ● SAMPLE-AND-HOLD

Fig. C10a Analog closed-loop speed controller

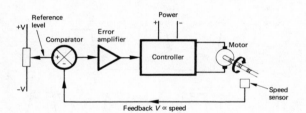

Fig. C10b Digital closed-loop speed controller

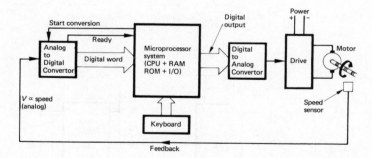

CMOS

Complementary Metal Oxide Silicon (field effect transistor logic) is a technology using combinations of p and n channel enhancement mode MOSFETS. This type of construction results in a number of particular advantages when compared with TTL and ECL. These unique features are

a) A very low power consumption (about 10 nW/gate static)
b) A wide operating supply voltage range (+3 V to +18 V)
c) A very high fan-out (at least 50)
d) Excellent noise immunity (45% of the supply voltage).

These properties show why CMOS is the logic chosen for low-cost low-power consumption systems, especially those used in electrically noisy environments and where speed of operation is not the prime consideration. The basic CMOS range

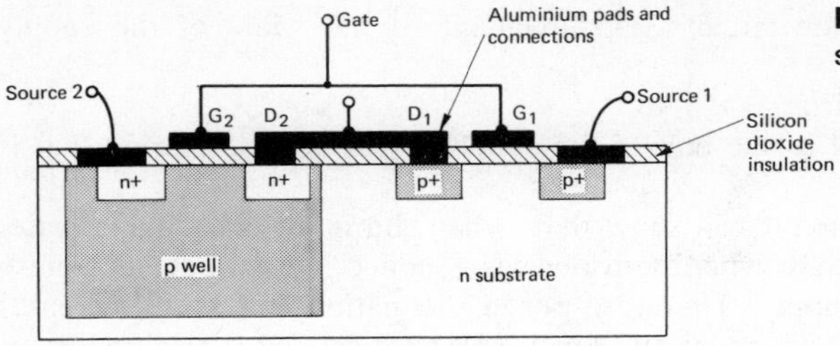

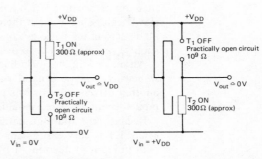

Fig. C11a Typical CMOS structure (invertor)

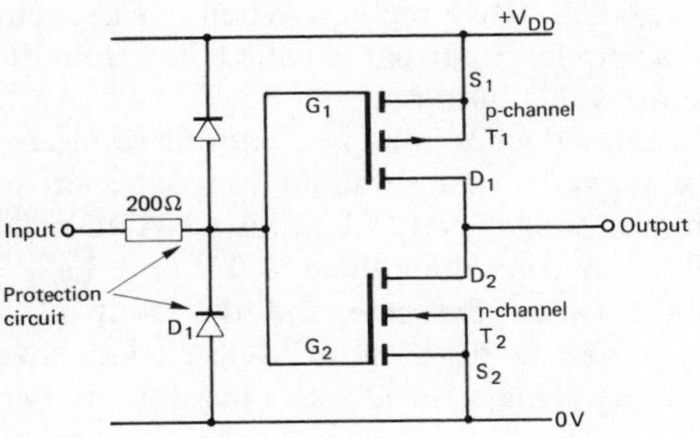

Fig. C11b CMOS invertor circuit

Fig. C11c Equivalent circuits for two input conditions

of devices is not as fast as TTL, a typical propagation delay being 35 nsec at a supply voltage of +5 V. However by using a supply of +10 V the switching speed improves to 20 nsec. One other disadvantage of CMOS is the relatively high output impedance, which means they cannot drive large capacitive loads and are more susceptible to current-injected noise.

To fully appreciate the unique features of CMOS it is useful to look at the operation of some basic gates. The structure and circuit of an *invertor* are shown in *fig. C11*. Both devices are enhancement mode MOSFETs. In this type of device there is no conducting channel between source and drain until a suitable bias voltage is applied to the gate. Then the layer beneath the gate inverts (changes from p to n for an n-channel) and conduction takes place. Consider the invertor circuit with V_{DD} applied and the input at 0 V. The n-channel MOSFET T_2 will be off, since there is zero volts between its gate and source. But the p-channel T_1 will be conducting and *on* because there is a large negative bias between its gate and source. The on-resistance of T_1 is about 300 Ω while the off-resistance of T_2 is very high at $10^9 \Omega$. The output is connected to $+V_{DD}$ via the low channel resistance of T_1.

If the input is now taken to $+V_{DD}$, the p-channel MOSFET T_1 is turned off, effectively disconnecting the output from $+V_{DD}$, and at the same time the n-channel device T_2 turns *on* connecting the output to 0 V via its conducting channel. The equivalent circuits for these two possible input states are shown in *fig. C11c*.

For CMOS gates   logic $\emptyset$ = 0 V to $0.3V_{DD}$
logic 1 = $+V_{DD}$ to $0.7V_{DD}$

From the description of operation it can be seen that

1 Since the gates of the MOSFETs are insulated from the substrate, the input impedance is extremely high ($10^{12} \Omega$ or greater). It is this high input impedance that gives CMOS such a high fan-out capacity.

2 In the static state, one device is on while the other is off. Thus the power taken from the supply is almost negligible.

3 The operation of the circuit is independent of the value of the supply voltage.

4 The output swings from $+V_{DD}$ to 0 V.

5 The input threshold is one half of the supply giving a noise margin that is typically 45% of V_{DD}.

A closer look at the circuit will show that, when the input is changing state, there must be a brief instant when both devices conduct. A small current pulse will be taken from the supply. Therefore power dissipation of CMOS increases with operating frequency and is typically 1 mW/MHz per gate. It is also important that inputs are not left open circuit, otherwise the small gate capacitance will slowly charge up and put the devices into their active regions. When this happens all devices in the package conduct and a very large current may be taken from the supply, causing the i.c. to overheat and possibly burn out.

All unused inputs, including those of unused gates in an i.c., *must be connected somewhere*. As a general rule, spare inputs to gates should be connected to another driven input or to an appropriate voltage level ($+V_{DD}$ for a NAND) and inputs to unused gates should be disabled by connecting them to 0 V or $+V_{DD}$.

Because the thin insulating region between the gate and the body of a MOSFET is very easily damaged by electrostatic discharge, CMOS circuits have built-in input protection—a typical example being a 200 Ω series resistor and two diodes as shown.

The CMOS NOR and NAND gates are simply extensions of the basic invertor. With the NAND gates (*fig. C12*) the output can only be low when both T_3 and T_4 conduct and both T_1 and T_2 are off. This condition only occurs when both inputs A and B are at logic 1 ($+V_{DD}$). The operation is more easily explained using a truth table.

The truth table for CMOS NAND, with logic $1 = V_{DD}$ and logic $\emptyset = 0$ V, is

| INPUTS | | STATE OF MOSFETs | | | | OUTPUT |
A	B	T_1	T_2	T_3	T_4	F
$\emptyset$	$\emptyset$	ON	ON	OFF	OFF	1
$\emptyset$	1	ON	OFF	OFF	ON	1
1	$\emptyset$	OFF	ON	ON	OFF	1
1	1	OFF	OFF	ON	ON	$\emptyset$

Similarly for the NOR gate:

| INPUTS | | STATE OF MOSFETs | | | | OUTPUT |
A	B	T_1	T_2	T_3	T_4	F
$\emptyset$	$\emptyset$	ON	ON	OFF	OFF	1
$\emptyset$	1	ON	OFF	OFF	ON	$\emptyset$
1	$\emptyset$	OFF	ON	ON	OFF	$\emptyset$
1	1	OFF	OFF	ON	ON	$\emptyset$

With the NOR gate (*fig. C13*) the output will go to $\emptyset$ if either input A or B is at logic 1.

Note that for clarity the protection circuits have been omitted from the diagrams. The two circuits are typical of the older A series type of CMOS. The later versions, called the B series, have two additional invertor stages to provide buffering. The B series give a sharp transfer characteristic and better drive than the A series.

● DIGITAL CIRCUIT ● ECL ● TTL

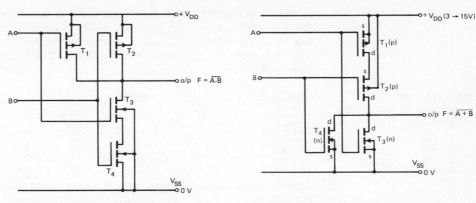

Fig. C12   CMOS NAND gate   **Fig. C13**   CMOS NOR gate

Comment (Field)

Although many of the mnemonics used for microprocessor instructions are self-explanatory, programs written in assembly language are made more intelligible by including a suitable *comment* on each line. The overall structure of the program is then made clearer, especially to other users.

The comments, usually limited to about 22 characters, are written as shown in the example, which is considered to be a portion of a program using 6809 mnemonics.

LINE NO.	LABEL	MNEMONIC OPERAND	COMMENTS
20.00	LOOP	LDX #$302F	SET POINTER TO TABLE
21.00		LDA Ø,X	GET DATA FROM TABLE
22.00		STA $E48Ø	OUTPUT TO PORT

● ASSEMBLY LANGUAGE   ● INSTRUCTION

Comparator

A comparator is any analog or digital circuit that carries out the process of comparing an input quantity against a reference level or against another input. The output signal is usually a change of state that indicates when one input exceeds or equals the other.

1   Analog types are usually formed from a high-gain differential input amplifier; for example, any i.c. op-amp (741, 531, 3130) can be used as a comparator. A simple example using a 741S op-amp is shown in *fig. C14a*, where the voltage level across a temperature sensor is compared with a reference level set by two resistors R_1 and R_2. While the temperature is low, the voltage across the thermistor will be higher than V_{ref}. The output voltage will therefore be at about $-5\,V$ (V_o^- sat). As the temperature rises, the thermistor resistance falls and a

Fig. C14a   Analog comparator using 741S op-amp

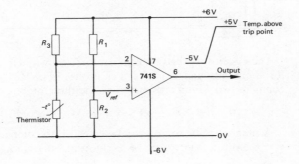

point will be reached where the voltage across it is just less than V_{ref}. Because of the very high gain of the op-amp (100 000 is typical), the output will switch rapidly to about +5 V (V_o^+ sat). The rise time of this signal will depend on the slew rate of the op-amp. After suitable shaping, the signal could be used to drive an indicator or to provide an interrupt to a microprocessor.

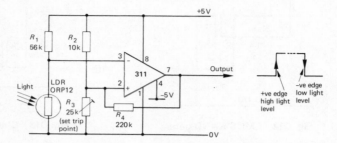

Fig. C14b Use of 311 comparator i.c. to generate an interrupt

Apart from using op-amps there are specialised i.c. comparators designed to have rapid switching action, low values of hysteresis and to give logic compatible outputs. The 311 shown in *fig. C14b* generating an interrupt or logic signal from a light sensor is one such i.c. The output can be applied directly to an interrupt line or port input of a microcomputer.

Analog comparators are used in applications covering level detection, interfaces, analog-to-digital convertors, and oscillators.

2 Digital comparators are logic circuits used to determine whether two binary numbers are equal or which has the greater magnitude.

INPUTS		OUTPUTS		
A	B	A = B	A > B	A < B
0	0	1	0	0
0	1	0	0	1
1	0	0	1	0
1	1	1	0	0

For $A = B$ $\quad F = A \cdot B + \bar{A} \cdot \bar{B}$
which is the exclusive-NOR function $F = \overline{A \oplus B}$

$$A > B \qquad F = A \cdot \bar{B}$$

$$A < B \qquad F = \bar{A} \cdot B$$

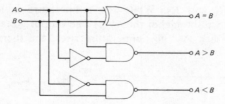

Fig. C15 Digital comparator for 2 bits

The circuit for a two-bit comparator is shown in *fig. C15*. This can be extended for more bits and a typical i.c. is the TTL 7485 4-bit comparator. This can compare two 4-bit words and gives the three output signals for

$$A = B \qquad A > B \qquad A < B$$

A number of these i.c.s can be cascaded to compare words of longer length.

● COMPARE INSTRUCTION   ● INTERRUPT   ● OPERATIONAL AMPLIFIER

COMPARE Instruction (CP or CMP)

This logic instruction has uses in decisions and branches within programs. It causes a comparison to be made between the contents of the processor's accumulator and another register, or between the accumulator and a memory location, and sets flags according to the result. The contents of both the accumulator and the other register or location are unchanged, which allows repeated comparisons to be made. The flags normally affected are

Z   set if the result of the comparison is zero
N   set if the result is negative
C   set if a borrow is required (since the comparison process is subtraction).

Thus an instruction such as:

CPA $3F   Compare Acc. with contents of address $3F

can be followed by one of a large range of branch instruction: BNE, BMI, BLE, and so on.

The normal set of addressing modes is usually available with the compare instruction. These include Immediate, Zero Page (or Direct), Absolute (or Extended) and Indexed.

● ADDRESSING MODE   ● BRANCH INSTRUCTION   ● LOOP

Compiler

This is system software that performs the task of translating a high-level language program into a machine code program. The *compiler* checks for errors in syntax and then converts the entire HLL program into the target machine language before the program is executed (*fig. C16*). Since each line of HLL may result in several machine code instructions, the compiler is a relatively complex program which requires a large area of memory; at least 16 K bytes is usual.

● CROSS-COMPILER   ● HIGH-LEVEL LANGUAGE   ● INTERPRETER

Fig. C16   Use of a compiler

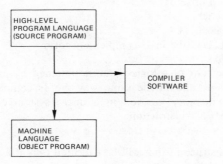

Complement

A complement, in number systems, is something that completes a number; for example in a 9s complement system the complement of a number is the value that has to be added to it to give a result of 9. Thus the 9s complement of 4 is 5. In the binary system two forms of complement exist

a) The 1s (ones) complement
b) The 2s (twos) complement

These are used in arithmetic operations and are essentially a method for representing negative numbers.

The 1s complement is obtained by simply changing all the 1s to Øs and all the Øs to 1s.

Thus the 1s complement of 1Ø11 is Ø1ØØ.

The 2s complement is obtained by changing all 1s to Øs and all Øs to 1s and then adding 1.

Thus the 2s complement of 1Ø11 is Ø1Ø1.

Note that the 2s complement form gives the true additive inverse of the number.

Example

$$5_{10} = \emptyset1\emptyset1$$

$$\frac{-5_{10} = 1\emptyset1\emptyset}{0 \quad \overline{1111}} \quad \text{in 1s complement form} \\ \text{result of addition does not} = \emptyset$$

$$5_{10} = \emptyset1\emptyset1$$

$$\frac{-5_{10} = 1\emptyset11}{0 \quad \emptyset\emptyset\emptyset\emptyset} \quad \text{in 2s complement form} \\ \text{result of addition} = \emptyset \\ \text{(carry is ignored)}$$

Therefore the 2s complement method is preferred since the result of a subtraction, by adding the 2s complement of the subtrahend, will give the correct result.

The 2s complement form is used for representing negative offsets in machine code programs when relative addressing is used, as in branch instructions. Suppose a branch-back is required as in the following program segment:

	ASSEMBLY LANGUAGE		ADDRESS	HEX. CODE
	LDX	#$30F$\emptyset$	$\emptyset\emptyset80$	CE 3$\emptyset$ F$\emptyset$
LOOP	LDA	$8\emptyset$,X	$\emptyset\emptyset83$	A6 $\emptyset\emptyset$
	INX		$\emptyset\emptyset85$	$\emptyset8$
	CMP	#$$\emptyset4$	$\emptyset\emptyset86$	81 $\emptyset4$
	BNE	LOOP	$\emptyset\emptyset88$	26 F9

2s complement off-set

The required offset is
7 places back

$$+ 7_{10} = \emptyset\emptyset\emptyset\emptyset\emptyset111$$
$$\therefore -7 = 11111\emptyset\emptyset1 \quad \text{in 2s complement form}$$
$$= \$F9$$

The complement of a logic signal is obtained by passing the signal through an invertor stage, and in the same way the 1s complement of the contents of a register or memory location in a micro system can be obtained by using a COMPLEMENT instruction.

● OFFSET ● TWOS COMPLEMENT ● V-FLAG

Conditional Branch (Jump)

A branch instruction that will be executed only if a certain specified condition is met.

Example

BCC OUT   Branch to OUT if the carry bit is clear

When this instruction is reached, the processor will cause a test to be made on the carry flag and if this flag is $\emptyset$ the branch will be made, otherwise the program will continue to the next instruction.

● BRANCH INSTRUCTION

Condition Code Register

This name is given to the STATUS or FLAG register by some microprocessor manufacturers [see 6800/6802]. It will contain the group of flags that are set or cleared according to the result of logic or arithmetic operations.

These flags (Z = ZERO; C = CARRY; N = NEGATIVE; V = OVERFLOW) are used mainly in conditional branching when the state of one, or a combination, of the flags is checked by the processor and a program branch is executed if the conditions are met.

● BRANCH INSTRUCTION   ● FLAG AND FLAG REGISTER

Configuring

A word used to describe the process of setting up or initialising devices such as interface adaptors, so that data lines are set as inputs or outputs and control lines are arranged to carry out appropriate handshake procedures.

● ASYNCHRONOUS COMMUNICATIONS INTERFACE ADAPTOR ● PERIPHERAL INTERFACE ADAPTOR

Constant-current Generator

A standard electronic circuit used, as its name implies, to supply a fixed value of current irrespective (within defined limits) of changes in its output voltage (*fig. C17a*).

One of the many uses of this circuit is in interfacing sensors such as thermistors and photoconductive cells to a micro system. With these types of sensor the resistance of the device changes with the input quantity, and by passing a fixed current through the sensor these changes of resistance can be converted into voltage signals suitable for input to an ADC.

Fig. C17 Constant-current generator

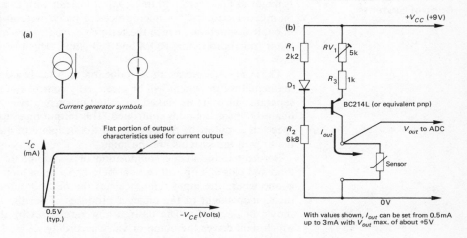

A typical circuit example (*fig. C17b*) uses the almost flat output characteristics of a transistor in common emitter mode to provide the constant current and high value of output resistance. The base voltage is set by the potential divider R_1R_2 and this then gives a fixed value of voltage across RV_1 and R_3. The emitter current, which is almost identical to the collector current in a modern high gain transistor, is then given by:

$$I_E = \frac{V_{CC} - V_E}{RV_1 + R_3}$$

Adjusting RV_1 sets the value of I_{out}.

Diode D_1 is included in the base circuit to compensate for changes in V_{BE} of the transistor with temperature.

● INTERFACE CIRCUITS ● SENSOR

Control Bus

The connections to and from a microprocessor can be divided into three groups:
  a) The Address bus
  b) The Data bus
  c) The Control bus

The *control bus* consists of a variety of important control and timing signals used between the microprocessor and the other devices which make up the system. These control lines can be further subdivided into:

Data transfer—such as R/$\overline{\text{W}}$ (read/write)
Bus state lines—Halt, Bus available
Interrupts—IRQ (interrupt request)
NMI (non-maskable interrupt)

The actual composition of the control bus varies from processor to processor and therefore the section dealing with the specific processor should be consulted.

● BUS ● MICROPROCESSOR

Control Character (Control Word)

1 A *character* in a program or within data used by the program that initiates a modification or halt.

2 A *control word* is a group of bits output from a microcomputer used to control the operation of a peripheral. Simple commands such as CLEAR, GO, READ, etc. can then be used to control a device that can only perform a limited set of operations.

Control System

It might at first seem odd that *control* is dealt with as a topic in a reference book on microelectronics, but microprocessor-based systems are being used extensively in control situations, hence the term *dedicated controller* to describe a microcomputer (microprocessor, ROM and I/O chips) which is used solely for one control task.

These notes serve as an introduction to what is a complicated subject and no mathematical treatment will be given. Any control system is essentially a group of separate sub-systems linked together in such a way that a process or output quantity of some kind is controlled. This output quantity might be liquid flow, the speed of a motor, or the position of the bedplate of a machine; but the essential features of the systems are the same.

Before looking at the composition of a system, the difference between open loop and closed loop will be considered. An **open loop system** (analog or digital) is one where the input reference sets the desired output level, but the output is then independent of the effect it produces. Take the liquid flow control system shown in *fig. C18a*. The desired flow rate is set by the input to the controller which then drives the pump or valve accordingly.

Fig. C18a Open loop control

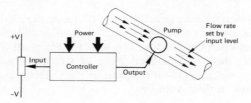

Fig. C18b Closed loop control

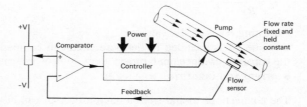

If, however, the liquid flow falls for some reason, say an increase in viscosity, the open loop system is unable to adjust the drive to the pump in order to compensate. When a flow rate transducer is introduced as in *fig. C18b*, it is possible to feed a signal proportional to output flow rate back for comparison with the input value. The error can then be used to adjust, via the controller, the drive to the pump. The introduction of the feedback connection gives **closed loop control**. These error-actuated systems are more complex than open loop and are in most cases more accurate, but they can suffer from instability problems. This is because the high gain required for fast response and good accuracy can make the system tend to overshoot or even oscillate about a desired position when a rapidly changing input is applied. Most closed loop systems therefore require stabilising networks of some kind.

Fig. C19a Analog position control system (servomechanism)

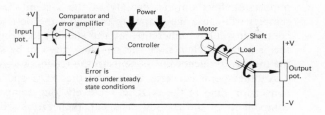

Fig. C19b Analog controller: example of a regulator system

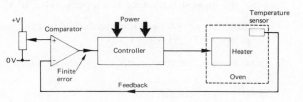

Fig. C19c Digital regulator

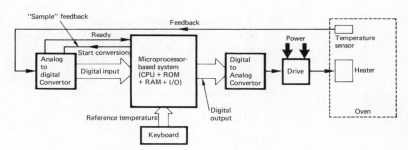

Closed loop control systems can be divided into many categories but the major divisions are between *servomechanisms* and *regulators*. A servo is any positioning control system in which, when the output is aligned correctly with the desired input, the steady state error is zero. An analog servo system is shown in *fig. C19a*.

A regulator is any form of controller where the output is some quantity that has to be maintained at a set value, for example the speed of a motor, the heat output from an oven, or flow rate in a pipe. In a regulator, a finite steady state error must exist in order to provide an input to the controller (see *fig. C19b*).

All forms of open and closed loop control systems can be created using a microprocessor as the controller. Such systems are usually more complicated than the analog form but they offer several distinct advantages. These are basically due to the micro's ability to store, process and manipulate data easily; it gives a digital system great flexibility over its actions; and the system can then be as versatile as the program demands. A digital version of *C19b*, the oven temperature regulator, is shown in *C19c*. The required temperature can be read from an input device such as a keyboard or it could be stored within the program. The output from the temperature transducer (assumed analog) must be converted into a suitable digital word via the ADC. This digital word, proportional to the actual temperature of the oven, can be compared with the reference word by the program, and a digital output dependent on the result of this comparison will be used via a DAC and interface circuit to adjust the power applied to the heater. This arrangement allows subtle automatic control of the oven's temperature.

One difference which is apparent between this digital controller and the analog form is that the microprocessor-based system has to sample the signal from the transducer. Thus, for the time between samples, the digital system switches from closed loop to open loop. The rate at which sampling is carried out will have an important effect on the stability of the system. Too long a period between samples will cause the output to overshoot the desired value. Any direct digital controller will have inherently inferior stability to an analog system. In most cases this is not a problem since the sampling rate can be set to be much higher than the highest frequency components of the feedback signal.

Another point concerns the use of the ADC and its conversion time. If the conversion time of the ADC is relatively long compared to the high frequency components of the transducer signal, then errors will occur in the conversion. Suppose the highest frequency has a peak value of V_p, then

$$1\,\text{LSB} = 2V_p/2^n \quad \text{where } n = \text{number of bits in the convertor}$$
$$\therefore \quad \text{an error of } 0.5\,\text{LSB} = V_p/2^n$$

If a sine wave is assumed, then $V = V_p \sin \omega t$ which has a rate of change of

$$r = \frac{dv}{dt} = \omega V_p \cos \omega t$$

This is a maximum value when $\cos \omega t = 1$.

$\therefore$ Maximum rate of change of feedback signal $= \omega V_p$

To avoid errors greater than $0.5\,\text{LSB}$,

$$rt < V_p/2^n$$

where t is the conversion time of the ADC

$$t \leqslant V_p/r2^n$$

$$t \leqslant \frac{1}{2^n \omega}$$

Put another way, this means the maximum frequency that can be followed by an ADC of n bits with a conversion time of t sec is

$$f_{max} = \frac{1}{2\pi t 2^n}$$

Suppose we have an 8-bit convertor with a conversion time of 0.5 msec, then the maximum frequency is

$$f_{max} = \frac{1}{2\pi \times 500 \times 10^{-6} \times 256} = 1.25\,\text{Hz}$$

If higher-frequency components, i.e. more rapid changes in output, are to be encountered, then either a faster ADC must be used or the analog signal from the sensor must be held constant during the conversion using a sample-and-hold circuit.

Assuming the sampling period (the time to carry out the conversion) is small compared to the sampling rate, the minimum sampling frequency is given by SHANNON's SAMPLING THEOREM and is twice the highest frequency component of the transducer signal. In practice the sampling rate will be set much higher than this to avoid possible instability.

For a closed loop system to have good accuracy and rapid settling time it is necessary to have high gain. Because of the negative feedback this high loop gain can, at some frequency, give positive feedback, leading to a loss of stability or even oscillations. Apart from electronic components causing phase shifts, there will be elements within the system that store energy (the heater in the oven or a revolving mass), which also represent lag networks. The classical methods of stabilising a system are to feed back a signal proportional to the rate at which the output is changing, and to mix this with the error signal to give a composite signal that retards the controller if the output changes too rapidly. Such methods are called VELOCITY FEEDBACK or OUTPUT DERIVATIVE FEEDBACK.

Methods like those above can also be used with the direct digital control using software techniques. The software could detect rapid changes in the output, compute the rate of change, and apply corrective action. It is also possible for the digital system to increase the sampling rate when a point of balance between required and actual output is being approached so that fine control is achieved and overshoot minimised.

● ANALOG-TO-DIGITAL CONVERTOR ● CLOSED LOOP ● DEDICATED CONTROLLER ● SAMPLE AND HOLD ● SENSOR ● STEPPER MOTOR

Convertor

This is a unit that takes an input signal in one coded form and outputs the equivalent value in another code. The main types of convertor used in microelectronic systems are *analog-to-digital* (ADC) and *digital-to-analog* (DAC). The number of bits used in the convertor determines the resolution, but high resolution does not necessarily imply high accuracy, for a convertor with a large number of bits may still have errors. These include:

Non-linearity   Offset error   Gain error

Fig. C20 Resolution for bits used in a convertor

Word length in bits (n)	Maximum number of possible combinations (2^n)	Decimal digits	Equivalent accuracy or resolution of least significant bit	
			percent	ppm
1	2	1	50.	500 000.
2	4	1	25.	250 000.
3	8	1	12.5	125 000.
4	16	2	6.25	62 500.
5	32	2	3.125	31 250.
6	64	2	1.562 5	15 625.
7	128	3	0.781 25	7 812.5
8	256	3	0.390 625	3 906.25
9	512	3	0.195 313	1 953.13
10	1 024	4	0.097 656	976.56
11	2 048	4	0.048 828	488.28
12	4 096	4	0.024 414	244.14
13	8 192	4	0.012 207	122.07
14	16 384	5	0.006 104	61.04
15	32 768	5	0.003 052	30.52
16	65 536	5	0.001 526	15.26
17	131 072	6	0.000 763	7.63
18	262 144	6	0.000 381	3.81
19	524 288	6	0.000 191	1.91
20	1 048 576	7	0.000 095	0.95
21	2 097 152	7	0.000 048	0.48
22	4 194 304	7	0.000 024	0.24
23	8 388 608	7	0.000 012	0.12
24	16 777 216	8	0.000 006	0.06

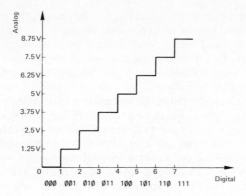

Fig. C21 Transfer characteristic of a convertor

Fig. C20 shows the value of resolution obtained for the number of bits used in a conversion. As a simple example consider a 3-bit convertor (A-to-D or D-to-A). The digital word of 3 bits can range from ØØØ up to 111 which gives 8 possible analog levels and a resolution of 12.5%. If the full-scale value of the analog signal is 8.75 V, each discrete step of the analog signal involved in the conversion will be separated from the next by 1.25 V. This is shown in the transfer characteristics in *fig. C21*. The 3-bit conversion can be expressed as a table:

| DIGITAL SIGNAL | | | ANALOG SIGNAL |
| MSB | | LSB | |
b2	b1	bØ	V
Ø	Ø	Ø	0
Ø	Ø	1	1.25
Ø	1	Ø	2.5
Ø	1	1	3.75
1	Ø	Ø	5
1	Ø	1	6.25
1	1	Ø	7.5
1	1	1	8.75

An 8-bit convertor on the other hand will have 256 possible states ($2^8 = 256$) and the resolution of the LSB, for a full-scale output of 10 V, is only 39 mV. When a fairly faithful conversion between analog to digital (and vice versa) is required, a large number of bits must be used.

● ANALOG-TO-DIGITAL CONVERTOR   ● DIGITAL-TO-ANALOG CONVERTOR

Counter

By linking bistables together so that they change state in a predetermined sequence, an electronic counter is formed. The sequence is called the *code* and the total number of different states is called the *modulo* of the counter.

1 The simplest of circuits, called **"ripple-through" counters** (*fig. C22*), are made up using either D or J-K bistables with each bistable connected so that it divides its input by two. For the D, this means connecting the $\bar{Q}$ output back to the D input and for the J-K it is necessary to connect both *J* and *K* to logic 1. The input is then applied to the clock. When several of these basic divide-by-two circuits are linked up we can make a ÷4, ÷8, ÷16 and so on. The only problem with this **asynchronous** type of counter is that a ripple-through delay builds up. In a ÷16 arrangement, as the counter overflows on the 16th input pulse the negative edge that appears at the output of the 4th bistable is delayed from the input by four propagation delay periods (see *fig. C22*).

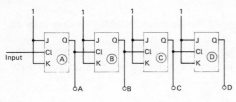

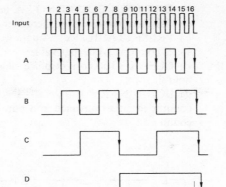

Dec.i/p	D	C	B	A
0	0	0	0	0
1	0	0	0	1
2	0	0	1	0
3	0	0	1	1
4	0	1	0	0
5	0	1	0	1
6	0	1	1	0
7	0	1	1	1
8	1	0	0	0
9	1	0	0	1
10	1	0	1	0
11	1	0	1	1
12	1	1	0	0
13	1	1	0	1
14	1	1	1	0
15	1	1	1	1
16	0	0	0	0

Fig. C23 Synchronous
divide-by-16 counter

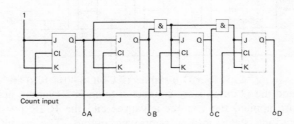

2 Synchronous counters (*fig. C23*) overcome the problem of cumulative delay by ensuring that, when bistables have to change state, they all change state at the same instant. In a synchronous ÷16 (8421) binary counter, the *Q* output of each bistable is connected to the *J* and *K* inputs of the next and so on, and all clock inputs are connected together. Extra AND gates are required to ensure that the counter changes state in the required sequence. In this way bistable *C* can only change state when both bistables *A* and *B* are at logic 1; this occurs after the 4th input pulse. Similarly, bistable *D* can only change state after the 8th input pulse because this is the first time that the *Q* outputs of bistables *A*, *B* and *C* are at logic 1. Synchronous counters allow dividers of large numbers to be created without generating long delays and are less prone to produce "glitches" when the circuit is decoded.

3 The count sequence of a pure binary counter can be altered by feedback techniques to give counters of other numbers, 3, 5, 7, 9, 10, etc. A few examples are given in *fig. C24*. Counters can be very useful in interfacing circuits, for **digital-to-analog convertors** for instance, and a simple low-cost example follows. A glance at the TTL or CMOS family of ICs will also show that there are several counter ICs available, most provided with useful extra facilities such as

Fig. C24 Synchronous
counters

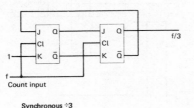

Synchronous ÷3

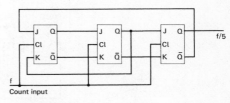

Synchronous ÷5

a) UP/DOWN COUNTING   A logic level on one pin controls the direction so that the counter either increments or decrements.

b) PRESETTABILITY   A data word can be loaded into the counter so that it starts counting from that value.

c) CLEAR   The correct pulse clears all the internal bistables so that they all hold ∅.

d) BCD/BINARY COUNT   A logic level applied to this pin causes the counter to either advance in a pure binary sequence or act as a decade (÷10) counter.

Fig. C25   Divide-by-16 counter circuit using four D bistables

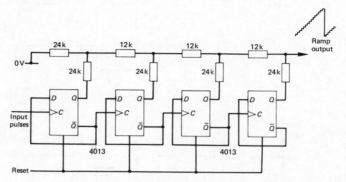

In *fig. C25*, four D bistables (2 CMOS 4013 ICs) are wired up as a ÷16 counter and the *Q* outputs are connected to an R-2R ladder network. When clock pulses are applied the counter advances and the R-2R resistor network converts the various states into a ramp-type output. The circuit is therefore a type of digital-to-analog convertor. If, for example, only one or two spare output ports from the micro system are available, it is possible to make a type of serial digital-to-analog convertor from this circuit. Initially the counter would be cleared by pulsing the reset line and then a fixed number of pulses would be directed to the counter from the main output port. The number of pulses from the micro under software-controlled output would be equivalent to the desired analog level. The pulses would be counted and the state of the counter decoded by the R-2R ladder network to give the analog output voltage.

Fig. C26   A basic analog-to-digital convertor

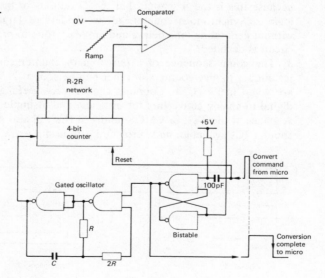

The basic circuit of *fig. C26* can also form the heart of an analog-to-digital convertor. For this, in addition to the counter and R-2R network, a comparator and a few CMOS gates will be needed. The clock pulses generated by the CMOS gated oscillator are applied to the counter just after the trailing edge of the reset pulse. The ramp output is compared with the analog input and, when the ramp just exceeds the analog value, the comparator output switches low and resets the control bistable to stop the clock. The total count achieved by the counter (4 bits in this case) will then be equivalent to the analog input.

● ANALOG-TO-DIGITAL CONVERTOR ● BISTABLE

Cross-Assembler

This is a program used on a computer to produce machine code output for another computer.

● ASSEMBLER

Cross-Compiler

A compiler converts high-level language programs into machine code and a cross-compiler is simply a compiler program run on one computer to produce machine code for another computer.

● COMPILER

Crosstalk

This refers to any unwanted signals imposed on a conductor by the signals travelling along an adjacent conductor. The level of crosstalk induced in the adjacent conductor (or communication channel) is a function of both the electrical coupling existing between the pair and the frequency components of the signal. Long runs of closely spaced conductors will have relatively high values of coupling capacitance and a greater amount of crosstalk. The unwanted signal level will also increase with frequency, so any ringing of the pulses that make up the valid signal will also increase crosstalk. The solution is to use a careful layout that avoids long runs of signal leads, to correctly terminate signal paths (this reduces reflection and ringing), and to provide a ground plane for the system. Unless the crosstalk is confined to a level within the noise margin of the logic being used, false switching will occur.

Reflections from unterminated lines will not be serious if the signal delay is much less than the signal rise and fall times. The maximum length for unterminated lines is generally:

$$l_{max} = \frac{tv}{k}$$

where t = rise time
v = velocity of propagation
k = an empirical constant which depends on the type of conductor.

For p.c.b. tracks $v = 2 \times 10^8$ m/sec
and typically $k = 4$.
Then for TTL, where $t = 10$ nsec, $l_{max} \simeq 50$ cm.

Current Loop

This is a serial link used to interface a microcomputer to peripherals such as a teleprinter.

Logic Ø is represented by zero current and logic 1 is represented by 20 mA. Connections are usually provided using standard 25-pin connectors as for the RS-232C, and in many cases the RS-232C and the 20 mA loop are provided in the same socket.

Typical connections are:

Pin connection at controller
1   Protective earth
18 Received data (+ve)
19 Received data (−ve)
21 Transmit data (+ve)
25 Transmit data (−ve)

● BUS SYSTEMS

Cycle Stealing

A method of DMA (Direct Memory Access) where a microprocessor's machine cycle is used to allow an external device to read or write to memory. Basically the DMA transfers occur during part of the instruction fetch cycle when the microprocessor is not accessing the memory. The clock signals are stretched during the DMA one-byte transfers, but the microprocessor is not completely halted.

● DIRECT MEMORY ACCESS

Daisy Chain Connection

A method in which peripheral devices are linked in series to a CPU, and in particular where interrupts are serviced from a number of series-linked peripherals (*fig. D1*) as an alternative to software polling. The peripherals are linked in priority order with the fastest device first in the chain and the slowest last. When an interrupt (request for service) is sent from any device, the interrupt

Fig. D1 Daisy chain connection

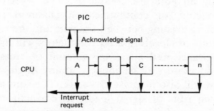

A is the fastest peripheral device
n is the slowest peripheral device

acknowledge signal is sent down the chain. The interrupt flag of each device is tested in turn and, if clear, the device controller passes the interrupt acknowledge on to the next device until the flag that is set is found. The interrupt service routine is then carried out. The method is more suitable for systems using a large number of peripherals where the additional hardware of a programmable interrupt controller (PIC) is then cost effective.

● INTERRUPT   ● POLLING

Darlington

A connection used in bipolar transistors to give a composite transistor pair with a high value of current gain and high input impedance (*fig. D2*). The two transistors are connected as cascaded emitter followers but the connection is also very useful in the common emitter mode. In this case the darlington is used as a switch. Because the overall current gain of the two transistors may be higher than 1000, it is possible for an input current of only 1 mA to switch 1 A at the output collectors.

The overall current gain is

$$A_i = 1 + h_{fe1} + h_{fe2} + (h_{fe1} \cdot h_{fe2})$$

or $A_i \simeq h_{fe1} \cdot h_{fe2}$

since $h_{fe1} \cdot h_{fe2} \gg 1 + h_{fe1} + h_{fe2}$

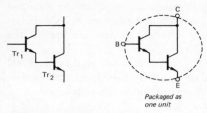

Fig. D2a The Darlington circuit

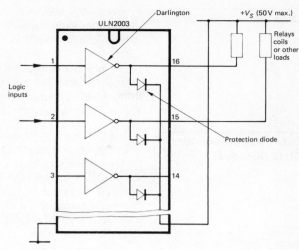

Fig. D2b Darlington i.c. driver to relays

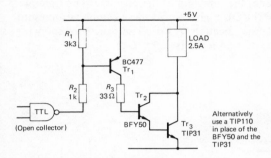

Alternatively use a TIP110 in place of the BFY50 and the TIP31

Fig. D3 TTL to high current using Darlington as interface

Many manufacturers package the circuit as a single discrete component with three leads (TIP110 NPN, TIP115 PNP for example) or several darlington devices are included in one i.c. (ULN2003, see *fig. D2*). Such devices and i.c.s have obvious applications in interfacing.

An example is shown in *fig. D3* showing how a darlington can interface from a TTL output or micro port to a 2.5 A load. When the TTL gate output is high, there is no base current taken from Tr_1 and this transistor is off. The darlington formed by Tr_2 and Tr_3 will also be off since the base drive to Tr_2 is derived from the collector of Tr_1. When the TTL output switches low (logic Ø), Tr_1 is turned on and passes current to the darlington forcing it to switch on also. To set up the required load current of 2.5 A, the emitter current of Tr_2 is about 250 mA and the collector current of Tr_1 is 8 mA. Consequently the TTL gate output or micro port has only to sink about 2 mA to ensure that the load is fully on.

● INTERFACE CIRCUITS

Data

A general term used for all the values operated on by a computer but not the program instructions or addresses. Data can consist of numbers, letters or symbols which are used to denote a value or condition. Data conveys information.

Two examples

1 LDX #$2EØ4   Load X reg. with data 2EØ4
   LDX = instruction (operator)
   $2EØ4 = data (operand)
2 LDA $3F2Ø   Load Acc. with data held at address $3F2Ø
   LDA = instruction
   $3F2Ø = address (data location)

● ADDRESSING MODE   ● INSTRUCTION

Data Bus

A group of conductors, usually 8 or 16 parallel tracks, along which the data and instructions within a micro system are moved as parallel binary words. A data bus is bidirectional and links all the main chips of a system to the data lines of the CPU.

The read/write line and other timing and control signals generated by the CPU normally control the direction in which the data flows by enabling tri-state buffers in the CPU, a memory chip or an I/O chip depending upon the instruction.

● BUS ● FETCH-EXECUTE CYCLE ● INSTRUCTION

Data Control Register (Data Direction)

A register used in programmable interface adaptor i.c.s to set up the ports as either inputs or outputs. During initialisation, this register would be loaded with a binary pattern which then determines the direction of the port line. For example, the 6821 PIA has two DATA CONTROL registers and these can be written into in exactly the same way as any memory location. A logic 1 sets the corresponding line as an output and a logic Ø sets it as an input (see *fig. D4*).

● PERIPHERAL INTERFACE ADAPTOR

Fig. D4 Setting the state of the peripheral data register

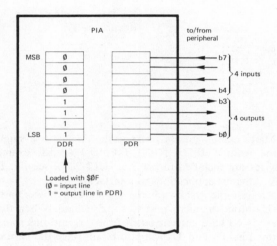

Data Transfer Instruction

The group of instructions within the instruction set of a microprocessor which are solely concerned with the movement of data.

Examples

Memory to accumulator (M → A)   Load accumulator
   LDA A   [6800]
   LDA   [Z80; 6502]
Accumulator to memory (A → M)   Store accumulator
   STA A   [6800]
   STA   [6502]
   LD (nn), A   [Z80]
where (nn) is the contents of memory address.

● INSTRUCTION ● INSTRUCTION SET

Dead Band (Dead Zone)

Used in both digital and analog control systems to describe the region in a transfer characteristic where a range of input values produces no change at the output (*fig. D5*).

● CONTROL SYSTEM

Fig. D5 Dead zone

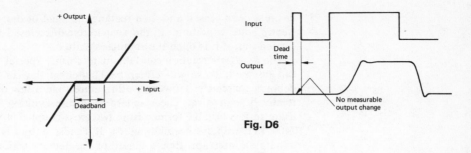

Fig. D6

Dead Time

The time interval in which a defined pulse input to a control system produces no measurable output from that system (*fig. D6*).

● CONTROL SYSTEM

Debounce

When a micro is used for control, many of its input signals will be from mechanical switches or contacts. These will be single push-button switches, keypads or keyboards, reed switches used for limit and position sensing, or thumbwheel switches for setting-up purposes. The problem with all these switches (apart from special types such as those with mercury wetted contacts) is that they are always subject to severe contact bounce. This bounce, illustrated in *fig. D7*, can take up several milliseconds as the contacts make and break before finally settling to the new position. All the variations will be treated as valid inputs to the system. Suppose a push switch is used to provide an interrupt as shown. The interrupt service routine may only last tens of microseconds and would therefore be triggered several times by one switch action unless the contact bounce is eliminated.

There are two possible solutions to this switch problem: to use either software to produce a delay or hardware to debounce the input edge to the micro. Consider the *software* approach first. The flowchart required is shown in *fig. D8* and basically consists of introducing a delay of, say, 20 msec after the switch input

Fig. D7 Contact bounce in system using a mechanical switch

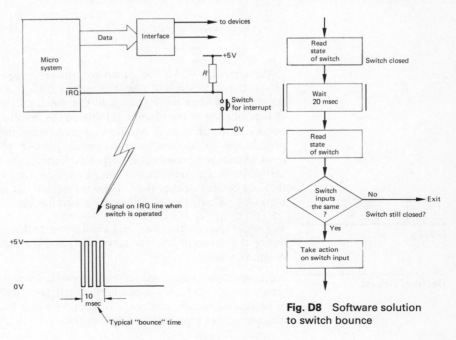

Fig. D8 Software solution to switch bounce

65

has first been sensed and then reading the state of the switch again to obtain the steady state condition. If the switch remains closed then the routine will be carried out; if it is open the routine is exitted.

The *hardware* solution can take many forms. Special "debounced" switch units can be used; these will either be Hall-effect devices or contain some built-in debounce circuitry. However, using more than a few of these types could prove relatively expensive. The standard hardware solution is to interface the switch using an R-S bistable formed from two cross-coupled NAND gates (2 gates from a 7400 TTL chip are normally used). If a pulse output is required, for example to initiate an interrupt, then a biased or momentary action changeover (single-pole double-throw) switch is necessary.

Fig. D9 Hardware solution to switch bounce using R-S bistable circuit

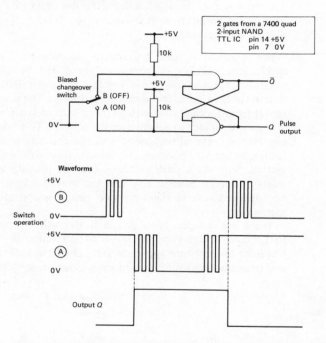

The connections for the circuit are shown in *fig. D9.* Assume the switch is biased OFF at position B. As it is moved from this position, the output of the bistable does not change state until the contact makes with position A. But the change of state of the bistable is initiated the first time A goes to logic Ø and the bounce of the contacts at A will be ignored. When the switch returns to its biased position, as the applied force is removed, B goes to logic Ø and the bistable is reset. Again any bounce at B is ignored because the bistable will respond to the first contact. The same circuit can be used to debounce latched switches—those that can be set to either A or B and will remain set until changed.

● DELAY ● INTERFACE CIRCUITS ● INTERRUPT

Debug

The technique of detecting and eliminating faults and errors which may occur during the design of software (programs) and hardware.

● BREAKPOINT

Decimal Adjust

An instruction used in many microprocessors when it is required to convert a binary result into binary coded decimal (BCD). The BCD notation is often used in arithmetic operations since it is naturally easier for humans to deal in decimal numbers rather than binary or hexadecimal.

The conversion from decimal to BCD is very straightforward, each digit of the decimal number being accorded a four-bit binary value. For example, the decimal number 396 would be written in BCD as follows:

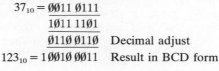

However a problem arises in the addition of BCD numbers (instructions like ADD and ADC) since invalid BCD codes can be generated. Suppose we have the addition of 86 and 37 in BCD:

$$86_{10} = 1000\ 0110 \quad \text{in BCD}$$
$$37_{10} = \underline{0011\ 0111} \quad \text{in BCD}$$
$$\underline{1011\ 1101} \quad \text{Result of addition}$$

Both the upper and lower 4 bits of this result are invalid.

The DAA instruction (Decimal Adjust Accumulator) adds 6_{10} (0110 in BCD) to each 4-bit result if an invalid code is generated and also corrects, if necessary, the state of the carry flag.

$$86_{10} = 1000\ 0110$$
$$37_{10} = \underline{0011\ 0111}$$
$$\underline{1011\ 1101}$$
$$\underline{0110\ 0110} \quad \text{Decimal adjust}$$
$$123_{10} = 1\ 0010\ 0011 \quad \text{Result in BCD form}$$

● ADD INSTRUCTION ● BINARY CODED DECIMAL ● DECIMAL MODE

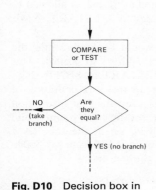

Fig. D10 Decision box in flowchart

Decimal Mode

A mode of operation used in some microprocessors to allow the device to automatically perform BCD arithmetic operations without using the decimal adjust instruction. The 6502 has for example an instruction SED (Set Decimal Mode) which sets a flag in the status register to allow corrections to be made to results automatically.

● DECIMAL ADJUST

Decision Box

A diamond-shaped flowchart symbol used to indicate where a choice in any program has to be made between two paths. A decision is often preceded by an instruction such as COMPARE or TEST which will be followed by a BRANCH instruction (see *fig. D10*).

● BRANCH INSTRUCTION ● COMPARE INSTRUCTION

Decoder

A logic circuit or combination of logic gates used to convert digital data from one form to another: for example, BCD to 7-segment code to drive a display device, binary to decimal, or address decoding.

● ADDRESS DECODING

Decrement

An instruction which reduces the content of a register or memory location by 1. For example:

Content of register *before*	1	0	1	0	0	1	1	1	= $A7

After DEC instruction	1	0	1	0	0	1	1	0	= $A6

If the register or memory location held all zeros ($00), the result after a DEC instruction will be ($FF) all ones.

● DELAY

Dedicated Controllers

In microelectronics this description refers to a microprocessor-based system that is solely used as the controller for some process or machine. A dedicated system will usually comprise a microprocessor chip, a small amount of RAM for data, some ROM or EPROM to hold the program, and input/output chips. Quite often such a system can be built up using one microcomputer chip such as the 6805 which has all the above requirements on one chip. Alternatively, a system as shown in *fig. D11* can be used. A 6802 processor, which has 128 bytes of RAM included on the chip, forms the heart of the system. A 2716 EPROM (2 K bytes) holds the program and the 6821 PIA gives 8 input lines and 8 output lines. This could be the controller for some industrial process with input data from switches and sensors taken in on port A lines and data output to control devices (motors, solenoids, etc.) via port B lines. The memory map shows that the PIA is located at address $3000 but, since address lines A_2 to A_{10} inclusive are not decoded, the overwrite is up to $37FF. Similarly the EPROM, located at $E000, is allowed to overwrite to $FFFF. This locates the vectored addresses for RESTART, NMI, SWI, and IRQ inside the EPROM itself.

The program for the machine or process control would be loaded into the EPROM via an EPROM programmer with its start address at $E000. This address must be set into the vectored address for RESTART at $E7FE (high byte) and $E7FF (low byte) during the programming. In this way operation of the RESET switch will cause the microprocessor to pick up the first instruction from $E000. The program must then initialise the PIA, set the stack pointer, and clear the IRQ mask bit (if required). The stack will be set at the top RAM address in the 6802, that is at $007F, and other locations in RAM from say $0000 to $0050 can be used for temporary data storage from the sensors.

● ADDRESS DECODING ● CONTROL SYSTEM ● PERIPHERAL INTERFACE ADAPTOR (PIA) ● VECTORED ADDRESS

Delay

There is often a need in electronic systems to delay a signal or to introduce a defined time delay between two events. There are both hardware and software approaches for this task.

1 Hardware Simple delay circuits can be made using an *RC* network with logic gates. Usually Schmitt types are preferred because of their "snap action" switching (see *fig. D12a*). If TTL gates are used, the value of *R* is limited to a maximum of about 390Ω, but with CMOS gates *R* can be a value up to several megohms. As an example, *fig. D12b* shows a TTL Schmitt gate with an *RC* delay used to debounce a normally closed switch. When the switch is opened, the capacitor charges via R_1 and R_2 and, as the voltage across the capacitor just exceeds the TTL gate threshold, the output is forced to change state. A similar arrangement is shown in *fig. D12c* using CMOS gates to generate an interrupt edge from a photocell. When the light beam is broken, the photocell resistance rises and the rising input voltage causes gate A output to switch low. The timing capacitor C_1 is now discharged via R_2, and only when the voltage across C_1 falls below V_T (the negative-going trip point) will the output of gate B switch to logic 1. A circuit like this will only generate an output change of state if the light beam is broken for longer than about 0.5 sec; shadows and sudden influctuations in light level will be ignored.

Monostable circuits, timers (555, 556 and ZN 1034) and other specialised i.c.s can also be used to generate delays. For really long delay periods a low-frequency oscillator is used, triggered by the input, to drive an *n*-stage counter. As the counter overflows on the final count, the output edge is generated. This principle is used in the ZN 1034.

● DEBOUNCE ● TIMER

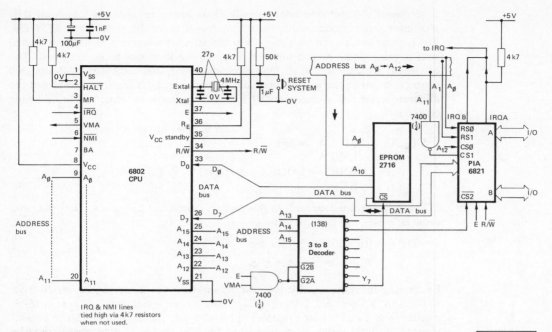

Fig. D11a Dedicated controller circuit

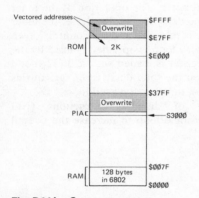

Fig. D11b System memory map

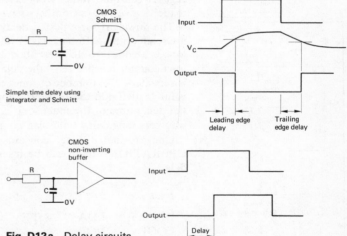

Simple time delay using integrator and Schmitt

CMOS non-inverting buffer

Fig. D12a Delay circuits

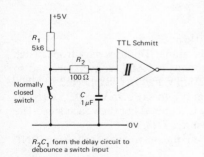

$R_2 C_1$ form the delay circuit to debounce a switch input

Fig. D12b Delay using TTL

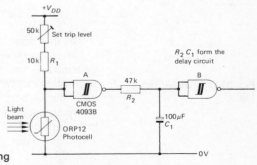

Fig. D12c Delay using CMOS

4093B quad 2 i/p NAND with Schmitt inputs

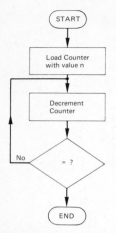

Fig. D13a Time delay flowchart

2 Software A software delay, usually a subroutine, consists of a loop formed by a counter and a conditional branch. The flowchart for this is shown in *fig. D13a*. The counter, which can be a register in the MPU or a memory location, is loaded with a value equal to the number of times the loop has to be executed. The counter is then decremented until it reaches zero, and until it does the branch instruction causes the loop to be made. Suppose an 8-bit register is used and the microprocessor has a cycle time of 1 μsec, a typical subroutine would be (using 6800 code):

Usual number of cycles

```
DELAY    LDA A    #$FF
LOOP     DEC A            2 cycles ⎫
         BNE      LOOP    4 cycles ⎭ Loop
         RTS
```

The loop takes 6 μsec and, in this case, is completed 255 times. Thus the total delay is:

$$\text{Delay} = [(6 \times 255) + 2 + 4]\ \mu\text{sec}$$
$$= 1536\ \mu\text{sec or } 1.536\ \text{msec}$$

By altering the value loaded into the accumulator the delay can be varied from 12 μsec to 1.536 msec. Longer delays can be achieved using either a 16-bit register (index register for example) or by using nested subroutines. Since a 16-bit register can hold values from zero to 65 536, the simple routine above could be made to give delays from 12 μsec up to 0.393 sec.

The flowchart for a nested delay loop is shown in *fig. D13b*. Delay multipliers are loaded into a 16-bit register and an 8-bit register. The operation of the inner loop is identical to that described and when one delay is completed, i.e. the inner loop counter reaches zero, the delay multiplier is reloaded and the counting down is repeated. The number of times the inner delay loop is operated is fixed by the value loaded into the register. Suppose the register is loaded with $20 ($32_{10}$) and the delay time of the inner loop is 0.3 sec, then the total delay is 9.6 sec. In this way very long delay times can be built up using three such nested loops.

One further point concerns the use of dummy instructions (NO OPERATION): these can be inserted into a single loop to increase the overall delay.

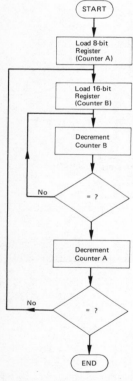

Fig. D13b Nested delay loops

Example

```
DELAY    LDA A    #$FF
LOOP     NOP              2 cycles ⎫
         DEC A            2 cycles ⎬ Loop time = 8 $\mu$sec
         BNE      LOOP    4 cycles ⎭
         RTS
```

The maximum delay possible with this is 2.046 msec.

Finally an example of the use of a delay subroutine. The uses vary from switch debouncing, waveform generation, to waiting loops for ADC conversions and so on. In this example we consider outputting a ramp via a DAC connected to 4 bits of an output port. The ramp has 16 states from 0 V to say 3.75 V in 0.25 steps. If the ramp time is 1 msec then a 62.5 μsec delay is required between each step. The program would be as shown on page 71 against *fig. D14*.

If a continuous ramp output is required then the instruction following BNE should be:

BRA   START

The subroutine delay labelled WAIT, using accumulator B, would be in the form described earlier.

● BRANCH INSTRUCTION   ● LOOP

Fig. D14 Use of delay subroutine in generating a ramp output via a DAC

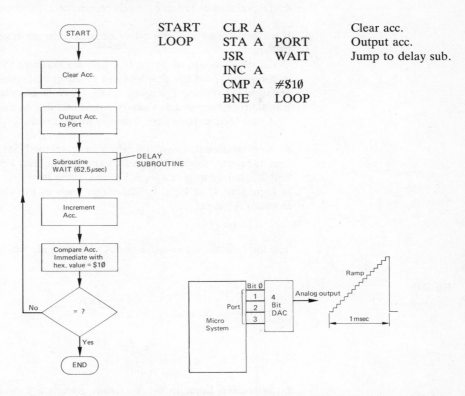

```
START   CLR A              Clear acc.
LOOP    STA A   PORT       Output acc.
        JSR     WAIT       Jump to delay sub.
        INC A
        CMP A   #$10
        BNE     LOOP
```

Digit

Any one of the ten Arabic numerals Ø to 9. A binary digit or BIT can have values of Ø or 1 only.

Digits are grouped to form data, but note that a digit is not the same as a character. Take the number 2622; this has four digits but only two characters.

● BIT   ● CHARACTER   ● DATA

Digital Circuit

Circuits, usually microelectronic, which use, process, or depend for their operation on digital signals. These digital signals are binary having two possible states which are

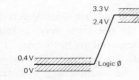

Fig. D15 TTL logic levels

Ø (low state)   or   1 (high state)

This assumes *positive logic* convention. Digital microelectronic circuits are built up using perhaps tens of thousand of two-state electronic switches. Such a switch is either ON or OFF and gives either a LOW or HIGH state output. The low state for a positive logic system will be near zero volts and the high state will be a few volts positive. Typical values for TTL gates are between 0 V to +0.4 V for the low state and between +2.4 V to +3.3 V for the high state (*fig. D15*). Other logic families may have differently defined levels but what is important in digital systems is that these levels are within specified limits.

Some of the important advantages of digital systems in comparison to analog are:

1 They are less susceptible to noise and interference signals.
2 A switch is either on or off and there is then less uncertainty about output.
3 Digital data can be easily stored without degradation.
4 Digital signals are more easily transmitted, processed and manipulated.

If a digital pulse is distorted or degraded during transmission it can readily be reshaped.

The disadvantage of digital-type systems in comparison to analog is the increase in complexity, but the development of integrated circuit technology removes this apparent weakness. By using VLSI (very large scale integration) more than 100 000 transistor switches can be fabricated in one chip.

Digital logic circuits have basically three forms:

1 Combinational Logic in which a combined set of input conditions are simultaneously required to give a particular output. For example, suppose a logic unit is required to give a logic 1 output when its inputs *ABCD* are *A* and *B* and *C* at logic 1 or *D* at logic 1. Statements such as this are best written down using Boolean Algebra:

$$F = A \cdot B \cdot C + D$$

The logic circuit is therefore one AND gate followed by an OR gate (*fig. D16*).

Fig. D16

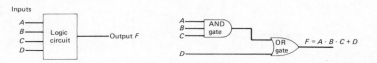

2 Sequential Logic in which circuits possess a memory and give an output, in response to an input, that is dependent upon the circuit's previous state. Typical examples of sequential logic circuits are counters and shift registers; and the basic building block is the bistable.

3 Program Controlled Logic combines all the features of the previous two with the powerful facility of preprogrammed control. The microprocessor and micro-computer are typical of this form of logic. The circuits are very complex but the system that results is relatively uncomplicated. The program capability gives the system great flexibility over its actions since a larger number of instructions such as OR, ADD, COMPARE, SHIFT and so on can be used to manipulate the internal logic circuits.

Apart from switch contacts the inputs to digital logic units are usually derived from an analog source, i.e. a sensor of some kind. In the same way, outputs (unless simple ON/OFF control is used) are often required to be analog (i.e. continuous over a defined range) so that smooth control is possible. This means that convertors, ADC on the input and DAC on the output, are essential. Suppose the temperature inside an oven has to be controlled. The output from the temperature sensor, perhaps a thermocouple, is converted into a digital word by the analog-to-digital convertor. For an 8-bit system the weighting for various temperatures might be as follows:

    20°C   00000010   or $02
    800°C   10000000   or $80
    670°C   01100111   or $67

The digital input could be stored, displayed, compared with a reference value and thereby used to generate a signal from the digital system to control the heat output to the oven. The system will be complex but is capable of very subtle control of the oven.

● CMOS   ● CONTROL SYSTEM   ● ECL   ● TTL

Digital-to-Analog Convertor (DAC)

The essential link between a digital system and output devices which require an analog drive. *Fig. D17* shows the block diagram and part of the transfer characteristic for a 3-bit DAC.

Fig. D17   Principle of digital-to-analog conversion

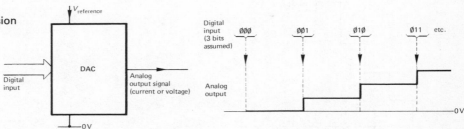

The principle of a DAC is that, when a digital input is applied, the analog output, which may be a current or voltage, takes a value according to the weight of the digital input. This is usually called a multiplying digital-to-analog convertor because it gives a way of obtaining the continuous multiplication of the digital input value; the product being represented by the varying analog output.

If a unipolar voltage output and normal binary coding for the digital input are assumed, then the transfer function of a DAC can be written using an equation. For the example in *fig. D17* the equation will be

$$V_{out} = V_{ref} \cdot \left(\frac{B_2}{2} + \frac{B_1}{4} + \frac{B_\emptyset}{8} \right)$$

where B_2 is the most significant bit (MSB) and $B_\emptyset$ is the least significant bit (LSB). A general equation takes the form

$$V_{out} = V_{ref} \cdot \left(\frac{B_{(n-1)}}{2} + \frac{B_{(n-2)}}{4} + \frac{B_{(n-3)}}{8} + \ldots + \frac{B_\emptyset}{2^n} \right)$$

where n = the number of bits used in the convertor.

Various errors can occur in a DAC. **Errors**, however small, will arise because of the mismatch of resistors and because the electronic switches inside the DAC will not have zero "on" resistance. As shown in *fig. D17*, as the digital input code to the DAC is increased by one LSB at a time, the analog output should also increase uniformly giving a "staircase" type waveform. As long as the output does increase in this manner, the DAC is said to be monotonic. Errors can, of course, force the output to be non-monotonic. This could happen if the working temperature increased beyond the specification limits. *Fig. D18* illustrates a non-monotonic DAC, where the analog output for the digital input code 1$\emptyset$1 falls instead of rising. This example is an obvious case of a nonlinear transfer function.

For a DAC, **nonlinearity** is defined as the maximum amount by which any point on the transfer characteristic deviates from the ideal straight line. Nonlinearity is usually expressed as a fraction of an LSB. Typically, the value is $\pm\frac{1}{2}$LSB and a nonlinearity of this size will mean that the DAC remains monotonic. Another type of nonlinearity that can occur, called differential nonlinearity, is an error between the value or height of any one of the analog step outputs compared to the others.

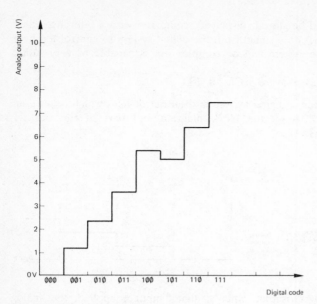

Fig. D18 Non-monotonic response

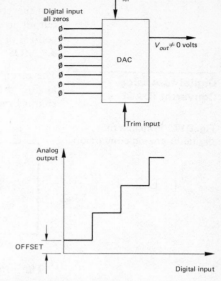

Fig. D19 Offset error in a DAC

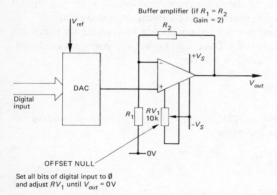

Fig. D20 Removal of offset error

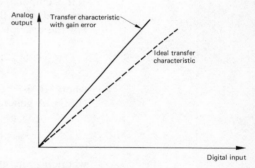

Fig. D21 Gain error in a DAC

Apart from nonlinearity two other errors occur:

1 Offset error: the small value of output voltage (or current) which appears at the output when all the DAC digital inputs are at logic Ø (*fig. D19*). This can be readily trimmed out by a simple circuit modification (*fig. D20*).

2 Gain error: caused primarily by a change in the reference voltage; this is the difference between the slope of the actual transfer characteristic and the ideal (*fig. D21*).

The parameter used as a measure of the speed of a DAC is *settling time*: the value specifying the time taken for the analog output to settle within $\pm\frac{1}{2}$LSB following a change in the digital input code. The worst-case change is when all the bits switch from 1 to Ø (1111 to ØØØØ or vice versa for a 4-bit DAC). A typical settling time is 1 μs.

Practical DACs

The simplest method of building a DAC is to use a **weighted-resistor network**, a summing amplifier, and a set of electronic switches (*fig. D22*). Each of the resistors has to be weighted in value in a binary sequence, i.e. R, 2R, 4R, 8R, etc.

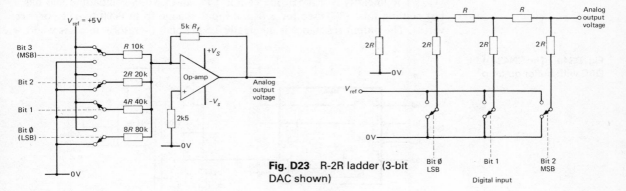

Fig. D23 R-2R ladder (3-bit DAC shown)

Fig. D22 Four-bit DAC using a binary weighted network (shown with the input set to 1010)

The digital word to be converted is used to operate the electronic switches to connect these resistors to V_{ref} if the bit is 1 and to 0 V if the bit is 0. Suppose the digital input for the 4-bit DAC example is 1010; then switches 1 and 3 are operated to connect two of the resistors to the 5 V reference. The output from the summing op-amp will be

$$V_o = \frac{R_f}{R} \cdot V_{ref}(1 + \tfrac{1}{4}) = 3.125 \text{ V}$$

Similarly if the digital input changes to 0110, then

$$V_o = \frac{R_f}{R} \cdot V_{ref}(\tfrac{1}{2} + \tfrac{1}{4}) = 1.875 \text{ V}$$

and $\quad V_{FSO} = \frac{R_f}{R} \cdot V_{ref}(1 + \tfrac{1}{2} + \tfrac{1}{4} + \tfrac{1}{8}) = 4.375 \text{ V}$

The only problem with this simple circuit is that the range of resistor values required for a high resolution convertor will be quite large. For a 12-bit convertor the resistor range is more than 2000:1. To achieve good linearity, accuracy, and monotonic operation, the resistors chosen must be close tolerance and must all track together with temperature. This becomes very difficult for DACs of more than a few bits. Therefore, although this simple circuit is useful for low resolution convertors, another method of conversion is preferred.

The most commonly used system for DACs is based on the **R-2R ladder network** shown in *fig. D23*. The output voltage is generated by switching sections of the ladder to either V_{ref} or 0 V corresponding to a 1 or 0 of the digital input. The switches are electronic and are usually incorporated in the DAC IC.

There are several advantages of the R-2R ladder compared to the weighted-resistor network:

1 Only two values of resistors are used.

2 It can easily be extended to as many bits as desired.

3 The absolute value of the resistor is not important, only the ratio needs to be exact.

4 The resistor network can be fairly readily manufactured as a film network or in monolithic form. In this way the temperature characteristics of the resistors will all be very similar.

DAC Circuit Examples

1 *ZN434 (Ferranti) (fig. D24)*

This is a 4-bit DAC IC consisting of bipolar switches, an R-2R ladder, and a built-in amplifier and attenuator which provides a reference voltage of nominally $\frac{1}{2}V_{CC}$. The linearity is $\pm\frac{1}{4}$LSB; the chip is TTL and CMOS compatible and has a fast settling time (300 nsec for a digital input change from 0000 to 1111 or vice versa). The output resistance is nominally 2.5 kΩ and, therefore, in cases where a

Fig. D24*a* The ZN434 4-bit DAC with buffer op-amp

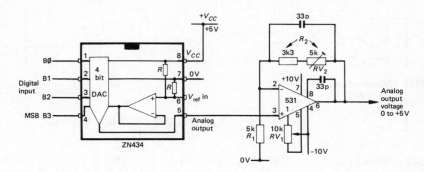

relatively heavy load is used (less than say 50 kΩ), a buffer amplifier must be used. This has the added advantage that an analog output of greater than $\frac{1}{2}V_{CC}$ is possible, and also that the small zero offset can be trimmed out, thus ensuring that the analog output for a digital input of 0000 is exactly zero volts. A 531 op-amp is used in a non-inverting configuration with offset null provided by RV_1 and gain adjust by RV_2. The gain is given by

$$A_v = \frac{R_1 + R_2}{R_1}$$

and R_1 in parallel with R_2 should equal the output resistance of the DAC in order to reduce drift with temperature. Therefore with $R_1 = R_2 = 5$ kΩ, the gain is 2 and the analog output will have a full-scale value of nearly 5 V. The amplifier circuit gives unipolar output, i.e. the analog output increases from zero to +5 V as the digital input is increased. For bipolar operation, giving a ±5 V output, the amplifier is modified by connecting a third resistor (*fig. D24b*) to the inverting input from the V_{ref} of the DAC. For all input codes where the MSB is 0, the output voltage will be negative but, when the digital input has the MSB = 1 (from 1000 through to 1111), the analog output becomes positive. For this type of DAC the input code is referred to as *offset binary*. Using a DAC in this way to give bipolar outputs enables true alternating signals to be generated at the analog output. These can be at very low frequencies determined by the rate at which digital words are output to the DAC.

2 *ZN429 (fig. D25)*

This is an 8-bit DAC of similar type to the ZN434 except that an external reference supply (V_{ref}) is required. This voltage reference should be between 2.0 V and 3.0 V, well regulated and decoupled with capacitors as shown to reduce noise. The manufacturers state that the slope resistance of the reference should be less than 2 Ω, therefore the circuit shown with *fig. D25* would be suitable. The ZN429 E-8, with an 8-bit accuracy, has a maximum nonlinearity of ±0.5LSB and a settling time of typically 2 μsec. The output buffer matched to the output resistance of the DAC (10 kΩ) uses a 741S op-amp to give a unipolar output. As for the previous example the circuit can be simply modified to give a bipolar output.

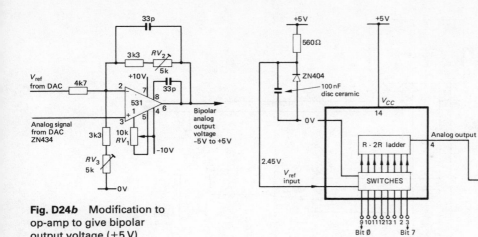

Fig. D24b Modification to op-amp to give bipolar output voltage (±5 V)

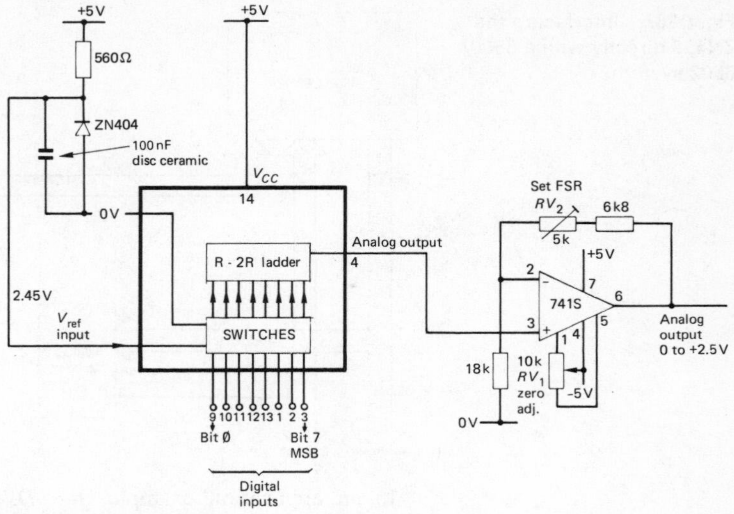

Fig. D25 The ZN429 8-bit DAC and buffer amplifier

Fig. D26a The ZN428 8-bit DAC

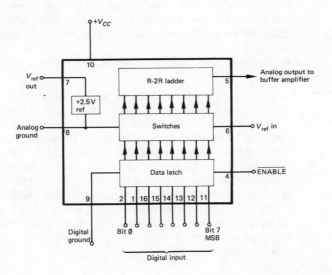

3 ZN428 (fig. D26a)

For micro systems it is often useful to have a data latch built into the DAC since this allows the DAC to be updated direct from the data bus. The ZN428, an 8-bit DAC, has this extra facility. A control input (on pin 4) called $\overline{\text{ENABLE}}$ allows data to be set or held. The action is shown in the table.

ENABLE	RESULT
Low 0	Latch is transparent
High 1	Data held

Fig. D26b Interfacing the ZN428 directly with a 6800/6802 system

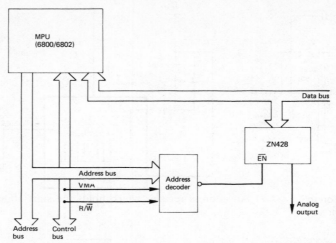

In an application example (*fig. D26b*), the ZN428 data inputs are directly connected to the microprocessor's data bus and the $\overline{\text{ENABLE}}$ signal can be obtained from address decoder logic. When the DAC address is called up, and the VMA (Ø2 of the clock on the M6800) and the WRITE signals are present, then a negative going pulse is applied to the $\overline{\text{ENABLE}}$ pin of the ZN428 to allow the word on the data bus to be transferred into the latches inside the DAC. This data will be held in the DAC until the DAC is again addressed. A system like this is termed *Memory Mapped I/O* and has obvious advantages when several DACs are required.

● ANALOG-TO-DIGITAL CONVERTOR ● CONTROL SYSTEM ● INTERFACE CIRCUITS

Direct Addressing

An addressing mode in which the address of the operand is listed as a single byte following the op code [6800 family of processors] (see *fig. D27*):

    LDA A $50   Load Acc A from address $0050

Only the low byte of the address has to be specified and the high byte is assumed to be ØØ; in other words the address is on zero page. In the 6800/6802 microprocessors the Direct Addressing mode is therefore the same as Zero Page addressing in other machines (see 6502). Using this mode, which saves program space, the memory that can be accessed is from $0000 to $00FF.

The 6809 has a direct page register which is used to hold the high byte of an address and to point to any page. This then enables the direct mode to be used on any page in memory.

● ADDRESSING MODE

Fig. D27 Direct addressing mode [6800]

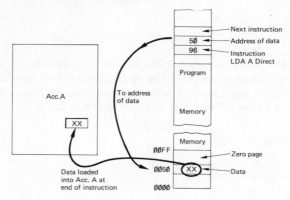

Direct Memory Access (DMA)

A method used to carry out high-speed transfer of data directly between a peripheral (I/O device) and memory (RAM). The process of data transfer for a microprocessor system is usually from the I/O port via the MPU and then to the memory or vice versa, but this is rather a slow process. With DMA, the MPU is effectively bypassed and data transfers between RAM and the peripheral can be speeded up. This is particularly useful for transfers of blocks of data between RAM and bulk storage devices such as a floppy disk. When DMA transfers are taking place, the MPU is disconnected from the address and data bus and is put into a wait mode. The disconnection is carried out by a control input to the MPU which puts the MPU tri-state buffers for the address and data bus into a high impedance state.

Extra hardware is required for DMA, and this is usually provided in the form of a chip called a DMA controller. This i.c. will probably include:

a) An address register which holds the start address of the RAM location of the data block.

b) A word counter holding the number of words to be transferred.

c) Read/write control logic.

d) A status register giving "flags" to show the state of the DMA circuits.

The various steps in a DMA sequence are as follows:

1 When required, the DMA controller sends a request to the MPU.

2 The MPU completes its current instruction and then sends an acknowledge signal to the DMA controller. At the same time, the MPU puts its bus drivers into a high Z state.

3 *a*) To read: The DMA controller sends the start address and Read signal to RAM.

or *b*) To write: The DMA controller sends the start address and Write signal to RAM.

4 The first word is transferred, the address register incremented, and the word counter decremented.

5 The end of transfer is detected by a flag in the status register, the DMA signals that transfer is complete, and bus control is taken by the MPU.

If a block of data is transferred without a break, the DMA is said to be operating in the *burst mode*. This naturally reduces the time available to the MPU for other operations. Another technique is called *cycle stealing* where the transfers are one byte at a time. With this mode the DMA controller is designed to detect the states of the clock cycles just before the MPU completes a machine cycle, to stretch these clock times and then use the time available to directly access RAM.

DMA controllers are fairly complex, typical being the 6844 and 8257, and require an initialisation routine, which is (from the MPU):

1) Load start address in DMA address register.

2) Set word counter.

3) Set read/write bit, mode bit and increment/decrement bit in the control register.

● CYCLE STEALING ● HALT ● INITIALISATION ● TRI-STATE

Directive

An instruction used to direct the operation of an assembler program but which will not be changed into object code. Essential directives are usually:

NAM (NAME)   so that the file can be formed for editing and so on.

ORG (ORIGIN)   the start address of the assembled program

END   the last statement

Other, non-essential, but useful directives include EQU, FCC, FCB and FDB.

● ASSEMBLER

Dummy Instruction	A "do-nothing" instruction, usually called NO OPERATION (NOP). This is useful for creating short delays, since an NOP usually takes one or two machine cycles, and in making spaces in programs so that other instructions can be inserted at a later date. For example, the main part of a program could be tested and debugged by replacing any jump to subroutine instructions and their specified addresses by NOPs. ● DELAY ● NO OPERATION
Duplex System	A data channel in which information can be transmitted simultaneously in both directions.
Dynamic (Circuit or Cell)	A word used to describe any microelectronic (or other) circuit that must be continually supplied with some form of clock signal in order to retain its information and/or operate correctly. Typical circuits, such as MOS dynamic memory chips (DRAM), would require a regular refresh pulse signal at a few kilohertz so that the tiny electrical charges held on gate capacitors are not allowed to leak away. These tiny charges make up the stored binary data in a dynamic RAM chip. The big advantage of a dynamic RAM is that the basic cell structure is very simple, making it easy for large-volume memory chips to be manufactured. In addition, a dynamic circuit consumes very little power. ● MEMORIES
EAROM	Acronym for Electrically-Alterable Read-Only Memory. This is a memory device, similar to the EEPROM, that can be erased and programmed by an electrical pulse. This process can be carried out while the chip is still in circuit. An EAROM is non-volatile (data is not lost when the power is switched off) and it can be used in the same way as RAM except that it is relatively slow in the write mode. It is therefore sometimes called a "read mostly memory" and finds applications in development work and where word or block alterability of stored data is required. ● EEPROM ● EPROM ● MEMORIES ● ROM
Editor	A program, usually of several thousand bytes and held on disc, used to assist in the construction of an error-free assembly language program. A text editor is therefore an essential back-up for an Assembler. The editor would be used to correct errors in the text of the source file, and with it it is possible to change, delete, or insert single characters, statements, lines or whole blocks of text. Other features would be to renumber lines and provide print-out of the listing. ● ASSEMBLER
EEPROM (or E²PROM)	Abbreviation for Electrically-Erasable and Programmable Read-Only Memory. This is a semi-permanent non-volatile store used where it is necessary to erase and reprogram individual locations (cells) or blocks without removing the device from the circuit board. The electrical erasing is achieved by applying a voltage pulse for a few milliseconds, which means that erasure can be carried out more quickly than for an EPROM. The device, however, is relatively more expensive than an EPROM. ● EAROM ● EPROM ● MEMORIES ● ROM
Emitter Coupled Logic (ECL)	This is a family of logic gates (10 000 series) which has one of the fastest operating speeds. The basic type has a propagation delay of 2 nsec and the newer type (Motorola MECL 10KH) has a typical gate propagation delay of only 1 nsec. The basic gate is the OR/NOR shown in *fig. E1*. The operation of the gate depends on the fact that Tr_1 in parallel with Tr_2 form a differential switch with Tr_3. These transistors do not saturate. A reference voltage of -1.29 V is developed in the i.c. and is applied to Tr_3 base. If the two inputs are at logic $\emptyset$

Fig. E1 ECL logic gate

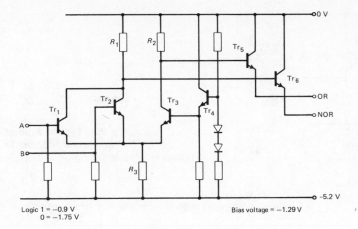

Logic 1 = −0.9 V
0 = −1.75 V

Bias voltage = −1.29 V

(−1.75 V) then the current through R_3 is supplied by Tr_3. This follows since the voltage at Tr_3 base at −1.29 V is more positive than the base voltages of Tr_1 and Tr_2. There will be a voltage drop of 0.85 V across R_2 making the OR output from emitter follower Tr_5 −1.75 V (logic Ø). The emitter voltage of Tr_6, the NOR output, will be at −0.9 V (logic 1).

If a logic 1 level (−0.9 V) is applied to either A or B input, then either Tr_1 or Tr_2 respectively will conduct. This diverts current away from Tr_3 causing a volt drop of 0.85 V to appear across R_1. The OR output will change to −0.9 V (logic 1) and the NOR output to −1.75 V (logic Ø).

The noise margin of ECL is not high, typically about 400 mV, but the circuit has the advantage of high fan-out. This is because of the emitter followers on the output circuit. Another advantage over other types of logic (TTL and CMOS) is the fact that power supply noise generation is virtually eliminated since the current taken from the supply remains almost constant even when switching occurs.

The later range (MECL 10KH) is a modified circuit. R_3 is replaced by a current source and the simple bias voltage generator has been changed to a voltage regulator circuit. These modifications, although making the i.c. more complex, give the improved performance.

Typical data for MECL 10KH:

Propagation delay	1.0 nsec
Power dissipation	25 mW per gate
Power supply	−5.2 V
Fan-out	30
Logic 1	−0.9 V
Logic Ø	−1.75 V

ECL is used in high-performance minicomputers, in frequency synthesizers, and in high-speed test systems.

● CMOS   ● TTL

Emitter Follower

This is the usual name given to the common collector connection of a bipolar transistor (*fig. E2*). It is a circuit that has near unity voltage gain (0.98), a moderately high input impedance, and a low output impedance. These features make it a good circuit for interfacing applications.

There is no signal inversion between the output on the emitter and the input on the base and, since the voltage gain is close to unity, the emitter "follows" the input; hence the name "emitter follower".

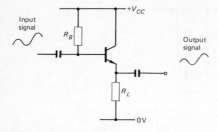

Fig. E2 Basic emitter
follower circuit

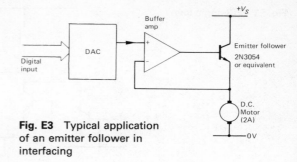

Fig. E3 Typical application
of an emitter follower in
interfacing

Basic formulae

Current gain $A_i \simeq 1 + h_{fe}$

Input resistance $R_i \simeq h_{ie} + h_{fe}R_L$

Voltage gain $A_v \simeq \dfrac{h_{fe}R_L}{h_{ie} + h_{fe}R_L}$

Output resistance $R_o = \dfrac{R_L(h_{ie} + R_s)}{R_s + h_{ie} + h_{fe}R_L}$

R_s is the source resistance and the above formulae take no account of the effect of any bias resistors.

The circuit has a wide range of applications. An example of a matching circuit using an emitter follower is shown in *fig. E3*. Here the digital word from a micro output port is converted by a DAC into an analog voltage and used to drive a d.c. motor. The op-amp would not be capable of driving the motor directly but can easily supply the base current required by the transistor. A larger current can then be taken from the emitter to drive the motor.

● BUFFER ● DARLINGTON ● INTERFACING

Emulate/Emulator

This is a "mimic" technique where hardware and software built into a microcomputer are used to test the operation of an external microprocessor-based system. To do this the microprocessor chip of the external system is removed and replaced by a plug connected to the machine performing the emulation. An arrangement such as this is of great assistance during the design and development stage of a new system and also in fault location and testing.

The *in-circuit emulator* usually has facilities such as monitoring, register examine, break-point insertion, and in halting or single-stepping the program. In some arrangements the emulator is based on the same family of processors; others called "universal emulators" can mimic several different types of processor. In this case a "personality card", which gives the required timing and control signals, is plugged into the emulator.

Enable

A word used in microelectronics to indicate the removal of an inhibiting signal. For example, the 8080 has an Enable Interrupt (ENI) instruction and most microprocessor support chips have an Enable input (E) which is connected to the master system clock and/or an address decoder circuit.

All tri-state gates and buffers (bus drivers) have an Enable input. When this input is low at logic Ø, the gate is disabled (inhibited) and the output assumes a high impedance state which effectively disconnects it from the line to which it is wired. Only when the Enable signal is high at logic 1 will the signal be transmitted through the gate.

● CHIP SELECT ● TRI-STATE

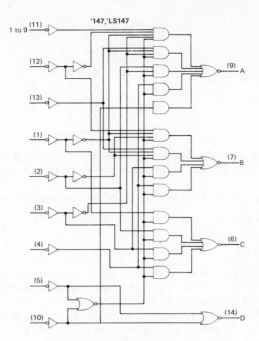

Fig. E4 Encoder [Texas Instruments]

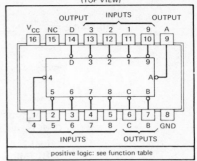

SN54147, SN54LS147 . . . J OR W PACKAGE
SN74147, SN74LS147 . . . J OR N PACKAGE
(TOP VIEW)

positive logic: see function table

NC—No internal connection

FUNCTION TABLE

INPUTS									OUTPUTS			
1	2	3	4	5	6	7	8	9	D	C	B	A
H	H	H	H	H	H	H	H	H	H	H	H	H
X	X	X	X	X	X	X	X	L	L	H	H	L
X	X	X	X	X	X	X	L	H	L	H	H	H
X	X	X	X	X	X	L	H	H	H	L	L	L
X	X	X	X	X	L	H	H	H	H	L	L	H
X	X	X	X	L	H	H	H	H	H	L	H	L
X	X	X	L	H	H	H	H	H	H	L	H	H
X	X	L	H	H	H	H	H	H	H	H	L	L
X	L	H	H	H	H	H	H	H	H	H	L	H
L	H	H	H	H	H	H	H	H	H	H	H	L

H = high logic level, L = low logic level, X = irrelevant

Encoder	The terms encoder and decoder are often used to describe the same device. However a **decoder** converts from one code into another, whereas an **encoder** is a logic circuit or device that takes an uncoded value and converts it into a binary coded form. A circuit example is the TTL 7414 9-to-4 line priority encoder. The input decimal pattern is converted into (8-4-2-1)BCD with only the highest order line encoded; in other words the highest line activated takes priority (*fig. E4*). ● DECODER
EPROM	Acronym for Erasable Programmable Read-Only Memory, sometimes referred to as a (UV)EPROM because the cells within the device are erased by exposure to ultra violet. The erasing takes between 10 to 20 minutes and is complete. PROMs like these are extremely useful for development systems since the program can be altered, although, after erasure, the whole program must be reloaded. ● DEDICATED CONTROLLER ● EAROM ● EEPROM ● MEMORIES
Exclusive-OR Gate	A digital logic gate, usually with only two inputs, that gives a logic 1 output if either of its inputs is at logic 1 but not when both inputs are logic 1 or logic Ø simultaneously (*fig. E5a*). The Boolean expression for this is:

$$F = A \cdot \bar{B} + \bar{A} \cdot B \qquad \text{usually written as } F = A \oplus B$$

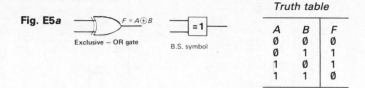

Fig. E5a

Exclusive — OR gate

B.S. symbol

Truth table

A	B	F
Ø	Ø	Ø
Ø	1	1
1	Ø	1
1	1	Ø

The function is provided in i.c. form, the most commonly used types being the CMOS 4070 and the TTL 7486 (each contain four independent exclusive-OR gates).

By following an exclusive-OR by an invertor we get the exclusive-NOR (*fig. E5b*):

$$F = \bar{A} \cdot \bar{B} + A \cdot B \qquad \text{or } F = \overline{A \oplus B} \quad \text{(CMOS 4077)}$$

● COMPARATOR   ● GATE

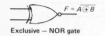

Exclusive — NOR gate

Fig. E5b

Exclusive-OR Instruction

Bits being EORed

B	A	Result
Ø	Ø	Ø
Ø	1	1
1	Ø	1
1	1	Ø

This instruction is useful in bit modification. It performs the logical exclusive-OR function between each bit of a register and corresponding bits of another register or memory location, placing the result in the original register.

For an exclusive-OR the result for each bit of the logic function will be logic 1 only if either of the two bits being exclusive-ORed are 1. The result is Ø if both bits are 1 or when both bits are zero.

Instruction mnemonic   EOR   [6502/6800]
                       XOR   [Z80/8080]

Example of use: changing the sign of a number held in an accumulator:

EOR   A   #$8Ø   Exclusive-OR Accumulator Immediate with Hex.
                    Num. = 8Ø

Assumed contents of accumulator
before EOR instruction

1	Ø	Ø	1	1	Ø	1	1

Instruction EOR A   #$8Ø

1	Ø	Ø	Ø	Ø	Ø	Ø	Ø

Result in accumulator

Ø	Ø	Ø	1	1	Ø	1	1

The sign has been changed while the magnitude of the number remains the same.

This instruction will therefore always complement a bit or bits where the number used in the EOR instruction contains logic 1s.

Suppose address $Ø1ØØ holds $FØ (111ØØØØØ), the accumulator holds $37 (ØØ11Ø111), and the following instruction is executed:

EOR A $Ø1ØØ   Exclusive-OR Accumulator with the Contents of Address
                   $Ø1ØØ

Contents of accumulator
before EOR instruction

Ø	Ø	1	1	Ø	1	1	1

Contents of address $Ø1ØØ

1	1	1	1	Ø	Ø	Ø	Ø

Result in accumulator following
instruction EOR A $Ø1ØØ

1	1	Ø	Ø	Ø	1	1	1

The upper 4 bits in the accumulator (bit 4 to bit 7 inclusive) have been complemented.

● LOGICAL INSTRUCTIONS AND LOGICAL OPERATIONS

Extended Address

Similar to Absolute Address but often used to distinguish between addresses on zero page and the rest of the memory. Thus an extended address is any address not on page zero; in other words, an address (for a system with 16-bit wide address bus) that is from $0100 to $FFFF.

● ABSOLUTE ADDRESS

Extended Addressing Mode

An addressing mode that is used to access an extended address, i.e. an address from $0100 up to $FFFF. An instruction using this mode will be 3 bytes; byte 2 being the high part of the address and byte 3 the lower portion. (*Note*: in some processors these bytes are reversed—see 6502 addressing.)

Examples [6800 systems]

MNEMONIC	OPERAND	COMMENT	MACHINE CODE
LDA	$32F0	Load Acc. from $32F0	B6 32 F0
JSR	$043A	Jump to subroutine	BD 04 3A

This addressing mode, as in absolute addressing, allows the user to specify any address in memory including the first 256 locations on page zero. But in the latter case, the leading zeros (the high byte of the address) must be included in the instruction, i.e.

   STA $0080   Store Acc. at $80   B7 00 80

Although the code in this case is correct it is wasteful of program space and time since direct or zero page addressing, requiring only 2 bytes for the instruction, can be used.

   STA $0080   Store Acc. at $80   97 80

● ABSOLUTE ADDRESSING MODE ● ADDRESSING MODE ● DIRECT ADDRESSING

FAMOS

The Floating-gate Avalanche-injection MOS cell is the basic element used in EPROMs. The structure is shown in *fig. F1* for the one cell and consists of an n-substrate with two p-regions diffused in to form the drain and source. Apart from the metal connections to these regions, the top surface is covered with silicon dioxide (an insulator). Above the gap between the drain and source and "floating" inside the silicon dioxide, a gate region is formed. When this gate region is uncharged, as it is after manufacture or erasure, there is no conducting

Fig. F1 Structure of FAMOS cell

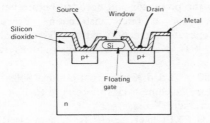

path between drain and source and the cell stores a logic 1. A cell is programmed to logic 0 by applying a voltage pulse (typically 20 V to 30 V) for about 50 msec between the drain and source. An avalanche effect then causes electrons to be injected into the gate and it becomes negatively charged. The gate charge, which cannot leak away, then sets up a conducting channel between drain and source. The cell then holds a logic 0. In this way a pattern of logic 1s and 0s can be stored in an array of FAMOS cells to make a ROM.

Cells within an EPROM are erased by exposure through the window to strong ultra violet light for up to 20 min. This effectively discharges the floating gate.

● EPROM ● MEMORIES ● MOS

Fast Interrupt Request

$\overline{\text{FIRQ}}$ (active low). An additional interrupt input provided on some high-performance processors, such as the 6809, that allows an interrupt to be serviced more rapidly than the normal interrupt request (IRQ). This is possible because, during the $\overline{\text{FIRQ}}$, only the contents of the program counter and status register are saved on the stack. This requires less time than saving the contents of all the registers as is required in the standard interrupt request.

$\overline{\text{FIRQ}}$ is maskable under software control by setting or clearing the F-bit in the flag register.

● INTERRUPT

Feedback

This exists in any analog or digital system when a portion of the output quantity is connected back and mixed with the original input (*fig. F2*). If the feedback signal is added to the input we get positive feedback which is the basis of all oscillator circuits, but when the feedback is subtracted from the input to give a negative feedback, a controlling effect is achieved. Applying negative feedback to systems or amplifiers enables gains to be accurately set and wide bandwidths (i.e. fast response in a system) to be given.

● CLOSED LOOP ● CONTROL SYSTEM ● OPERATIONAL AMPLIFIER

Fig. F2 Feedback principle

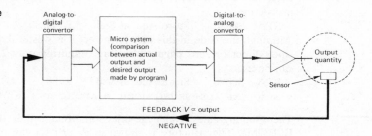

Fetch-Execute Cycle

The program on any computer, however complicated the programming task, is made up of a series of discrete instructions. These instructions, binary patterns carried along the data lines, are carried out in a defined sequence one after another until the program is completed. The program is held in memory, with instructions followed by data or addresses holding data, and each instruction must be fetched by the processor and decoded before being executed. In this way the machine works on a fetch instruction → execute instruction, fetch next instruction → execute instruction pattern. This is called the FETCH-EXECUTE CYCLE (*fig. F3*). Naturally, some instructions take longer than others, for example:

LDX $4000   Load X reg. from address $4000

would take more machine cycles to execute than

INX   Increment X reg.

The FETCH-EXECUTE cycle is synchronised by the master clock and controlled by signals generated by the processor. As long as the program starts with the valid code for an instruction, and the code is correct throughout the program, the machine will not get out of step.

● CLOCK SIGNAL ● INSTRUCTION ● MACHINE CYCLE

Field

This is used to describe a defined area in a program line. A field, consisting of a fixed number of characters, is used for a specific purpose; for example, the source statements in an Assembler format will consist of five fields as follows:

LINE NUMBER□LABEL□MNEMONIC□OPERAND□COMMENT

Each of these distinct fields is separated from the next by a space.

● ASSEMBLER ● ASSEMBLY LANGUAGE

Fig. F3 Fetch-Execute cycle for a microprocessor

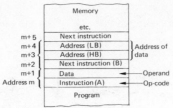

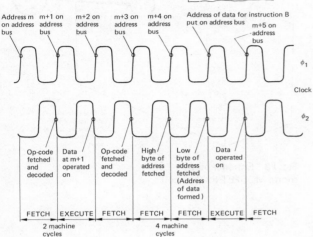

FETCH EXECUTE FETCH FETCH FETCH EXECUTE FETCH

2 machine cycles   4 machine cycles

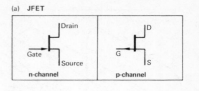

(a) JFET

n-channel   p-channel

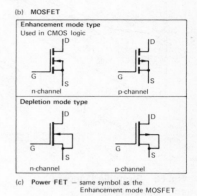

(b) MOSFET

Enhancement mode type
Used in CMOS logic

n-channel   p-channel

Depletion mode type

n-channel   p-channel

(c) **Power FET** — same symbol as the Enhancement mode MOSFET

Fig. F4 Field effect transistors

Field Effect Transistor (FET)

An electronic amplifying and switching device that relies for its operation on an electric field. The current flowing through two terminals of the FET, the drain and source, is controlled by the input voltage (the field) applied between the gate and source. This type of action requires hardly any input current and is therefore a distinct advantage in applications where the available power to drive a device is limited. Field effect devices are therefore used extensively in microprocessor and memory chips.

There are a number of different types of FET and sometimes several names are used for the same type of device. The commonly used types, which have the symbols shown in *fig. F4*, are:

1 The JUNCTION FET or FJET (sometimes called a JUGFET).

2 The MOSFET or metal oxide silicon field effect transistor (sometimes referred to as a MOST or IGFET or more simply as MOS). From this we get NMOS and PMOS.

3 The POWERFET with special names such as VMOS, TMOS and HEXFET.

1 The JFET construction and operation is illustrated in *fig. F5*. Because of the reverse bias applied between the p-type gate and the n-type source, a depletion region is set up around the gate that restricts the width of the conducting channel between source and drain. By increasing the negative gate-to-source voltage, the depletion region gets wider and causes a further narrowing of the channel, making the drain current fall. If a sufficiently high negative voltage is applied (usually a few volts), the channel is cut off altogether and the drain current ceases. The important point to note is that hardly any input gate current is required for this controlling action.

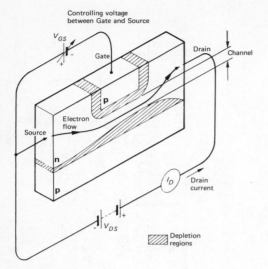

Fig. F5 Simplified view of an n-channel JFET

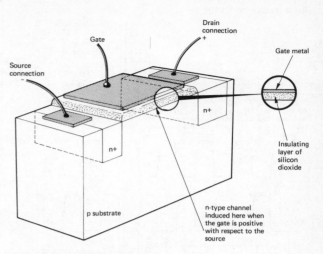

Fig. F6 Enhancement-mode MOSFET (n-channel)

2 The MOSFET (enhancement mode type) operates by the controlling voltage applied between gate and source inducing a channel in the silicon beneath an insulated gate region (*fig. F6*). For NMOS devices, a positive voltage on the gate sets up a conducting path between source and drain as electrons are attracted to the region just beneath the gate. The operation of PMOS is the same except that a negative voltage is required to turn it on. These devices make excellent switches and are used in large numbers to make CMOS logic ICs, microprocessor chips, and all types of memories.

3 The enhancement mode POWERFET operates in the same way as a MOSFET. The structure of one type, the vertical FET (VFET), is shown in *fig. F7*. The cross-section shows that the geometry is similar to a planar transistor except that a V-groove is etched through the top n and p regions. On top of this V-groove is a coating of silicon dioxide which acts as the insulator between the metal of the gate and the body of the device. With the drain positive with respect to the source, a positive voltage on the gate will induce the regions in the p material opposite the groove (both sides) to invert to n-type. A large current will then flow from drain to source. The short thick channels created enable the VFET to pass the high values of drain current and this is controlled by the input voltage between gate and source.

● CMOS   ● FAMOS   ● INTERFACING   ● POWER CONTROL

Firmware

The name given to any program when the instructions and data are held in a semi-permanent form in ROM or on disc or tape. The monitor program for a system will be firmware.

● HARDWARE   ● MONITOR PROGRAM

Flag and Flag Register

Flags are single-bit memory units used in a microprocessor to indicate conditions immediately following an instruction. A flag is set or reset according to the result of the latest instruction executed by the microprocessor. Flags, which are bistables, although unlinked are grouped together inside the processor in what is

Fig. F7 Structure of the VFET

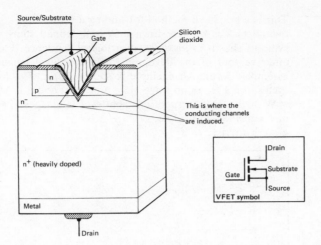

called the FLAG REGISTER (other names used are STATUS REGISTER and CONDITION CODE REGISTER) (*fig. F8*). The following conditions are indicated by flags:

a) A carry out (or borrow)   C flag
b) Negative result (Sign flag)   N flag or S flag
c) Zero result   Z flag
d) Overflow   V flag

The flag register will probably also contain interrupt and half-carry flags.

Fig. F8 Flag register

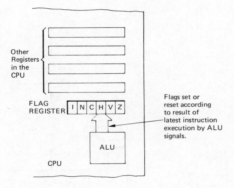

Suppose that the contents of a register is compared with the contents of a memory location. If the numbers are equal, the Z flag will be set (logic 1), otherwise it will be cleared (logic $\emptyset$).

A wide range of instructions, but not all, affect either one or a number of flags, and the state of a flag or combination of flags can then be used in further instructions such as in conditional branching or arithmetic operations.

● ARITHMETIC AND LOGIC UNIT   ● BRANCH INSTRUCTION   ● CONDITION CODE REGISTER

Flag Setting Instruction

These instructions are available to the programmer so that flags can be cleared or set at convenient points in a program. An obvious use is in the addition of several numbers when it would be necessary to initially clear the carry flag before adding the first two bytes.

● FLAG

Flowchart

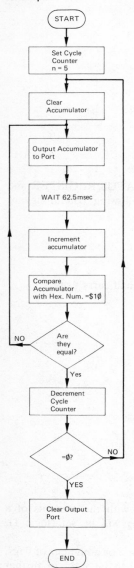

This is a graphical method for finding a solution to a problem. In a *flowchart* the overall task is broken down into well-defined steps and then drawn, using the symbols shown in *fig. F9a*, in a logical sequence. Flowcharting is a particularly effective tool in the development of low-level language programs; typically in assembler form. An example is shown in *fig. F9b* for the task of outputting 5 cycles of a 1 Hz ramp wave via a 4-bit port and a DAC.

With the more structured high-level languages (Pascal and C) flowcharts are now considered obsolete.

● ALGORITHM

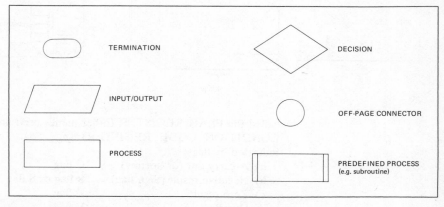

Fig. F9a Flowchart symbols

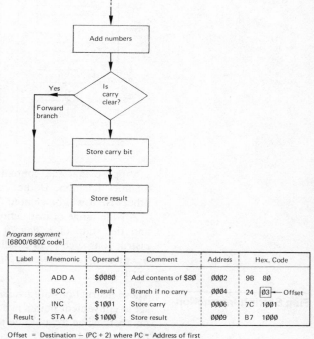

Fig. F10 Forward branch

Program segment
[6800/6802 code]

Label	Mnemonic	Operand	Comment	Address	Hex. Code
	ADD A	$0080	Add contents of $80	0002	9B 80
	BCC	Result	Branch if no carry	0004	24 03 ◄─ Offset
	INC	$1001	Store carry	0006	7C 1001
Result	STA A	$1000	Store result	0009	B7 1000

Offset = Destination − (PC + 2) where PC = Address of first
= 0009 − (0006) byte of branch
= 03 instruction

Format	A word used to describe the way in which programs and data are logically organised.		

Format

A word used to describe the way in which programs and data are logically organised.
- ASSEMBLER ● SERIAL DATA FORMAT

Forward Branch

A branch or jump instruction allows the program to change its location to either a lower (previous) or a higher (later) position. The latter situation is referred to as a forward branch and the effective address branched to will be given by the contents of the program counter plus an offset specified with the branch instruction (*fig. F10*). The offset is normally in twos complement form allowing a forward branch of +128 places, although the exact value and offset calculation method depends on the machine being used.
- BRANCH INSTRUCTION ● CONDITIONAL BRANCH ● RELATIVE ADDRESSING MODE

Fusible-link PROM

A standard type of PROM which is supplied to the user in blank form. It is then programmed by "blowing" the fuse links. The PROM consists of a matrix of FETs or diodes each with a series fusible link attached. These fusible links, made of nichrome, polycrystalline silicon or other material, are blown by passing a high current pulse for a short duration. Once programmed in this way the programming is complete and cannot be reversed.
- MEMORIES

Gate

A gate is any circuit that allows the transmission of a signal when an appropriate switching input is applied. In CMOS, for example, special analog transmission gates are available that have this facility. More particularly the word "gate" is assumed to mean a digital logic element, one that gives a certain logical output as long as a particular set or combination of states exists on its inputs. Such gates are the building blocks of digital logic systems. In the majority of logic circuits the logic levels have two states and the most positive level is called logic 1 (positive logic).

	TTL	CMOS at 10 V	ECL
Logic 1 High most-positive level	2.4 V	+9.5 V	−0.9 V
Logic Ø Low most-negative level	0.4 V	+0.5 V	−1.75 V

The types of logic gate used in combinational logic are (*fig. G1*):

    AND, OR, NOT, NAND, NOR, Exclusive-OR

and their operation can be described by Boolean algebra. The following assumes positive logic.

The **AND gate** gives a logic 1 output only when all its inputs are at logic 1. In other words, for a three-input gate, the output will be high only when input A *and* input B *and* input C are all high. The output will be logic Ø and low for all other input combinations.

The **OR gate** will give a logic 1 output if there is a logic 1 on any one of its inputs. For a three-input OR gate, the output will be high if input A *or* input B *or* input C is high.

The **NOT gate** is simply a circuit that always inverts and is therefore often referred to as an invertor. If its input is logic 1 then its output will be logic Ø and vice versa.

By following an AND gate by a NOT gate we get the NAND function (NOT-AND). A **NAND gate** will give a logic Ø output only when all of its inputs are at logic 1. For a three-input gate the output will be logic Ø only if input A *and* input B *and* input C are logic 1.

Fig. G1 Logic gates

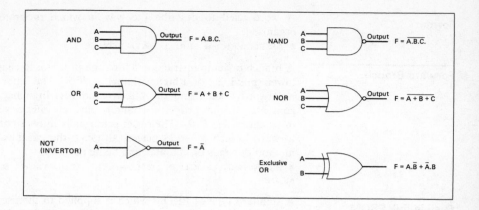

A **NOR gate** is the result of following an OR gate by a NOT gate (NOT-OR). A NOR gate will give a logic Ø output if any input is at logic 1. For a three-input gate, the output will be logic Ø if A *or* B *or* C is at logic 1.

The **Exclusive-OR** is a special circuit which only gives a logic 1 output if either of its inputs are at logic 1 but not when they are both 1 or both Ø.

The operation of logic gates can be followed from a truth table. Only two input gates are assumed for simplicity.

INPUTS	AND	OR	NAND	NOR	EXCLUSIVE-OR
A B	$F = A \cdot B$	$F = A + B$	$F = \overline{A \cdot B}$	$F = \overline{A + B}$	$F = A \oplus B$
Ø Ø	Ø	Ø	1	1	Ø
Ø 1	Ø	1	1	Ø	1
1 Ø	Ø	1	1	Ø	1
1 1	1	1	Ø	Ø	Ø

Simple circuits using discrete components can be used to make up any of the gates but this would be totally impractical for most digital systems where hundreds of gates may be required. The integrated circuit versions in such families as TTL, CMOS and ECL are the types most commonly used.

The common properties and parameters used in specifying gates are:

FAN-IN   The number of inputs that can be accommodated on one gate.

FAN-OUT   The ability of a gate to drive several inputs of similar gates simultaneously.

PROPAGATION DELAY TIME   The speed at which the logic switches.

NOISE MARGIN   The measure (in volts) of a noise signal that can be accepted without causing a change of state at the output.

POWER CONSUMPTION   The amount of power taken by one gate during static, i.e. steady state, and dynamic (switched) conditions.

Groups of gates are connected together usually of the same family (i.e. all TTL or all CMOS) to create a logic system.

● CMOS   ● DIGITAL CIRCUIT   ● ECL   ● TTL

Glitch

Whenever the inputs to logic circuits change state there is always the possibility that an unwanted "spike" will be generated at the output. This "spike" is referred to as a glitch. Take the case of a simple 2-input AND gate with input signals that do not change state at exactly the same moment. Because of this slight timing error (caused by some delay to one signal), the output produces a glitch (*fig. G2*).

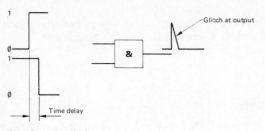

Fig. G2 A glitch

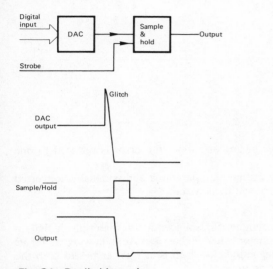

Fig. G4 Deglitching using sample and hold

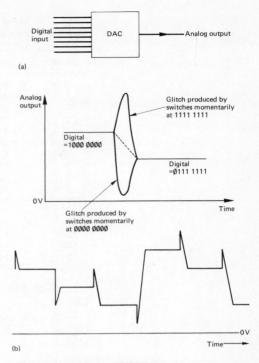

Fig. G3 Glitches in a DAC

Circuits such as decoders and digital-to-analog convertors are particularly prone to glitch generation. In a DAC, the internal switches cannot all change at exactly the same instant, with the result that spurious outputs are generated. This is shown in *fig. G3a* when the input to a DAC switches from 1000 0000 to 0111 1111. In the worst cases the switches might be either all zeros or all logic 1s for a brief instant, causing a large amplitude glitch as shown. The output from a DAC if viewed by a fast CRO would appear as shown in *fig. G3b*. If the DAC is driving a relatively slow device, these fast glitches will be ignored, but if the device has fast response then the glitches will produce errors. This is the case when the output from a DAC is used to drive a display; the glitches will produce a blurring of the image.

The effect can be reduced by using a low pass filter, usually a capacitor, connected across the output of the DAC. But this increases response time with the result that information may be lost. A preferred method of deglitching uses the sample-and-hold technique, where the DAC output is sampled for a brief time after its output has settled. In this way the glitch is almost ignored and eliminated. (See *fig. G4*.)

● DIGITAL-TO-ANALOG CONVERTOR   ● SAMPLE-AND-HOLD

Gray Code

A useful code for encoding data on angular or linear positions from machines. Coded discs or plates are used with the Gray code pattern printed on and with detection via a light source and opto-devices.

The main point with the code is that only one binary digit changes at any one time, this being true whether the count is moving up or down. For this reason Gray is often called a "reflected code". There are sixteen combinations:

DECIMAL	BINARY	GRAY
0	0000	0000
1	0001	0001
2	0010	0011
3	0011	0010
4	0100	0110
5	0101	0111
6	0110	0101
7	0111	0100
8	1000	1100
9	1001	1101
10	1010	1111
11	1011	1110
12	1100	1010
13	1101	1011
14	1110	1001
15	1111	1000

Because only one digit changes at any one time, the error is reduced to one LSB.

Gray code cannot be used for arithmetic operations and is usually converted (by software) immediately it is received by a system.

● SENSOR

Hall Effect Device

The *Hall Effect*, which is most pronounced in semiconductor materials, is that an e.m.f. will appear across a conductor when it has a current flowing along its length and when it is within a magnetic field which is at right angles to both the current and the e.m.f. This is shown in *fig. H1*.

Fig. H1 Hall effect

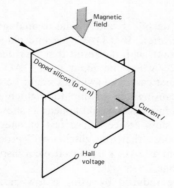

Various sensors are made based on this effect. These include proximity switches, where the output switches from low to high when a magnetic field is present; and vane switches which will detect the presence of a ferrous metal vane passing through a gap provided between the sensor and a fixed magnet. The big advantage of Hall effect switches is that they are bounce free.

● DEBOUNCING

Halt

1 *Input* A control input provided on some microprocessors that is used to stop the processor and effectively disconnect it from the bus system. This input is particularly useful in DMA (Direct Memory Access) when an external device needs to bypass the processor and to write to or read data from memory. The

Halt line is activated, the processor completes its current instruction, and then puts the address bus, the data bus and the R/W̄ line into a high impedance state. Following this, the processor signals that direct transfers can commence by a change of state on the Bus Available (BA) line.

2 *Instruction* (Mnemonic HLT) Used with some microprocessors [see 8080] to stop the processor and force it into an idle state so that it can either service a direct memory access request or an interrupt. The instruction, under user software control, is similar in operation to a Wait for Interrupt (WAI) used in the 6800 series since its basic purpose is to allow the processor to stop activity while waiting for an interrupt signal from a peripheral. It would only be used when there is nothing of further use that the processor can carry out until the interrupt occurs.

● DIRECT MEMORY ACCESS ● INTERRUPT

Handshake

This describes a way in which data transfers between peripherals and a micro system are synchronised; necessary because of the differing speeds of operation between peripherals and microprocessors. Handshaking is usually achieved via an interface adaptor such as a PIA, PIO or VIO where additional control lines are used for signalling between the system and peripherals. Suppose an ADC with a conversion time of tens of microseconds is linked to the input port of a system as shown in *fig. H2*. Input data transfer can be arranged by two control lines: one from the micro to the ADC to initiate conversion, the other from the ADC to the micro to signal that the conversion is complete and that valid data can be input.

● ANALOG-TO-DIGITAL CONVERTOR ● ASYNCHRONOUS COMMUNICATIONS INTERFACE ADAPTOR ● INTERFACE CIRCUITS ● PERIPHERAL INTERFACE ADAPTOR

Fig. H2 Handshake example

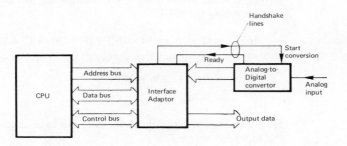

Hardware

The name given to the actual solid components (ICs, transistors, display devices, switches and so on) that are wired together to make up a complete microelectronic system.

● FIRMWARE

Heuristic

A trial-and-error approach to problem solving, so that an heuristic program is one designed to adapt and improve its performance. This implies that some learning occurs as the program is run and successively solves the problem.

● ALGORITHM

Hexadecimal Numbers

Binary numbers used by a micro system for addresses, instructions, and data tend to be cumbersome and error-prone when used by human operators. Hexadecimal numbers, numbers to the base of 16, are a very convenient way of representing these binary patterns.

In hexadecimal, the letters A, B, C, D, E and F are used to represent values 10, 11, 12, 13, 14 and 15 as shown in the table.

DECIMAL	BINARY	HEXADECIMAL
0	0000	0
1	0001	1
2	0010	2
3	0011	3
4	0100	4
5	0101	5
6	0110	6
7	0111	7
8	1000	8
9	1001	9
10	1010	A
11	1011	B
12	1100	C
13	1101	D
14	1110	E
15	1111	F

To express a binary number in hexadecimal, the binary bits are arranged in groups of four starting from the right, and the hexadecimal value for each group is then assigned:

Binary number $\quad 1101\ 1001\ 0011_2$

Hexadecimal equivalent $\quad$ D $\quad$ 9 $\quad$ 3_{16}

Conversion from hexadecimal to binary is just as simple:

Hex. $\quad$ F $\quad$ 3 $\quad$ A $\quad$ 2_{16}

Binary $\quad 1111\ 0011\ 1010\ 0010_2$

Conversion from hexadecimal to decimal is achieved by assigning the appropriate weight to each hexadecimal digit, multiplying this by the value of that digit, and then summing the total.

$$16F2_{16} = (1 \times 16^3) + (6 \times 16^2) + (F \times 16^1) + (2 \times 16^0)$$
$$= (1 \times 4096) + (6 \times 256) + (15 \times 16) + (2 \times 1)$$
$$= 4096 + 1536 + 240 + 2$$
$$= 5874_{10}$$

Hex. numbers are used in generating machine code and are indicated in one of the following ways:

$\quad$ $F20A

or $\quad$ F20AH

or $\quad$ $F20A_{16}$

● BINARY AND BINARY CODED DECIMAL $\quad$ ● MACHINE CODE $\quad$ ● OCTAL NUMBERS

High-level Language

At machine level the program instructions and the data for a microcomputer must be in binary form, but writing software is made easier and much more efficient if a language nearer to human thought and speech is used. This type of language, referred to as a high-level language (HLL), has several advantages over both machine code and assembly mnemonics. These include:

1 The written program is shorter.

2 It is more understandable (at least to others who know the language).

3 It is portable in that a program written in Pascal on a Z80-based system can be run on machines that are 8085 or 6800 based.

4 An HLL can be more easily maintained and debugged.

Because of these points there is a trend away from assembly language and many of the more advanced processors have a structure designed to support HLLs.

Two main disadvantages of HLLs are:

1 An HLL occupies a large area of memory.

2 The running time is usually longer than the equivalent assembly language program.

When a program is written in an HLL, the source code has then to be converted into the appropriate machine code. A COMPILER performs this task.

Popular high-level languages for microprocessor-based computers are:

BASIC   PASCAL   FORTH   C

● ASSEMBLER   ● ASSEMBLY LANGUAGE   ● COMPILER

HMOS

An abbreviation for High-density MOS, a MOS technology using scaled-down NMOS switches thus increasing the density. In addition, an HMOS switch gives an approximate fourfold increase in operating speed compared with a conventional NMOS switch. HMOS is used in memories and some microprocessor chips.

● MOS

Immediate Addressing

One of the basic addressing modes of a microprocessor for loading (setting) a register to a specific value, comparing the contents of a register with a set value, or for adding and subtracting a fixed value to or from a register. With this mode of addressing, the data to be used follows on immediately after the code for the instruction.

Example (see *fig. I1*)

LDA   #$B9   Load Accumulator Immediate with the Number B9

The # sign is often used to signify that the immediate addressing mode is being used. This addressing mode can only be used with registers contained within the processor, not for memory locations.

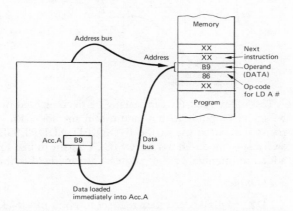

Fig. I1 Immediate addressing

Other examples

MVI A,3FH   Load Acc Immediate with $3F [8080,Z80]
ADD A #$0F   Add $0F Immediate to Acc
LDX #$32F8   Set X register to hex. value $32F8
CPX #$4FFF   Compare X register Immediate with hex. value 4FFF

● ADDRESSING MODE

Implied Addressing

Also called Inherent Addressing (see 6800 range), this is an addresssing mode used for those instructions to a microprocessor which require neither an operand nor an address to be specified; the destination will be in the processor itself and is implicit in the instruction. For example, CLC (clear carry), SEI (set interrupt bit), INX (increment the index register), and DAA (decimal adjust accumulator). An instruction using implied addressing is therefore single byte.

● INHERENT ADDRESSING

Index Register and Indexed Addressing

The Index Register within a microprocessor is used mainly as a memory pointer, when for example it could hold the start address of a look-up table, although it is also useful as a counter. Most processors are provided with at least one 16-bit Index Register which can then be set to point to any address in the range $0000 to $FFFF. All that is required to cause the register to "point" to a particular location is to load it with the hex. number of that address.

Example

LDX #$25A0   Set Index reg. to point to address $25A0

With this instruction the Index Register is loaded immediately with the value $25A0 and it then points to that location (see *fig. I2*).

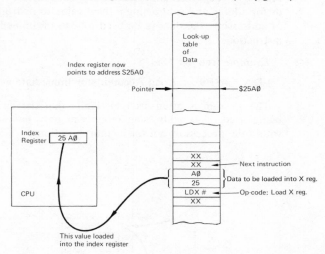

Fig. I2 Loading an index register so that it points to a particular memory location

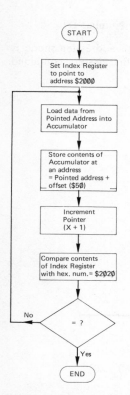

Fig. I3 Flowchart for program example using indexed addressing

The Index Register can usually be decremented or incremented so that it can be made to point to any address in memory. But the real advantage of this register is in the use of the INDEXED ADDRESSING MODE. This powerful addressing mode allows an OFFSET in the range $00 to $FF (0 to 255) to be added to the number (i.e. address) already held in the index register.

Example

LDX #$1500   Index reg. set to point to $1500
LDA 00,X   Acc. loaded from "pointed" address
                (i.e. from $1500 since offset is zero)
STA 05,X   Contents of Acc. stored at $1505
                (i.e. at address = pointed address + offset)

In order to further illustrate the use of this addressing mode, the program example, using 6800 code, is given below for the task of moving a block of data from one area of memory to another. Assume the block begins originally at address $2000, consists of 32 locations (this is 20 in hex.), and is to be moved to a new start address of $2050. The flowchart is shown in *fig. 13*. Initially the index register is loaded with the hex. number of the address of the first byte of data ($2000). An arbitrary start address of $1000 is used for the program and no address is specified for the monitor. The program is as follows:

	Assembly language			*Machine code*	
LABEL	MNEMONIC		COMMENT	ADDRESS	HEX. CODE
	LDX	#$2000	SET POINTER	1000	CE 2000
LOOP	LDA A	$00X	LOAD DATA	1003	A6 00
	STA A	$50,X	STORE DATA	1005	A7 50
	INX		INCREMENT X REG	1007	08
	CPX	#$2020	COMPARE	1008	8C 2020
	BNE	LOOP	BRANCH BACK	100B	26 F6
	JMP	MON	RETURN TO MON	100D	7E XXXX

● ADDRESSING MODE   ● OFFSET

Inherent Addressing

The name used in the 6800 range of microprocessors for IMPLIED ADDRESSING, where the single-byte instruction (for example TAB transfer accumulator A to accumulator B) requires no address or data to be specified.

● IMPLIED ADDRESSING   ● MICROPROCESSOR [6800]

IN/OUT Instruction

Not all microprocessors are arranged to have memory input/output (I/O) ports, the Z80 being one of the main examples, but have instead what is called *isolated I/O*. With the Z80, IN and OUT instructions are then necessary for arranging data transfers between the processor and external devices. These instructions activate an $\overline{IORG}$ (input/output request) signal to indicate that the lower 8 bits on the address bus constitute a port address. This address is decoded separately from memory (see *fig. 14*).

● MICROPROCESSOR [Z80]   ● PORT

Fig. I4 Isolated I/O arrangement in the Z80 system

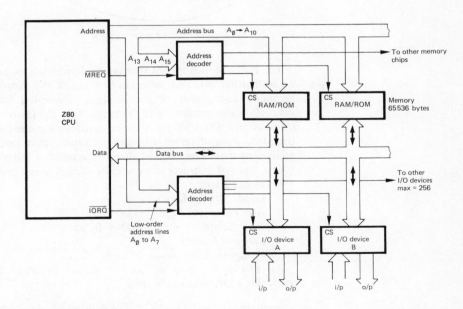

Initialisation

A word used to describe the programming steps or instructions required to set up some primary or opening conditions; for instance, setting up a counter for a program with a loop or to configure an interface adaptor.

● INTERFACE CIRCUITS (ADAPTOR)   ● LOOP

Instruction

Any program for a microprocessor-based system is made up of a series of discrete commands or INSTRUCTIONS. These, at machine level, are binary patterns which are fetched from memory, routed via the data bus to the instruction register, and then decoded within the microprocessor (*fig. 15*). The microprocessor then carries out the operation required by the particular instruction. In assembly language the instructions are given easy-to-remember mnemonics such as:

LD	LOAD
ST	STORE
INC	INCREMENT
CLR	CLEAR

Fig. I5 Fetching the op code of a two-byte instruction

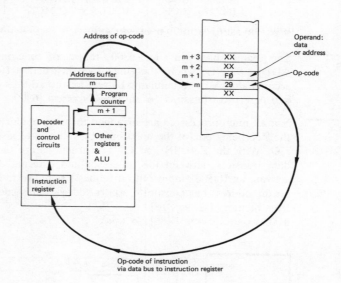

The range of instructions that can be carried out by a processor is referred to as its **instruction set**, and generally the larger the instruction set the greater the flexibility and power of the machine. Typically, 8-bit microprocessors have instruction sets numbering in the range 50 to 100 instructions, but this is increased substantially when all the possible variations caused by addressing modes are included. Four different instructions result from loading a register using the addressing modes immediate, direct, extended or indexed.

The types of instruction are usually classed under three headings:

1 *Data transfer*
   Load, Store, Move
2 *Arithmetic and logic*
   Add, Subtract, Shift, AND, OR, etc.
3 *Test and branch*
   Compare, Test, Jump, Branch

An instruction may be single, double or triple byte, depending on the particular addressing mode used.

Single byte	CLC, NOP, DAA using implied (inherent) addressing		
Double byte	LDA	#$F0	Immediate
	LDA	$F0	Direct (zero page)
Triple byte	LDX	#$3FF0	Immediate
	LDX	$3FF0	Extended

The number of machine cycles, and hence the time taken to fetch and execute an instruction, also varies with the complexity of the operation required. Using the 6502 as an example, the instruction CLC (clear carry—implied addressing) takes 2 cycles; whereas a JSR (jump to subroutine—absolute addressing) requires 6 cycles. The instruction-set table for a microprocessor will have a column showing the number of cycles for each instruction.

● ADDRESSING MODE ● FETCH-EXECUTE CYCLE ● MICROPROCESSOR

Interface Circuits and Interfacing Techniques

An interface can be defined as:

The area in which the interactions take place between any two connected parts of a system.

Thus interface circuits are the essential linking elements between the input/output devices and the microelectronic chips in a system. An interface accepts a signal from one part of the system and adjusts it so that the resulting output is fully compatible with another part of the system. Interface circuits perform one or more of the following functions:

Electrical buffering
Conversion
Timing and synchronising
A change in the number of lines

A whole host of circuits and devices come within the description of "interface": matching circuits for input sensors, A-to-D and D-to-A convertors, drive circuits, and linking units from one type of logic to another. But even if a circuit seems unique in its design it will probably be using techniques that are similar to other interface circuits. In microprocessor-based systems these techniques can be listed as follows:

1 *Matching or buffering*—adjusting the power and voltage levels of a signal and preventing excessive loading to a device.

2 *Multiplexing and sampling*—where a number of signals are switched in turn using an electronic switch to provide input data to one ADC.

3 *Conversion*—analog to digital (ADC) at the input and digital to analog (DAC) at the output.

4 *Power control and isolation*—methods of coupling the small power output available from the micro to drive motors, solenoids, heaters or other devices connected to an external high voltage supply. Electrical isolation is often essential to prevent possible damage to the micro system.

The general principle of these techniques is illustrated in *fig. I6* where a micro controller samples data from four input sensors and uses this data with its program to adjust the power delivered to two output devices. Each sensor has a matching circuit of some kind that adjusts the sensor's output signal to be within

Fig. I6 Block diagram of interfacing requirements in a system

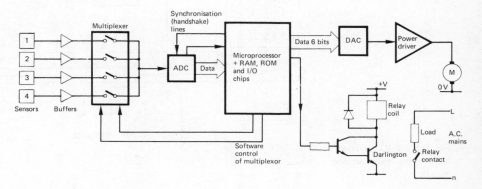

101

the range of the analog-to-digital converter and also serves as an impedance match. The multiplexor, an electronic switch, then connects each sensor output in turn to the ADC. The rate at which the switching action occurs can either be set by an external timer or be software controlled by the microprocessor. The ADC takes an analog level and converts it into digital, then signals to the microprocessor via handshake lines that valid data is available. Synchronisation of data transfers, to avoid the possibility of errors if the microprocessor accepted data before the ADC had finished the conversion, is an essential feature of most input interface circuits.

At the output, one bit of the 8-bit digital word is used for on/off control while 6 bits are shown being converted into analog to give smooth speed control for a d.c. motor.

To take this illustrated example further, some possible circuits for a selected group of these interfaces are shown in *fig. 17*.

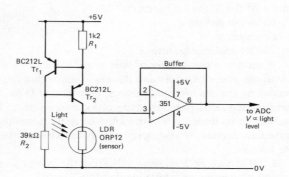

Fig. 17a Light intensity detector

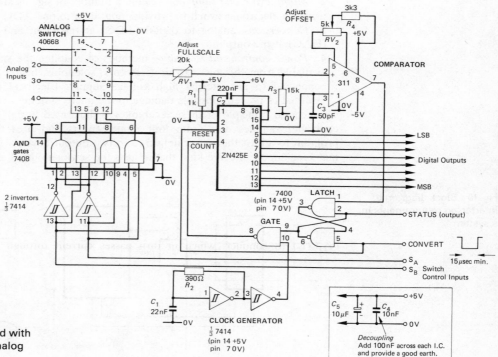

Fig. 17b ADC board with four multiplexed analog inputs

Fig. 17c Output interface circuit

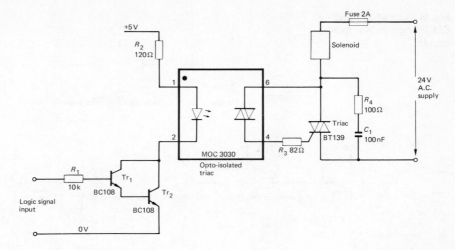

A) *Light-intensity detector*

A light-dependent resistor (LDR) is used as a light level sensor to supply a voltage signal to the ADC of a system. The sensor, an ORP12, or similar type, is supplied with a constant current of about 0.5 mA from the two-transistor arrangement of Tr_1 and Tr_2. The voltage developed across the LDR, which will fall as the light intensity is increased, is then transferred to the ADC by an op-amp wired as a unity-gain amplifier. An op-amp connected in this way has a very high input impedance and a low output impedance and therefore prevents the signal generated at the sensor from being excessively loaded.

B) *Multiplexor*

Four analog inputs can be switched in turn by this circuit which uses some TTL gates and a CMOS 4066B quad analog switch i.c. Switch control is by the pins labelled S_A and S_B which are decoded using two invertors from a 7414 and the four AND gates of a 7408. The sequence, to ensure that only one switch is on at any one instant is shown by the table:

INPUTS		DRIVE TO OPERATE SWITCHES			
S_A	S_B	1	2	3	4
0	0	1	0	0	0
0	1	0	1	0	0
1	0	0	0	1	0
1	1	0	0	0	1

C) *Output interface to switch a.c. power*

This circuit allows a logic signal from a micro output port to switch power to a load connected to the a.c. mains supply. A high logic level forces the darlington (Tr_1/Tr_2) to conduct, which in turn passes current through the LED in the opto-isolator. The light-sensitive triac inside the opto-device switches on and causes the main triac, a BT 139 or similar type, to conduct and switch power to the a.c. load. The a.c. supply is completely isolated from the micro output port by the use of the opto-device; electrical isolation is obviously an important feature of an interface circuit such as this.

There are also situations in microelectronic systems where it is necessary to use a mix of TTL and CMOS logic (*fig. 18*). Depending on the voltage supplied to the CMOS (TTL is always +5 V) the following rules apply:

Fig. 18 Mix of TTL and
CMOS logic in interface
circuits

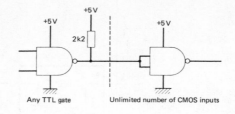

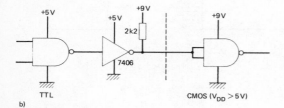

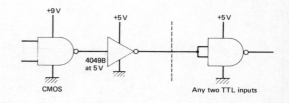

Any TTL gate   Unlimited number of CMOS inputs

a)

b)   TTL   7406   CMOS ($V_{DD} > 5$ V)   CMOS   4049B at 5 V   Any two TTL inputs

1 If the CMOS is running from a +5 V supply, then any TTL gate provided with a 2k2 pull-up resistor will drive an unlimited number of CMOS gate inputs.

2 Usually the CMOS will be running at a higher voltage, say +9 V, and then a TTL open collector output gate (7406 is an example) can be used with the pull-up resistor connected to the +9 V CMOS supply.

3 Any CMOS gate output, with a supply of +5 V, will drive *one* low power Schottky TTL input. Otherwise the CMOS (at a supply of +5 V or higher) must be interfaced to the TTL via a 4049B or 4050B buffer. These will drive any two TTL inputs.

● CONTROL SYSTEMS   ● OPTO-DEVICE   ● POWER CONTROL

Interpreter

Software which carries out the task of checking a high-level language program and translating it into machine language. An interpreter does this checking and translation process for each statement of the source language and outputs error messages to assist the programmer; it is therefore slower than a compiler.

● ASSEMBLER   ● COMPILER   ● HIGH-LEVEL LANGUAGE

Interrupt

Most microprocessors are provided with one or more interrupt inputs. These are supplied so that the main program (the one currently being executed) can be temporarily halted to allow some external condition to be acknowledged and to force the processor to take some sort of action. Interrupts are therefore an important feature in servicing peripherals especially when a microprocessor is used in a control set-up. There are two main types of interrupt:

1 NON-MASKABLE INTERRUPT (NMI) which is used for emergency conditions such as imminent power supply failure, overheating of some external device and so on. A logic signal on this input will force the processor to break from its current program. The instruction being executed is completed and processor status (the contents of selected register in the processor) is saved on the stack. The address of a service routine is loaded into the program counter from the interrupt vector and the required action, which could be sounding an alarm or switching to a standby power unit, can be executed. When the interrupt service routine is completed, the processor status will be restored and the main program can be continued if that is required.

2 INTERRUPT REQUEST (IRQ) (*fig. 19*) This is the standard interrupt request facility for servicing a wide range of peripherals. It is used to synchronise

Fig. l9a The situation at the instant an interrupt occurs

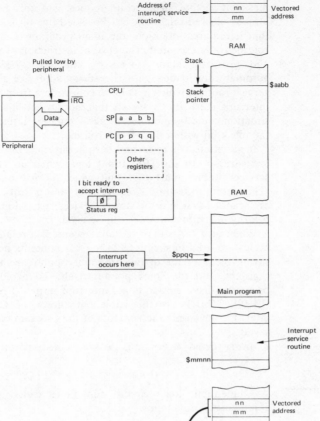

Address of interrupt service routine → | nn |
| mm | ← Vectored address

RAM

Pulled low by peripheral

Stack

Stack pointer → | | ← $aabb

IRQ

CPU

SP | a a b b |

PC | p p q q |

Other registers

I bit ready to accept interrupt

| | Ø | |
Status reg

Data

Peripheral

RAM

Interrupt occurs here → $ppqq → |

Main program

Interrupt service routine

$mmnn

Fig. l9b The situation when the interrupt request has been accepted

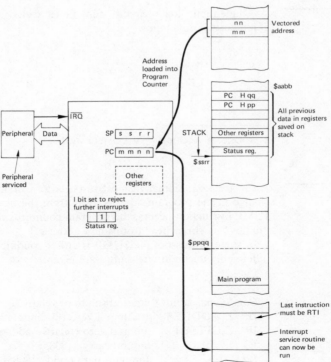

| n n |
| m m | ← Vectored address

Address loaded into Program Counter

| | ← $aabb
| PC H qq |
| PC H pp |
All previous data in registers saved on stack

IRQ

Peripheral

Data

SP | s s r r |

PC | m n n n |

STACK

| Other registers |
| Status reg. |

$ssrr

Other registers

I bit set to reject further interrupts

| | 1 | |
Status reg.

Peripheral serviced

$ppqq → |

Main program

Last instruction must be RTI

Interrupt service routine can now be run

data transfers and to save processor time. The IRQ is controlled by means of a mask bit so that an interrupt request can only be accepted if the program has already cleared this mask bit. Provided this bit is clear when a peripheral signals that it requires attention, the main program is interrupted to allow the service routine to be executed. The current instruction of the main program is completed and processor status saved on the stack before the program counter is automatically loaded with the start address of the service routine. While the service routine, which may be to collect data from a sensor, is being executed, the interrupt mask bit is set so that no further interrupts can be accepted. This situation could be modified to allow multiple interrupts by an instruction to clear the mask bit within the service routine.

In situations where several peripherals must use the IRQ input, the peripherals are wired-or to the IRQ input and, when an interrupt is detected, the IRQ service routine must first find which device requires attention. This can be achieved by *software polling*, usually on a priority basis where the fastest devices are scanned first and the slower devices last. Alternatively a special chip called a *priority interrupt controller* can be used.

When an IRQ is detected and accepted, a relatively large number of machine cycles are used in saving CPU register contents on the stack. This could involve saving the contents of the program counter, accumulators, index registers, flag registers, and the stack pointer itself. To avoid this time delay, some later processors have an additional interrupt termed FAST INTERRUPT REQUEST (FIRQ). This is also maskable but allows the CPU to respond rapidly to an interrupt since only the contents of the program counter and the flag register are saved.

● HANDSHAKE ● POLLING ● STACK AND STACK POINTER

Invertor

A single-input logic circuit, sometimes called a NOT gate, that gives the complement of its input.

Input	Output
A	F
Ø	1
1	Ø

$F = \bar{A}$

● BOOLEAN ALGEBRA ● COMPLEMENT

JUMP Instruction

An instruction, similar in most respects to a branch instruction, which causes a change in the program address away from the next sequential location. When a JUMP instruction occurs, the program counter is reloaded and the program then "jumps" or "branches" to this new address.

In some processors the JUMP is either conditional or unconditional, while in others only unconditional jumps are given.

Examples

Conditional jumps (either absolute or relative)
JP Z,ADDRESS   Jump if zero (absolute addressing) [Z80]
JP Z,OFFSET   Jump if zero (relative addressing) [Z80]
JC LABEL1   Jump on carry [8085]
JPO LABEL2   Jump on parity odd [8085]

JMP   ADDRESS   Jump (absolute addressing) [Z80, 8085]

JMP   ADDRESS   Jump (extended or indexed) [6800]

In some texts, conditional relative jumps are referred to as branch instructions with the name jump reserved only for instructions in which an absolute address is specified.

● BRANCH INSTRUCTION ◖ CONDITIONAL BRANCH ● SUBROUTINE

Karnaugh Map

An aid in logic simplification where the Boolean function to be simplified is displayed in diagram form. The map consists of a square or rectangular grid, where each cell within the grid represents a minterm of the logic expression.

Karnaugh maps for two, three and four variables are shown in *fig. K1* together with very simple examples which cannot be further reduced. The process of simplification is to examine the marked cells and to "couple" together those that are adjacent. Adjacent cells are those which differ by one variable. Cells must be grouped in binary combinations (2, 4, 8) and edge "couples" can be included.

Fig. K1 Karnaugh maps

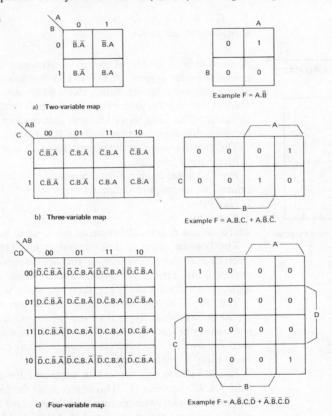

a) Two-variable map

Example $F = A.\bar{B}$

b) Three-variable map

Example $F = A.B.C + A.\bar{B}.\bar{C}$.

c) Four-variable map

Example $F = A.\bar{B}.C.\bar{D} + \bar{A}.\bar{B}.\bar{C}.D$

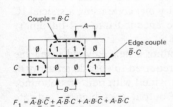

Couple $= B \cdot \bar{C}$

Edge couple $\bar{B} \cdot C$

$F_1 = \bar{A} \cdot B \cdot \bar{C} + \bar{A} \cdot \bar{B} \cdot C + A \cdot B \cdot \bar{C} + A \cdot \bar{B} \cdot C$

$= B \cdot \bar{C} + \bar{B} \cdot C$

Fig. K2

Example (fig. K2)

$$F_1 = \bar{A} \cdot B \cdot \bar{C} + \bar{A} \cdot \bar{B} \cdot C + A \cdot B \cdot \bar{C} + A \cdot \bar{B} \cdot C$$

This gives four cells with logic 1s as shown and two couples. The variables common to the couple in the top row are $B \cdot \bar{C}$, while the edge couple have the variables $\bar{B} \cdot C$ in common. Therefore the expression F_1 can be simplified to:

$$F_1 = B \cdot \bar{C} + \bar{B} \cdot C$$

Fig. K3

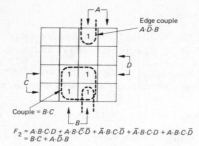

$$F_2 = A \cdot B \cdot C \cdot D + A \cdot B \cdot \bar{C} \cdot \bar{D} + \bar{A} \cdot B \cdot C \cdot \bar{D} + \bar{A} \cdot B \cdot C \cdot D + A \cdot B \cdot C \cdot \bar{D}$$
$$= B \cdot C + A \cdot \bar{D} \cdot B$$

Example (fig. K3)

$$F_2 = A \cdot B \cdot C \cdot D + A \cdot B \cdot \bar{C} \cdot \bar{D} + \bar{A} \cdot B \cdot C \cdot \bar{D}$$
$$+ \bar{A} \cdot B \cdot C \cdot D + A \cdot B \cdot C \cdot \bar{D}$$

This requires a four-variable map which when drawn gives five cells filled and two couples. From this, the simplified expression is

$$F_2 = B \cdot C + A \cdot \bar{D} \cdot B$$

● BOOLEAN ALGEBRA

Keyboard and Encoding

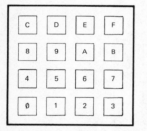

Fig. K4 Layout of a typical hex. keypad

A *keyboard* is a set of switches arranged so that data can be input to a microcomputer system. A QWERTY keyboard, the standard typewriter format, allows the user to input the full alphanumeric set together with other useful control characters, but often in a small system a Hex. keypad (*fig. K4*) is sufficient. This uses 16 switches to give the hexadecimal numbers Ø to F and may include additional switches such as RS (reset), EX (exit), and G (go).

The switches used in keyboards/keypads are usually one of the following:
Mechanical contacts
Reed switches operated by a magnet
both of which require debouncing, or
Hall effect
Capacitive
which do not require debouncing but tend to be expensive.

The bounce effect is pronounced in mechanical contacts on both on and off operation as the contacts close and open several times before finally taking up a new position. Special debounce circuits, which are often included in any encoding logic, or a software delay are then necessary to avoid false inputs to the system.

The output of any keyboard or keypad has to be *encoded* into a suitable logic signal before being applied to the microcomputer input. A QWERTY keyboard will usually be encoded into 8-bit ASCII (plus 1 parity bit) code using a special IC with built-in ROM, whereas a hex. keypad can be encoded into a 4-bit binary word using a relatively simple chip.

Fig. K5 shows one typical arrangement for encoding a hex. keypad using the MM 74C922 encoder IC. This contains all the logic required to encode an array of 16 push-to-make switches into 4-bit binary and is provided with built-in debounce and an interval clock oscillator. A Data Available output goes high to indicate that a key has been operated and returns to a low when that key is released, even if another key is depressed. In this way, key rollover is provided between any two switches. The diagram also shows how input data from the encoder can be synchronised to the micro system data bus using Data Available output to set a D-type bistable. The microprocessor will respond with a Data Accept signal connected to the output enable of the encoder.

● DEBOUNCE ● INTERFACE CIRCUITS

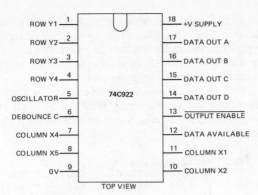

Fig. K5a Pinout of the 74C922

1	ROW Y1
2	ROW Y2
3	ROW Y3
4	ROW Y4
5	OSCILLATOR
6	DEBOUNCE C
7	COLUMN X4
8	COLUMN X5
9	0V
18	+V SUPPLY
17	DATA OUT A
16	DATA OUT B
15	DATA OUT C
14	DATA OUT D
13	$\overline{\text{OUTPUT ENABLE}}$
12	DATA AVAILABLE
11	COLUMN X1
10	COLUMN X2

74C922

TOP VIEW

Fig. K5b The 74C922 connections for decoding a hex. keypad

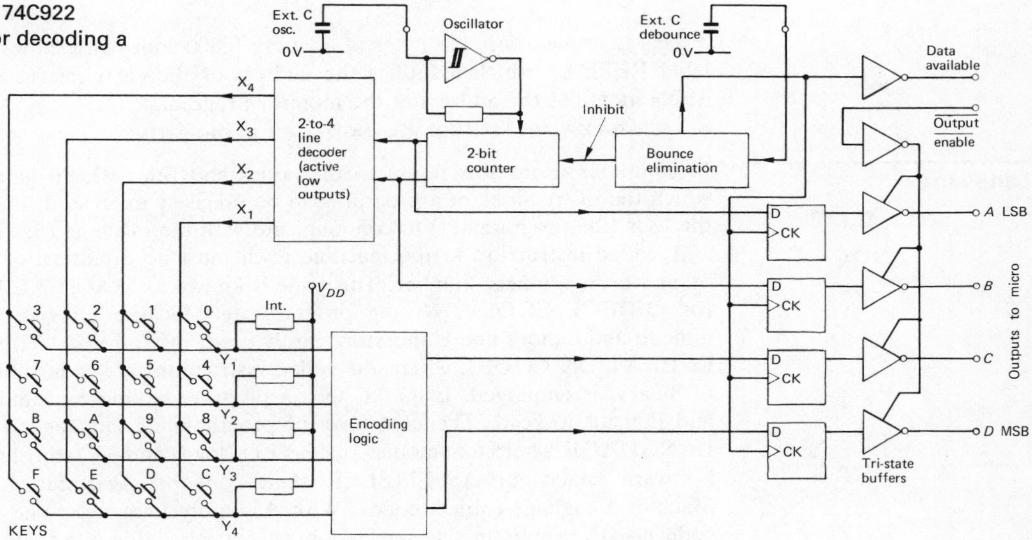

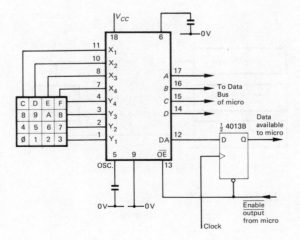

Fig. K5c One method of interfacing the keypad and the 74C922 to a microprocessor (synchronous handshake)

109

Label

A "nametag" made up of a group of characters, and attached to an instruction or statement in a program. This name then identifies the address of the object code produced from the instruction or statement.

For example, PAUSE could be a label to identify the address of the first instruction of a time delay subroutine.

A label, which is optional and referred to as a symbolic address, is most useful in identifying addresses which have to be used repeatedly in programs, i.e. those programs containing loops or subroutines. Program example in assembly language:

LABEL FIELD	MNEMONIC	OPERAND	COMMENT
	LDX	#$3000	SET POINTER
REPEAT	CLR	$00,X	CLEAR POINTED ADDRESS
	INX		INCREMENT POINTER
	CPX	#$3080	CHECK IF POINTER AT END
	BNE	REPEAT	IF NOT BRANCH BACK
	JMP	MON	

This example clears 128 bytes of memory (6800 code) and shows the use of the label REPEAT which identifies the address of the clear instruction. The label MON identifies the address of the monitor program.

● ASSEMBLER   ● ASSEMBLY LANGUAGE   ● DIRECTIVE

Language

In computer terms this refers to the codes and rules which define the way in which the instructions of a program can be precisely expressed, thereby allowing the user (the programmer) to communicate with the machine (*fig. L1*).

A coded instruction to the machine itself must be a pattern of Øs and 1s—in other words, a binary number. This code is known as MACHINE LANGUAGE (or OBJECT CODE). Writing programs in Machine Language is obviously difficult and tedious and is therefore rarely used. Instead, MACHINE CODE (or OPERATION CODE), where the coded instructions are in hexadecimal instead of binary, is employed. Even so, such a program is time-consuming to produce and difficult to read. The next level of programming language is ASSEMBLY LANGUAGE where mnemonics such as LD (load) and ST (store) are employed. Software called an ASSEMBLER then converts Assembly Language into Machine Language (object code). With Assembly Language, one line of source code usually results in one line of object code but this one-to-one relationship does not exist with a HIGH-LEVEL LANGUAGE. An HLL such as PASCAL, BASIC, C, FORTRAN, etc. is a language designed for programming ease and is

Fig. L1 Levels of language in a microcomputer

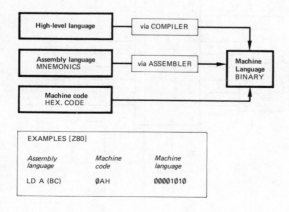

110

therefore capable of being run on different machines. A COMPILER is software in the system that then converts a High-Level Language into Machine Language.

- ASSEMBLY LANGUAGE ● ASSEMBLER ● COMPILER ● HIGH-LEVEL LANGUAGE ● MACHINE CODE ● MACHINE LANGUAGE

Large-scale Integration (LSI)

A monolithic integrated circuit where the density is equivalent to more than 100 gates.

Microprocessor, memory and interface ICs are examples of LSI devices.

- CHIP

Latch

Used to describe the operation of bistable-type memory circuit, as in: "The circuit latched to a new state." A *latching circuit* is one that retains its logic state even when the input that caused the change of state is removed.

A group of D bistables (data latch types) can be used to create a simple interface port for a micro system. The array is addressed on the clock line and the data then present on the data bus will be latched into the bistable and held until a new word is required to be written in.

- BISTABLE ● MEMORIES ● PORT

Light-emitting Diode (LED)

A semiconductor diode which emits light when it is forward biased (*fig. L2*). In a pn junction, energy is released when an electron recombines with a hole. When this happens in a semiconductor junction, particularly gallium arsenide, the energy is released as infra-red radiation. By mixing other substances with gallium, LEDs can be made that emit visible light.

Typical LED data

| MATERIAL | FORWARD CHARACTERISTICS | | |
	COLOUR	V_F at	I_F
Gallium arsenide phosphide (GaAsP)	Red	2.0 V	10 mA
Gallium phosphide (GaP)	Green	2.2 V	10 mA
Gallium indium phosphide (GaInP)	Yellow	2.4 V	10 mA

I_F max is usually 40 mA and V_R max is usually 5 V.

All that is required to get an LED to emit light is to forward bias it and set the current to a few milliamps. Unless the LED is driven from a constant current

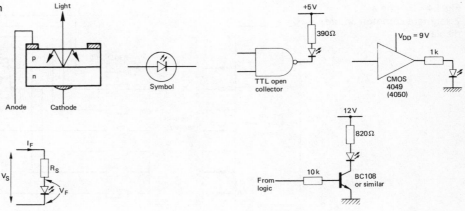

Fig. L2 LED construction and operation

source, a resistor R_S must be wired in series with the diode:

$$R_S = \frac{V_S - V_F}{I_F}$$

where V_S is the supply voltage, V_F is the forward volt drop of the diode, and I_F is the forward current (usually 10 mA to 20 mA). If the supply is +5 V then R_S is about 150 Ω.

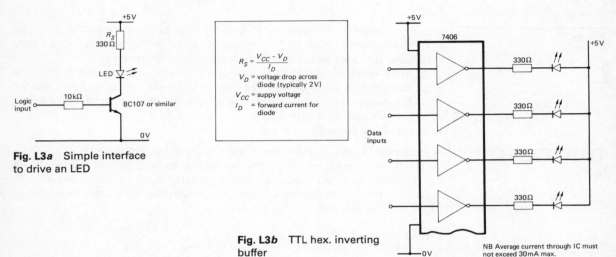

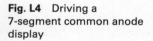

Fig. L3a Simple interface to drive an LED

Fig. L3b TTL hex. inverting buffer

A single LED makes a useful ON/OFF indicator in microelectronic systems but cannot normally be driven directly from output ports; some sort of interface is required. Typical arrangements are shown in *fig. L3*. If two or more LEDs are used it may be better to use an i.c. to perform the buffer action. A TTL hex. inverting open collector i.c. such as the 7406 is suitable but again series resistors must be used to limit the current through each diode.

Seven-segment displays with either common anodes or common cathodes (*fig. L4*) can also be driven via transistor or i.c. buffers from a micro 8-bit port.

● INTERFACE CIRCUITS ● SEVEN-SEGMENT DISPLAY

Fig. L4 Driving a 7-segment common anode display

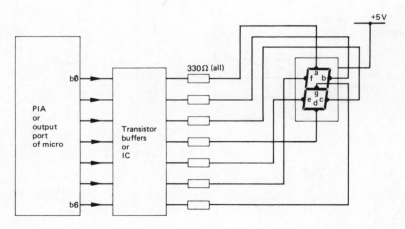

Literal and Literal Mode

A *literal* (a numerical constant) in a source language instruction is an operand which is data rather than an address at which data is stored.

In the statement

LD(r)   AFH   [Z80]

AF is a literal.

This instruction would load the data byte AF_{16} into the register. Hence, the literal addressing mode is identical to immediate mode.

● IMMEDIATE MODE

LOAD Instruction (LD)

A data transfer instruction which loads into a register or accumulator the data held at the address specified in the instruction.

Example

LD A   3F∅∅H   [Z80]

Load (LD) accumulator (A) from address 3F∅∅.

The data will not be lost from the memory location and any previous data held in the accumulator will be overwritten.

Various addressing modes can be used with the LD instruction: Immediate, Direct (or zero page), Extended (or absolute), and Indexed.

● ADDRESSING MODE   ● INSTRUCTION

Logic Instructions and Logical Operations

Instructions such as AND, OR, EXCLUSIVE-OR, COMPLEMENT and LOGICAL SHIFT are examples of logical operations that can be executed by a microprocessor. Usually the logic operation is performed, on a bit-for-bit basis, between the contents of a selected memory location and the accumulator. The result is then placed in the accumulator. Addressing modes such as immediate, absolute (extended), zero page (direct) and indexed are normally available for use with logic instructions.

1   The AND instruction is most useful for masking: that is, clearing selected bits to zero.

Example

Accumulator originally holds $73

∅	1	1	1	∅	∅	1	1

AND accumulator Imm. with $∅F

∅	∅	∅	∅	1	1	1	1

Result left in accumulator = $∅3

∅	∅	∅	∅	∅	∅	1	1

The upper four bits have been cleared to zero.

2   The OR instruction can be used to set selected bits in the accumulator to 1.

Example

Accumulator originally holds $39

∅	∅	1	1	1	∅	∅	1

OR accumulator Imm. with $8∅

1	∅	∅	∅	∅	∅	∅	∅

Result left in accumulator = $B9

1	∅	1	1	1	∅	∅	1

The M.S.B. has been set to 1.

3 The EXCLUSIVE-OR instruction can be used to complement (invert) selected bits in the accumulator.

Example

Accumulator originally holds $9A

1	0	0	1	1	0	1	0

XOR accumulator Imm. with $81

1	0	0	0	0	0	0	1

Result left in accumulator = $1B

0	0	0	1	1	0	1	1

Both the MSB and LSB have been complemented.

● COMPARE INSTRUCTION

Look-up Table

A list of data arranged sequentially in memory so that any part can be readily retrieved. For an example see ● SEVEN-SEGMENT DISPLAY.

Loop

Whenever a program requires a certain operation or set of operations to be repeated several times, a loop is necessary. The *loop* is a return path that allows the program to branch back and pick up the instructions again and again until the required number of passes is completed.

A program with a loop contains three sections:

a) *Initialisation*: when a loop counter will be loaded with the required number of passes or cleared to zero.

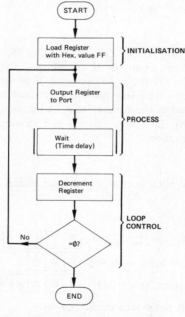

Fig. L5*a* Section of a program with a loop

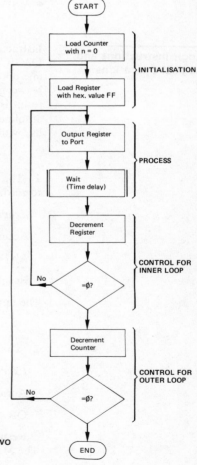

Fig. L5*b* Program with two loops

b) The *process*.

c) *Loop control*: this will include incrementing (or decrementing) the counter, testing the value of the counter, and a branch instruction that will cause the program to repeat the process until the number of passes required has been completed.

A typical program with one loop to output a ramp waveform to a port could be as shown in *fig. L5a*. This is modified at *fig. L5b* so that 10 such ramp outputs can be generated.

● BRANCH INSTRUCTION ● DELAY ● LABEL

Machine Address

This has the same meaning as ● ABSOLUTE ADDRESS.

Machine Code

These are programs written using hexadecimal numbers to represent the instructions and data used by a microcomputer. Although hexadecimal numbers are commonly used for machine code, these codes can also be expressed in octal or decimal.

A typical instruction such as LDA $84 [6502] would be represented by A9 84 in machine code.

● ASSEMBLER ● ASSEMBLY LANGUAGE ● HEXADECIMAL
NUMBERS ● LANGUAGE ● MACHINE LANGUAGE

Machine Cycle

The basic time unit for a microprocessor, measured in microseconds and derived from the periodic time of the master clock. The exact way in which it is specified differs between processors, but usually during a machine cycle an address is placed on the address bus allowing an op-code to be fetched or data to be transferred. This is illustrated for the 6502 in *fig. M1* showing how, in one machine cycle, the op-code for Load Accumulator immediate is fetched and then, in the second machine cycle, the data byte (3F in this case) is loaded into the accumulator. If the system clock is running at 1 MHz then this instruction would take 2 μsec to fetch and execute.

Fig. M1   The 6502 timing
diagram

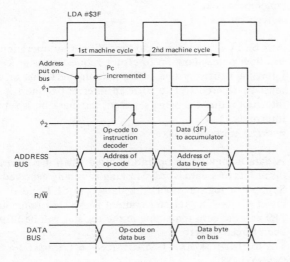

The number of machine cycles required for any instruction depends upon the complexity of the instruction and the addressing mode used. For example, the instruction LDA $3F6∅ (load the accumulator from address 3F6∅) would therefore use more machine cycles than the previous instruction.

● CLOCK SIGNAL ● FETCH-EXECUTE CYCLE

Machine Language

These are the binary numbers at machine level that represent the instruction codes and data used by a microprocessor.

Hence LDA $84 is

10101001 10000100

in 6502 machine language.

● LANGUAGE ● MACHINE CODE

Macro

A *macro* is a single statement in a source listing which is used to generate a small group of machine instructions. The macro can then be converted into machine code using a *macro assembler* and in this way the programmer can replace a short sequence of instructions with a single instruction name. This macro name can then be used as many times as required in the program and this saves programming time and reduces errors. Macros are used where a small program segment has to be repeated several times, say for an I/O routine, but where the use of a subroutine is not warranted.

Example

MACRO NAME: GET

LABEL	MNEMONIC	
GET	MDEF	
	LDA $C004	Program segment to load
	STA 0,X	accumulator from an input;
	INX	store the value at a
	MEND	location pointed at by
		the index register; and
		then increment the pointer

Here. MDEF = Macro define
and   MEND = Macro end   Assembler directives

Thereafter the macro can be called by using the label GET, placed in the mnemonic field.

● ASSEMBLER

Mask Bit and Maskable Interrupt

Any bit in a register used to "mask" out an operation. A typical mask bit is used to allow or disallow an interrupt request to a processor. The mask bit for the interrupt is usually one of the bits in the status or condition code register and must be cleared (set to 0) if an interrupt request is to be serviced. Whilst one interrupt request is being serviced, the mask bit is set to 1, preventing any further interrupts.

● INTERRUPT ● MASKING

Masking

A data manipulation operation, used when it is necessary to blank off a selected bit or bits of a data word. Masking is usually achieved using the AND instruction. Suppose a register holds the data byte $E7 and it is required to mask off the lower 4 bits. The register content is ANDed immediately with the hex. number $F0 and the data remaining in the register will be $E0. The lower 4 bits will have been forced to zero.

● AND GATE ● AND INSTRUCTION ● LOGICAL INSTRUCTIONS AND LOGICAL OPERATIONS

Memories

A memory of some kind is an essential part of any microprocessor-based system. It is used to store data and programs, as patterns of 1s and 0s, in a temporary, semi-permanent or permanent form. A memory has two main properties:

1 Every location must have a unique address.
2 It has to be possible to read out the state of every location.

Apart from ROM stores, write facilities must also be provided so that the state of any location can be changed.

The main features of a memory are characterised by:

a) Capacity—the total number of bits that can be held.

b) Organisation—the arrangement of the locations. For example 256 bits can be organised as:

$$256 \times 1 \qquad 128 \times 2 \qquad 32 \times 8 \qquad 16 \times 16$$

c) Addressing method—the way in which the locations are accessed. This can be random, serial or cyclic.

d) Access time—the speed with which a location can be read.

e) General use—either to hold data (scratch-pad), current program, fixed program and/or data, or as a bulk back-up store.

There are two main categories of semiconductor memory. Both use random access, where any location can be accessed in the same time as any other. Access is rapid, typically less than 500 nsec.

RAM: random access memory, or more accurately READ/WRITE memory, in which data can be read out or new data written in. A control pin $R/\bar{W}$ or $\overline{WE}$ (write enable), set by the microprocessor according to the instruction being executed, determines the data direction. RAM is used for current program and data.

ROM: read only memory, a memory chip in which the data is fixed and not erasable. Used for fixed program (such as the monitor for a system), holding constants, and for character tables. ROM is mask-programmed by the i.c. manufacturer to the user's specification and cannot be changed. No $R/\bar{W}$ line is required.

Greater flexibility for the user is allowed using:

PROM: user programmable or field programmable read only memory. Once programmed they also cannot be changed.

EPROM: electrically programmable read only memory. The stored pattern can be erased by exposing the memory cells to ultra-violet light through a transparent quartz window. The process usually takes 20 to 30 minutes. All cells are erased, and a new pattern can then be set up by applying suitable electrical signals to the required cells. An EPROM programmer is the standard machine for this task.

EEPROM or E^2PROM: electrically erasable and programmable read only memory. Individual locations can be erased and changed by applying suitable electrical voltages.

EAROM: electrically alterable read only memory, sometimes termed a read mostly memory. Used in applications where word or block changes are required.

A memory is referred to as **volatile** if the stored data is lost when the power supply to the memory is switched off. Most semiconductor RAM is therefore volatile, but ROM stores which have a fixed pattern are non-volatile.

A further distinction has to be be made between STATIC and DYNAMIC memories. **Static** memories will hold data as long as d.c. power is applied, but the **dynamic** types must be provided with clock pulses in order to keep the stored pattern refreshed. The dynamic types have the advantage of higher density and lower power consumption. Dynamic RAMs are sometimes referred to as DRAMs.

IC memory chips are made using the following technologies: TTL, ECL, I^2L, NMOS and CMOS.

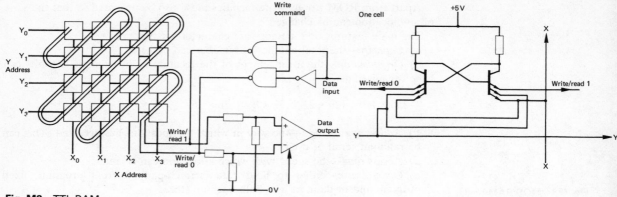

Fig. M2 TTL RAM

TTL and I^2L are fast low-density types whereas NMOS and CMOS are lower in speed but have the advantage of higher density, reasonable power consumption and low cost.

The basic cell structures for TTL and CMOS RAM are shown in *fig. M2* and *fig. M3* and consist of a bistable circuit formed by two cross-coupled transistors. X and Y address lines are used to activate a cell and its state can be either read out or overwritten by suitable signals applied to the R/$\bar{\text{W}}$ line. In both cases, readout is non-destructive and the memory is volatile.

Access time   TTL (Schottky) 50 nsec
                CMOS   200 nsec

The internal organisation of a static RAM is made up of address decoders, the memory array, sense and control logic, and a tri-state data input-output section. *Fig. M4* shows the basic arrangement for a CMOS 16 K-bit static RAM (5516 type) which is organised as 2048 words of 8 bits. A total of 11 address lines are necessary to allow any group of 8 cells in the array to be accessed ($2^{11} = 2048$). The lower-order address lines ($A_\emptyset$ to A_5) are decoded inside the chip to identify the required row and the next higher group of address lines (A_6 to $A_{1\emptyset}$) are decoded to identify a particular column. The chip select pins (active low) are used to allow external decoding of the remaining high-order address lines (A_{11} to A_{15}). When an address is applied with the R/$\bar{\text{W}}$ line high, the content of 8 cells will be transferred via the tri-state data buffers to the data bus. If the R/$\bar{\text{W}}$ line were taken low, then data would be written into the 8 cells overwriting the previous stored pattern.

Fig. M5 shows how this CMOS memory chip can be given a unique range of addresses by fully decoding the remaining high-order address lines. A_{11} and A_{12} must be $\emptyset$ and 1 respectively while A_{13}, A_{14}, and A_{15} are required to be $\emptyset1\emptyset$ in order to give a logic $\emptyset$ via the 3-to-8 line address decoder to $\overline{\text{CS2}}$.

A ROM is a fixed logic array which can also be manufactured in bipolar or MOS form. The bipolar type is usually very fast with access times as low as 50 nsec. *Fig. M6* shows one form of NMOS ROM. A cell containing a transistor holds a logic 1 and those without a logic $\emptyset$. The address lines (not shown in this case) are connected to each cell. With no address signal applied, all the series output transistors Tr_0 to Tr_3 will be conducting and the output on the bit line will be low at logic $\emptyset$. Suppose an address is applied to 2.1. The transistor at this cell will conduct taking the gate of Tr_2 low, Tr_2 turns off, and the output rises to logic 1. If a new address is applied to say 2.2, where there is no transistor, Tr_2 remains conducting and the output remains low.

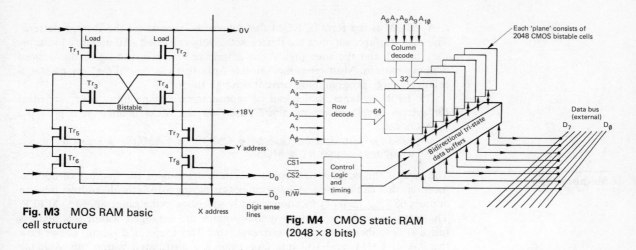

Fig. M3 MOS RAM basic cell structure

Fig. M4 CMOS static RAM (2048 × 8 bits)

Fig. M5 Address range for CMOS RAM (typical)

A_{15}	A_{14}	A_{13}	A_{12}	A_{11}	A_{10}	A_9	A_8	A_7	A_6	A_5	A_4	A_3	A_2	A_1	A_0
0	1	0	1	0	0	0	0	0	0	0	0	0	0	0	0
					1	1	1	1	1	1	1	1	1	1	1

$5000 to $57FF

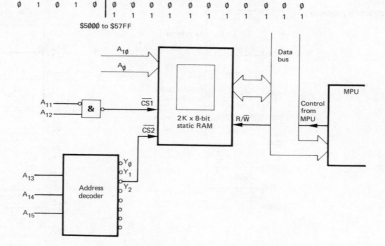

Fig. M6 Principle of MOS ROM

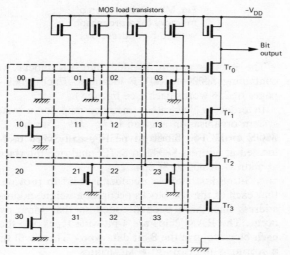

119

A PROM is the form of ROM that allows the user to set the storage pattern. The manufacturer supplies the device with every cell filled. All memory locations then hold 1 and the user then removes selected transistors to give the desired memory pattern. Most types have fusible links that can be "blown" by passing a relatively large programming current through them.

The EPROM types, which can be reprogrammed many times over, are ideal for system development; most are based on the MOS floating gate principle FAMOS cell.

● ADDRESS ● ADDRESS DECODING ● CMOS ● FAMOS ● MEMORY MAP ● MICROPROCESSOR ● MOS

Memory Map

The size of the address bus within a system determines the number of address locations that can be used. A microprocessor having a 16-bit-wide address bus can address $65\,536_{10}$ memory locations, that is addresses in the range $\$0000$ to $\$FFFF$. The way in which the various memory chips are arranged within this address range is described as a *system memory map*. This map, or diagram, shows how the RAM, ROM, and I/O interface chips are distributed within the available space (*fig. M7*).

Fig. M7 A system memory map

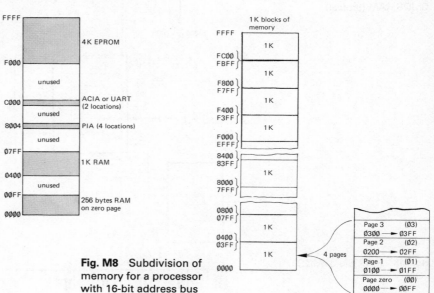

Fig. M8 Subdivision of memory for a processor with 16-bit address bus

The map is usually divided into 1 K blocks with each of the 64 K-blocks containing $\$0000$ to $\$03FF$ locations. Each block is further subdivided into 4 pages of 256 words each (see *fig. M8*).

In order to illustrate a memory map for a system, an example of memory system organisation is given in *fig. M9*. This has 1 K RAM blocks at addresses $\$0000$ to $\$03FF$, $\$2000$ to $\$23FF$, and $\$4000$ to $\$43FF$. An EPROM (2 K) is located at address $\$8000$ to $\$87FF$ and one interface adaptor chip (PIA or VIA) at address $\$C000$ to $\$C004$.

A 3-to-8 line address decoder is used to provide chip enable (CE) signals so that each of the 1 K blocks occupies a unique address, but in this example not all address lines have been decoded so that some overlap or "overwrite" would occur. The RAM chips are 4-bit-wide types and therefore two must be used for each block to give the 8-bit data word. These will then share the same address.

● ADDRESS DECODING ● MEMORIES

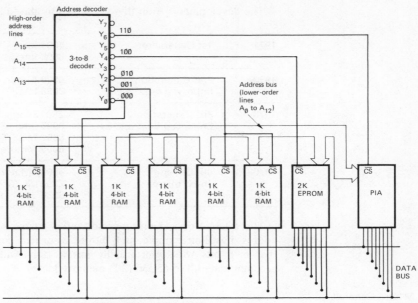

Fig. M9 Memory system organisation

Address decoder

High-order address lines

A_{15}

A_{14}

A_{13}

3-to-8 decoder

Y_7
Y_6 — 11Ø
Y_5
Y_4 — 1ØØ
Y_3
Y_2 — Ø1Ø
Y_1 — ØØ1
Y_0 — ØØØ

Address bus (lower-order lines A_0 to A_{12})

CS — 1K 4-bit RAM
CS — 1K 4-bit RAM
CS — 1K 4-bit RAM
CS — 1K 4-bit RAM
CS — 1K 4-bit RAM
CS — 1K 4-bit RAM
CS — 2K EPROM
CS — PIA

DATA BUS

1K RAM   ØØØØ to Ø3FF and 2ØØØ to 23FF and 4ØØØ to 43FF
EPROM at   8ØØØ to 87FF PIA at CØØØ to CØØ4

Microcomputer

A system, based on a microprocessor, which in its simplest form is made up of:
    a central processor unit (CPU)
    some memory (RAM ROM)
    and input/output circuits.
These can be assembled and interconnected on printed circuit boards or manufactured as a single integrated circuit.

Microinstruction

Instructions stored in ROM inside a microprocessor which are used by and within the processor itself in order to carry out its various machine instructions. Microinstructions are the basic steps required at a level lower than program instructions and are not available to the programmer. A **microprogram** is simply a sequence of microinstructions necessary to carry out each machine instruction.

Microprocessor

Definition: a VLSI chip which can be used as the Central Processor Unit (CPU) for a digital computer. As such it contains the following sections:
    an arithmetic and logic unit (ALU).
    a set of registers (accumulator, program counter, status register, stack pointer) and an instruction decode and control unit.
    The first microprocessor was designed and developed by the Intel Company in 1971. Intel had been approached by a Japanese firm to design and produce a programmable calculator chip. The device produced, a 4-bit CPU, was marketed as the 4004 microprocessor. During this time Intel were also working on the design of a chip for Datapoint, a programmable device for use in an intelligent data terminal. The resulting micro circuit proved too slow for Datapoint's use but was marketed as the world's first 8-bit microprocessor—the 8008. These two devices represent what is now called the 1st generation.

121

The developments from these is shown by the following table:

1971	1st Generation	4004 Intel
		8008 Intel
1973–	2nd Generation Improved 8-bit micros	6800 Motorola 8080 Intel
1975–	3rd Generation Enhanced 8-bit micros	Z80 Zilog 8085 Intel 6502 MOS Technology 6809 Motorola
1979–	4th Generation 16-bit micros	68000 Motorola Z8001/2 Zilog 8086/8088 Intel

The *bit size* of a microprocessor refers to the width of its *data bus*, not its address bus. For example, an 8-bit processor (the common type) operates on data that is 8 bits wide, but usually has a 16-bit-wide address bus. It can then accommodate up to 65 536 (2^{16}) memory locations.

Fig. M10a Generalised microprocessor architecture

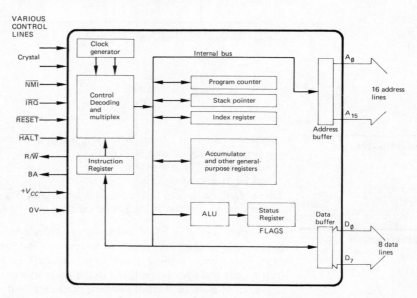

A microprocessor of any type can be represented by the generalised internal architecture as shown in *fig. M10a*. Connections are made to the necessary support chips (memory and I/O) via an address, data and control bus system (*fig. M10b*). These are the common features of all types.

Current program and data will be held in the memory (RAM or ROM) and will be fetched and executed by the microprocessor in sequence. An important difference between processors in the 8080 series and others such as the Z80, 6800 and 6502 is that the 8080 types do not have a dedicated data bus, but instead multiplex address, control and data information on the same lines (see 8080 series).

The function and operation of the registers and other sections within the processor are dealt with more fully in individual sections; but the way in which the various parts of the overall system operate and the use of the registers in

Fig. M10*b* Connections to other chips to form a system

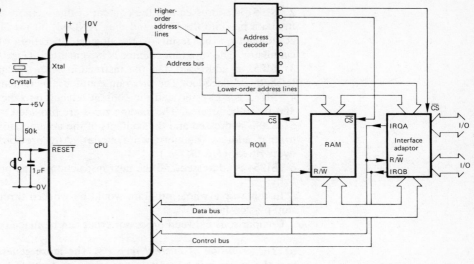

the processor can best be appreciated by considering the fetch and execution of simple instructions.

Example [6502 code used]:

AND   #$0F   AND the Accumulator with the hex. number $0F
              (*immediate addressing*)
STA $20   Store the Acc. content at address $20
              (*zero page addressing*)

The 1st instruction is considered to be at address $1050 (see *fig. M11*).

The program counter would first cause $1050 to be placed on the address bus. The PC is then automatically incremented. The sequence of events is now as follows:

1   The instruction (op-code $29 AND immediate) is fetched into the CPU via the data bus. The instruction is decoded. The program counter is incremented. (*Fig. M11a.*)

Fig. M11*a* Instruction AND # $0F fetched

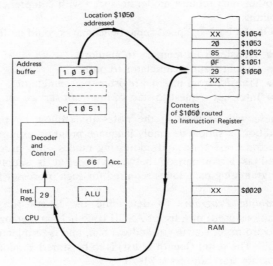

2 $1Ø51 is addressed and the content of this memory location ($ØF) is taken via the data bus into the CPU and then ANDed, bit for bit, with the content of the accumulator. The result of this logical operation will be placed in the accumulator. The program counter is incremented. (*Fig. M11b*.)

3 $1Ø52 is addressed and the instruction Store Accumulator (op-code $85) is fetched and decoded. The program counter is incremented. (*Fig. M11c*.)

4 $1Ø53 is addressed and the content fetched into the CPU so that the address $ØØ2Ø can be formed. The leading zeros are provided by the CPU. (*Fig. M11d*.)

5 $2Ø is addressed and the contents of the accumulator are sent via the data bus to that address (memory write mode). Any previous data at this address is overwritten. (*Fig. M11e*.)

6 $1Ø54 is addressed and the next instruction in the program is fetched.

In this way a whole program would be worked through to its conclusion in a step-by-step fashion.

Comparisons between processor types can be made considering:

a) *The provision of internal registers.* The more general-purpose registers there are, the easier it is for certain programming tasks to be carried out. Having two index registers, for example, is a very useful feature for data processing applications.

b) *The variety and size of the instruction set.* The instruction set is the list of operations that the processor can perform. The greater the list, the greater the flexibility of the machine.

c) *The range and variety of the addressing modes.* Again the more addressing modes, the greater the flexibility.

d) *The method in which I/O transfers are achieved.* I/O can have a specified address area which is isolated from the other memory or it can be memory mapped.

e) *The provision of interrupt facilities.* This may be important in control applications especially when fast response to an interrupt is required.

f) *The speed with which instructions can be fetched and executed.*

This list is not in order of importance since one application may require high speed and fast interrupt with only a limited use of an instruction set, whereas another may require moderate speed with comprehensive addressing/instruction facilities.

On the basis of speed some benchmarks could be the following applications:

- Transfer from memory to memory.
- Output from accumulator to port.
- Transfer from internal register to accumulator.
- Interrupt request to start of interrupt service routine.

These will be used in the notes that follow on popular microprocessors. In addition, a simple assembly language program example will be given in order to illustrate operation and addressing modes—this program is not intended to be used as a comparison between types, it is simply a demonstration of the programming techniques required for each processor (8-bit types only).

Example Program To determine the length (i.e. the number of memory locations used) of a list of ASCII code held in memory. The list is assumed to be on zero page, starting at address $5Ø, and is terminated with the ASCII code for EOT. The result (length of list) is to be stored at address $3ØØØ. In each case the program start address is $1ØØØ.

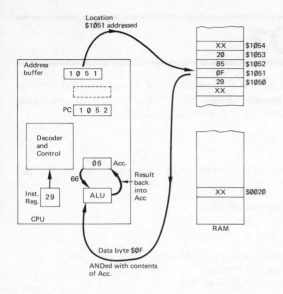

Fig. M11b Execution of instruction AND #$0F

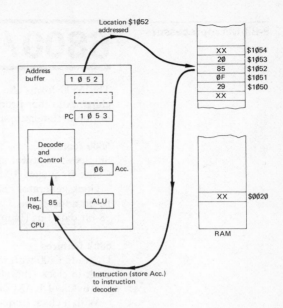

Fig. M11c Instruction Store Acc. (zero page) fetched

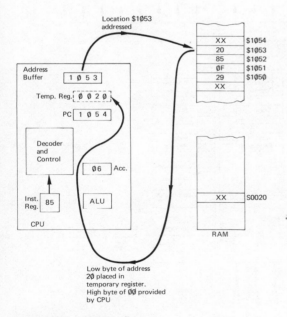

Fig. M11d Address (low byte) $20 fetched

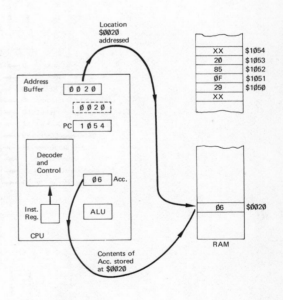

Fig. M11e Acc. stored at address $0020

125

6800/6802

The 6800 forms the starting point for a large family of processors and support chips. All other processors in the series (6801, 6802, 6803, 6805, 6809) are based on the architecture and instruction set of the 6800 (*fig. M12*).

6800 features

Single +5 V power supply.
Clock frequency 1 MHz, but the 2-phase clock must be supplied by an external clock generator chip (6875).
16-bit address bus
  8-bit data bus (bidirectional) } Dedicated lines

6802 features

Upgrade 6800 with identical features and in addition:
Built-in clock (therefore only requires crystal)
128 bytes of RAM on chip (address ØØØØ to ØØ7F).

    With a clock frequency of 1 MHz the machine cycle is 1 μsec. Faster versions of both processors at 1.5 MHz and 2 MHz are available. *Fig. M13* gives pinout and basic diagrams.

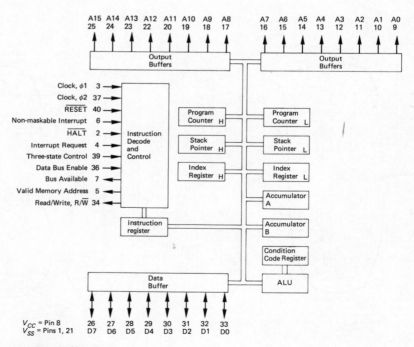

Fig. M12a Architecture of the **6800**

6800/6802

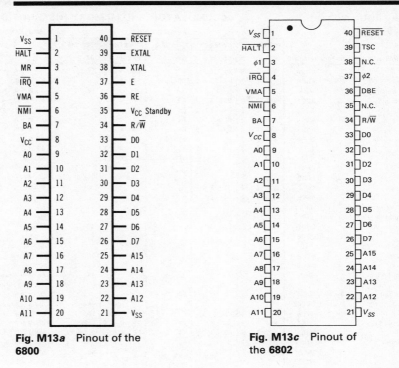

V$_{SS}$	1	40	$\overline{RESET}$
$\overline{HALT}$	2	39	EXTAL
MR	3	38	XTAL
$\overline{IRQ}$	4	37	E
VMA	5	36	RE
$\overline{NMI}$	6	35	V$_{CC}$ Standby
BA	7	34	R/$\overline{W}$
V$_{CC}$	8	33	D0
A0	9	32	D1
A1	10	31	D2
A2	11	30	D3
A3	12	29	D4
A4	13	28	D5
A5	14	27	D6
A6	15	26	D7
A7	16	25	A15
A8	17	24	A14
A9	18	23	A13
A10	19	22	A12
A11	20	21	V$_{SS}$

Fig. M13a Pinout of the **6800**

V$_{SS}$	1	40	$\overline{RESET}$
$\overline{HALT}$	2	39	TSC
ϕ1	3	38	N.C.
$\overline{IRQ}$	4	37	ϕ2
VMA	5	36	DBE
$\overline{NMI}$	6	35	N.C.
BA	7	34	R/$\overline{W}$
V$_{CC}$	8	33	D0
A0	9	32	D1
A1	10	31	D2
A2	11	30	D3
A3	12	29	D4
A4	13	28	D5
A5	14	27	D6
A6	15	26	D7
A7	16	25	A15
A8	17	24	A14
A9	18	23	A13
A10	19	22	A12
A11	20	21	V$_{SS}$

Fig. M13c Pinout of the **6802**

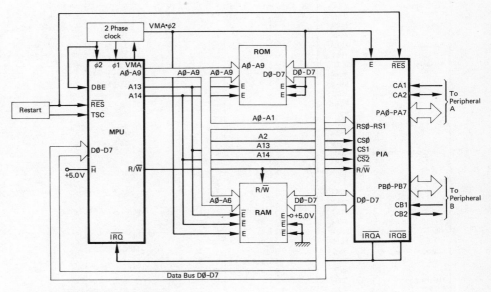

Fig. M13b Typical minimum system set-up [6800]

127

Fig. M12b Instruction set of the 6800

ACCUMULATOR AND MEMORY INSTRUCTIONS

OPERATIONS	MNEMONIC	IMMED OP	~	=	DIRECT OP	~	=	INDEX OP	~	=	EXTND OP	~	=	IMPLIED OP	~	=	BOOLEAN/ARITHMETIC OPERATION (All register labels refer to contents)	H	I	N	Z	V	C
Add	ADDA	8B	2	2	9B	3	2	AB	5	2	BB	4	3				A + M → A	↕	•	↕	↕	↕	↕
	ADDB	CB	2	2	DB	3	2	EB	5	2	FB	4	3				B + M → B	↕	•	↕	↕	↕	↕
Add Acmltrs	ABA													1B	2	1	A + B → A	↕	•	↕	↕	↕	↕
Add with Carry	ADCA	89	2	2	99	3	2	A9	5	2	B9	4	3				A + M + C → A	↕	•	↕	↕	↕	↕
	ADCB	C9	2	2	D9	3	2	E9	5	2	F9	4	3				B + M + C → B	↕	•	↕	↕	↕	↕
And	ANDA	84	2	2	94	3	2	A4	5	2	B4	4	3				A · M → A	•	•	↕	↕	R	•
	ANDB	C4	2	2	D4	3	2	E4	5	2	F4	4	3				B · M → B	•	•	↕	↕	R	•
Bit Test	BITA	85	2	2	95	3	2	A5	5	2	B5	4	3				A · M	•	•	↕	↕	R	•
	BITB	C5	2	2	D5	3	2	E5	5	2	F5	4	3				B · M	•	•	↕	↕	R	•
Clear	CLR							6F	7	2	7F	6	3				00 → M	•	•	R	S	R	R
	CLRA													4F	2	1	00 → A	•	•	R	S	R	R
	CLRB													5F	2	1	00 → B	•	•	R	S	R	R
Compare	CMPA	81	2	2	91	3	2	A1	5	2	B1	4	3				A − M	•	•	↕	↕	↕	↕
	CMPB	C1	2	2	D1	3	2	E1	5	2	F1	4	3				B − M	•	•	↕	↕	↕	↕
Compare Acmltrs	CBA													11	2	1	A − B	•	•	↕	↕	↕	↕
Complement, 1's	COM							63	7	2	73	6	3				$\overline{M} \to M$	•	•	↕	↕	R	S
	COMA													43	2	1	$\overline{A} \to A$	•	•	↕	↕	R	S
	COMB													53	2	1	$\overline{B} \to B$	•	•	↕	↕	R	S
Complement, 2's	NEG							60	7	2	70	6	3				00 − M → M	•	•	↕	↕	①	②
(Negate)	NEGA													40	2	1	00 − A → A	•	•	↕	↕	①	②
	NEGB													50	2	1	00 − B → B	•	•	↕	↕	①	②
Decimal Adjust, A	DAA													19	2	1	Converts Binary Add. of BCD Characters into BCD Format	•	•	↕	↕	↕	③
Decrement	DEC							6A	7	2	7A	6	3				M − 1 → M	•	•	↕	↕	④	•
	DECA													4A	2	1	A − 1 → A	•	•	↕	↕	④	•
	DECB													5A	2	1	B − 1 → B	•	•	↕	↕	④	•
Exclusive OR	EORA	88	2	2	98	3	2	A8	5	2	B8	4	3				A ⊕ M → A	•	•	↕	↕	R	•
	EORB	C8	2	2	D8	3	2	E8	5	2	F8	4	3				B ⊕ M → B	•	•	↕	↕	R	•
Increment	INC							6C	7	2	7C	6	3				M + 1 → M	•	•	↕	↕	⑤	•
	INCA													4C	2	1	A + 1 → A	•	•	↕	↕	⑤	•
	INCB													5C	2	1	B + 1 → B	•	•	↕	↕	⑤	•
Load Acmltr	LDAA	86	2	2	96	3	2	A6	5	2	B6	4	3				M → A	•	•	↕	↕	R	•
	LDAB	C6	2	2	D6	3	2	E6	5	2	F6	4	3				M → B	•	•	↕	↕	R	•
Or, Inclusive	ORAA	8A	2	2	9A	3	2	AA	5	2	BA	4	3				A + M → A	•	•	↕	↕	R	•
	ORAB	CA	2	2	DA	3	2	EA	5	2	FA	4	3				B + M → B	•	•	↕	↕	R	•
Push Data	PSHA													36	4	1	A → M_{SP}, SP − 1 → SP	•	•	•	•	•	•
	PSHB													37	4	1	B → M_{SP}, SP − 1 → SP	•	•	•	•	•	•
Pull Data	PULA													32	4	1	SP + 1 → SP, M_{SP} → A	•	•	•	•	•	•
	PULB													33	4	1	SP + 1 → SP, M_{SP} → B	•	•	•	•	•	•
Rotate Left	ROL							69	7	2	79	6	3				M	•	•	↕	↕	⑥	↕
	ROLA													49	2	1	A	•	•	↕	↕	⑥	↕
	ROLB													59	2	1	B	•	•	↕	↕	⑥	↕
Rotate Right	ROR							66	7	2	76	6	3				M	•	•	↕	↕	⑥	↕
	RORA													46	2	1	A	•	•	↕	↕	⑥	↕
	RORB													56	2	1	B	•	•	↕	↕	⑥	↕
Shift Left, Arithmetic	ASL							68	7	2	78	6	3				M	•	•	↕	↕	⑥	↕
	ASLA													48	2	1	A	•	•	↕	↕	⑥	↕
	ASLB													58	2	1	B	•	•	↕	↕	⑥	↕
Shift Right, Arithmetic	ASR							67	7	2	77	6	3				M	•	•	↕	↕	⑥	↕
	ASRA													47	2	1	A	•	•	↕	↕	⑥	↕
	ASRB													57	2	1	B	•	•	↕	↕	⑥	↕
Shift Right, Logic	LSR							64	7	2	74	6	3				M	•	•	R	↕	⑥	↕
	LSRA													44	2	1	A	•	•	R	↕	⑥	↕
	LSRB													54	2	1	B	•	•	R	↕	⑥	↕
Store Acmltr.	STAA				97	4	2	A7	6	2	B7	5	3				A → M	•	•	↕	↕	R	•
	STAB				D7	4	2	E7	6	2	F7	5	3				B → M	•	•	↕	↕	R	•
Subtract	SUBA	80	2	2	90	3	2	A0	5	2	B0	4	3				A − M → A	•	•	↕	↕	↕	↕
	SUBB	C0	2	2	D0	3	2	E0	5	2	F0	4	3				B − M → B	•	•	↕	↕	↕	↕
Subtract Acmltrs.	SBA													10	2	1	A − B → A	•	•	↕	↕	↕	↕
Subtr. with Carry	SBCA	82	2	2	92	3	2	A2	5	2	B2	4	3				A − M − C → A	•	•	↕	↕	↕	↕
	SBCB	C2	2	2	D2	3	2	E2	5	2	F2	4	3				B − M − C → B	•	•	↕	↕	↕	↕
Transfer Acmltrs	TAB													16	2	1	A → B	•	•	↕	↕	R	•
	TBA													17	2	1	B → A	•	•	↕	↕	R	•
Test, Zero or Minus	TST							6D	7	2	7D	6	3				M − 00	•	•	↕	↕	R	R
	TSTA													4D	2	1	A − 00	•	•	↕	↕	R	R
	TSTB													5D	2	1	B − 00	•	•	↕	↕	R	R

(Condition Code Register bits: 5 4 3 2 1 0 = H I N Z V C)

INDEX REGISTER AND STACK MANIPULATION INSTRUCTIONS

POINTER OPERATIONS	MNEMONIC	IMMED OP	~	#	DIRECT OP	~	#	INDEX OP	~	#	EXTND OP	~	#	IMPLIED OP	~	#	BOOLEAN/ARITHMETIC OPERATION	COND. CODE REG. 5 H	4 I	3 N	2 Z	1 V	0 C
Compare Index Reg	CPX	8C	3	3	9C	4	2	AC	6	2	BC	5	3				$X_H - M, X_L - (M + 1)$	•	•	⑦	‡	⑧	•
Decrement Index Reg	DEX													09	4	1	$X - 1 \rightarrow X$	•	•	•	‡	•	•
Decrement Stack Pntr	DES													34	4	1	$SP - 1 \rightarrow SP$	•	•	•	•	•	•
Increment Index Reg	INX													08	4	1	$X + 1 \rightarrow X$	•	•	•	‡	•	•
Increment Stack Pntr	INS													31	4	1	$SP + 1 \rightarrow SP$	•	•	•	•	•	•
Load Index Reg	LDX	CE	3	3	DE	4	2	EE	6	2	FE	5	3				$M \rightarrow X_H, (M + 1) \rightarrow X_L$	•	•	⑨	‡	R	•
Load Stack Pntr	LDS	8E	3	3	9E	4	2	AE	6	2	BE	5	3				$M \rightarrow SP_H, (M + 1) \rightarrow SP_L$	•	•	⑨	‡	R	•
Store Index Reg	STX				DF	5	2	EF	7	2	FF	6	3				$X_H \rightarrow M, X_L \rightarrow (M + 1)$	•	•	⑨	‡	R	•
Store Stack Pntr	STS				9F	5	2	AF	7	2	BF	6	3				$SP_H \rightarrow M, SP_L \rightarrow (M + 1)$	•	•	⑨	‡	R	•
Indx Reg → Stack Pntr	TXS													35	4	1	$X - 1 \rightarrow SP$	•	•	•	•	•	•
Stack Pntr → Indx Reg	TSX													30	4	1	$SP + 1 \rightarrow X$	•	•	•	•	•	•

JUMP AND BRANCH INSTRUCTIONS

OPERATIONS	MNEMONIC	RELATIVE OP	~	#	INDEX OP	~	#	EXTND OP	~	#	IMPLIED OP	~	#	BRANCH TEST	COND. CODE REG. 5 H	4 I	3 N	2 Z	1 V	0 C
Branch Always	BRA	20	4	2										None	•	•	•	•	•	•
Branch If Carry Clear	BCC	24	4	2										C = 0	•	•	•	•	•	•
Branch If Carry Set	BCS	25	4	2										C = 1	•	•	•	•	•	•
Branch If = Zero	BEQ	27	4	2										Z = 1	•	•	•	•	•	•
Branch If ≥ Zero	BGE	2C	4	2										$N \oplus V = 0$	•	•	•	•	•	•
Branch If > Zero	BGT	2E	4	2										$Z + (N \oplus V) = 0$	•	•	•	•	•	•
Branch If Higher	BHI	22	4	2										C + Z = 0	•	•	•	•	•	•
Branch If ≤ Zero	BLE	2F	4	2										$Z + (N \oplus V) = 1$	•	•	•	•	•	•
Branch If Lower Or Same	BLS	23	4	2										C + Z = 1	•	•	•	•	•	•
Branch If < Zero	BLT	2D	4	2										$N \oplus V = 1$	•	•	•	•	•	•
Branch If Minus	BMI	2B	4	2										N = 1	•	•	•	•	•	•
Branch If Not Equal Zero	BNE	26	4	2										Z = 0	•	•	•	•	•	•
Branch If Overflow Clear	BVC	28	4	2										V = 0	•	•	•	•	•	•
Branch If Overflow Set	BVS	29	4	2										V = 1	•	•	•	•	•	•
Branch If Plus	BPL	2A	4	2										N = 0	•	•	•	•	•	•
Branch To Subroutine	BSR	8D	8	2											•	•	•	•	•	•
Jump	JMP				6E	4	2	7E	3	3				} See Special Operations	•	•	•	•	•	•
Jump To Subroutine	JSR				AD	8	2	BD	9	3					•	•	•	•	•	•
No Operation	NOP										01	2	1	Advances Prog. Cntr. Only	•	•	•	•	•	•
Return From Interrupt	RTI										3B	10	1		─────── ⑩ ───────					
Return From Subroutine	RTS										39	5	1	} See Special Operations	•	•	•	•	•	•
Software Interrupt	SWI										3F	12	1		•	•	•	•	•	•
Wait for Interrupt *	WAI										3E	9	1		•	⑪	•	•	•	•

*WAI puts Address Bus, R/W, and Data Bus in the three-state mode while VMA is held lo

CONDITION CODE REGISTER MANIPULATION INSTRUCTIONS

OPERATIONS	MNEMONIC	IMPLIED OP	~	#	BOOLEAN OPERATION	COND. CODE REG. 5 H	4 I	3 N	2 Z	1 V	0 C
Clear Carry	CLC	0C	2	1	$0 \rightarrow C$	•	•	•	•	•	R
Clear Interrupt Mask	CLI	0E	2	1	$0 \rightarrow I$	•	R	•	•	•	•
Clear Overflow	CLV	0A	2	1	$0 \rightarrow V$	•	•	•	•	R	•
Set Carry	SEC	0D	2	1	$1 \rightarrow C$	•	•	•	•	•	S
Set Interrupt Mask	SEI	0F	2	1	$1 \rightarrow I$	•	S	•	•	•	•
Set Overflow	SEV	0B	2	1	$1 \rightarrow V$	•	•	•	•	S	•
Acmltr A → CCR	TAP	06	2	1	$A \rightarrow CCR$	─────── ⑫ ───────					
CCR → Acmltr A	TPA	07	2	1	$CCR \rightarrow A$	•	•	•	•	•	•

CONDITION CODE REGISTER NOTES: (Bit set if test is true and cleared otherwise)

1	(Bit V)	Test: Result = 10000000?
2	(Bit C)	Test: Result ≠ 00000000?
3	(Bit C)	Test: Decimal value of most significant BCD Character greater than nine? (Not cleared if previously set.)
4	(Bit V)	Test: Operand = 10000000 prior to execution?
5	(Bit V)	Test: Operand = 01111111 prior to execution?
6	(Bit V)	Test: Set equal to result of N⊕C after shift has occurred.
7	(Bit N)	Test: Sign bit of most significant (MS) byte = 1?
8	(Bit V)	Test: 2's complement overflow from subtraction of MS bytes?
9	(Bit N)	Test: Result less than zero? (Bit 15 = 1)
10	(All)	Load Condition Code Register from Stack. (See Special Operations)
11	(Bit I)	Set when interrupt occurs. If previously set, a Non-Maskable Interrupt is required to exit the wait state.
12	(All)	Set according to the contents of Accumulator A.

LEGEND:

OP   Operation Code (Hexadecimal);
~   Number of MPU Cycles;
=   Number of Program Bytes;
+   Arithmetic Plus;
−   Arithmetic Minus;
•   Boolean AND;
M_{SP} Contents of memory location pointed to be Stack Pointer;

+   Boolean Inclusive OR;
⊙   Boolean Exclusive OR;
$\overline{M}$ Complement of M;
→   Transfer Into;
0   Bit = Zero;
00   Byte = Zero;

Note – Accumulator addressing mode instructions are included in the column for IMPLIED addressing

CONDITION CODE SYMBOLS:

H   Half-carry from bit 3;
I   Interrupt mask
N   Negative (sign bit)
Z   Zero (byte)
V   Overflow, 2's complement
C   Carry from bit 7
R   Reset Always
S   Set Always
‡   Test and set if true, cleared otherwise
•   Not Affected

6800/6802

Register Set [6800/6802] (*fig. M14*)

Two 8-bit Accumulators (A and B).

16-bit Index Register (X), used as a memory pointer with indexed addressing.

16-bit Stack Pointer (SP): defines stack.

16-bit Program Counter (PC)

Condition Code Register (status or flag register).

Flags H Half-carry (not accessible to programmer)
         I   Interrupt request mask bit
         N Negative (sign)
         Z Zero
         V Overflow (2s complement)
         C Carry.

Although the register set may appear limited there are several instructions that operate directly on memory locations. In this way, any memory location can be treated as a general-purpose register.

Instruction Set (*fig. M12b*)

Modelled on the PDP11 minicomputer. There are 72 basic instructions but since there are seven addressing modes the total number of different instructions adds up to 197.

Addressing Modes (total 7)

Immediate (IMM)   Relative (REL)
Direct (DIR)   Inherent (INH) or Implied
Extended (EXT)   Accumulator (A and B)
Indexed (IND)

IMMEDIATE ADDRESSING allows a register to be loaded with a value.

> *Example*
> LDA B #$8F   Load AccB Immediate with hex. number 8F

DIRECT ADDRESSING is similar to zero page addressing in other processors, where a single-byte page zero address is specified as part of the instruction.

> *Example*
> LDA A $30   Load AccA from address $30

EXTENDED ADDRESSING (similar to absolute) enables any address in memory to be used. The instruction will be triple byte.

> *Example*
> LDA A $3030   Load AccA from address $3030

INDEXED ADDRESSING uses the X register as a memory pointer with an offset supplied with the instruction. The offset is positive in the range $00 to $FF (0 to 255).

> *Example* (assume X register has been loaded with the hex. value $4500).
> STA A 00,X   Store AccA at address pointed to by X reg. (offset = 00)
> or
> STA B $80,X   Store AccB at address = address pointed
>   to by X reg. + offset $80, i.e. address $4580

6800/6802

6800

Fig. M14 Register set of the **6800/6802**

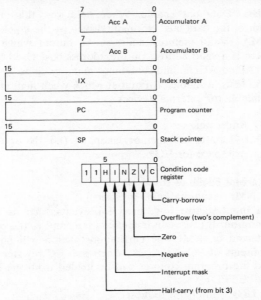

Since the X register can be made to point to any memory location and can be incremented (INX) or decremented (DEX), indexed addressing is a powerful mode in the 6800/6802.

RELATIVE ADDRESSING is used in branch instructions and allows both forward and backward branching relative to the value held by the program counter

$$D = (PC + 2) + R$$

where D = destination address
  PC = address of 1st byte of the branch instruction
  R = offset value (2s complement form).

Control Signals

RESET Input used to reset and start up the processor. Active low. When pulled low this input causes the processor to load the program counter with the address stored in the restart pointer ($FFFE and $FFFF). The contents of the address pointed to by this vector ($FFFE and $FFFF) must be the first instruction of the user's restart machine.

HALT Active low control input which allows an external device to take control of the address and data bus. When pulled low by a peripheral, the processor first completes its current instruction and then disconnects itself from the bus lines.

R/W̄ Output line used to signal direction of data on the data bus. High for read, low for write.

TSC Three-state control. An input which, when taken high, effectively disconnects the processor from the address bus. Both the address bus and R/W̄ line will be put into high impedance states and at the same time VMA and BA signals are taken low. This allows the address bus to be taken over by a peripheral. A necessary condition is that the ϕ_1 and ϕ_2 clocks must be held high and low respectively.

131

6800/6802

DBE Data bus enable. When held low, this input allows another device to control the data bus. Normally driven by the ϕ_2 clock signal.

VMA Valid memory address. An output which indicates to peripherals that there is a valid address on the address bus. Used for enabling interface adaptors (PIA and ACIA) and sometimes memory chips.

BA Bus available. An output which when high indicates that the address bus is available for external devices.

I/O Addressing

All I/O ports are memory mapped (no IN or OUT instructions or *separate* memory space for I/O).

Interrupt Facilities (total 2)

a) $\overline{\text{NMI}}$ (non-maskable interrupt)

An input, active low, used for events such as power failure or other fault condition. It causes an immediate interrupt to the processor. If a negative edge is detected on $\overline{\text{NMI}}$, the current instruction will be completed; processor status (contents of PC, X, AccA, AccB and CC registers) will be saved on the stack; and the program counter will be loaded from the $\overline{\text{NMI}}$ pointer (address $FFFC and $FFFD).

b) $\overline{\text{IRQ}}$ (interrupt request)

The normal interrupt for peripheral service routines. This interrupt can be masked out by setting the I-bit in the condition code register (instruction SEI). If the mask bit is clear ($\emptyset$), a negative edge on $\overline{\text{IRQ}}$ will initiate the interrupt. The $\overline{\text{IRQ}}$ pointer is at $FFF8 and $FFF9. *Fig.* M15 shows stack during an $\overline{\text{IRQ}}$ routine.

Benchmarks 1 MHz clock assumed

1. Transfer from memory to memory (using extended addressing)   9 μsec
2. Output accumulator to port   5 μsec
3. Transfer register to accumulator   2 μsec
4. $\overline{\text{IRQ}}$ to start of interrupt service routine (assuming current instruction completed)   10 μsec

Sample Program (see page 124)   Flowchart: *fig. M16*

	ASSEMBLY LANGUAGE			MACHINE CODE Address Code		(hex.)
	CLR B		Clear counter	1000	5F	
	LDX	#$0050	Set pointer	1001	CE	00 50
NEXT	LDA A	0,X	Load data	1004	A6	00
	INX		Increment pointer	1006	08	
	INC B		Increment counter	1007	5C	
	CMP A	#$03	= EOT?	1008	81	03
	BNE	NEXT	Branch	100A	26	F8
	STA B	$3000	Store result	100C	B7	30 00
	SW1		Stop	100F	3F	

Support Chips (extensive)   Examples: PIA 6821   ACIA 6850
Triple 16-bit Timer 6840   DMA controller 6844   Modem 6860

6800/6802

Fig. M15 How the microprocessor status is saved on the stack in the 6800

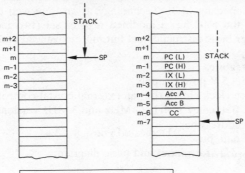

```
SP = stack pointer
PC (L) = program counter (low byte)
PC (H) = program counter (high byte)
IX (L) = index register (low byte)
IX (H) = index register (high byte)
Acc A = accumulator A
Acc B = accumulator B
CC = condition codes register
```

Fig. M16 Flowchart for **6800/6802** program to find the length of a list of ASCII code

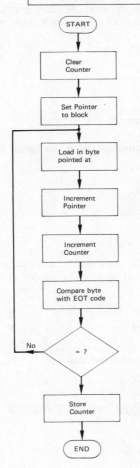

6502

Developed by MOS Technology as an improved 6800. Although based on the 6800, the 6502 has a modified register set (two index registers for example), a smaller basic instruction set but more advanced addressing modes.

6502 features

Single +5 V power supply.

2-phase clock circuit (but an external crystal-controlled oscillator is required).

Clock frequency 1 MHz (2 MHz and 3 MHz versions available).

16-bit address bus⎫
 8-bit data bus ⎬Dedicated lines

  Fig. M17 for pinout and basic diagram.

Register Set [6502] (*fig. M18*)

One 8-bit Accumulator (A).

Two 8-bit Index Registers (X, Y), used to hold values for instructions in the indexed addressing mode.

9-bit Stack Pointer (SP). The lower 8 bits are used to hold the next available space in the stack. The 9th bit (b8), which is permanently at 1, forces the stack to reside in page 1 of memory. (The stack must be within $0100 to $01FF of RAM.)

16-bit Program Counter (PC)

Flag Register (status registers)

Flags

  S Sign
  O Overflow (2s complement)
  * Unused
  B Break—a software interrupt using the break instruction (not accessible to programmer)
  D Decimal mode
  I Interrupt
  Z Zero
  C Carry

Instruction Set (*fig. M19*)

56 basic instructions, which may seem a small number compared to other processors, but the variety of addressing modes (13 in all) allows considerable programming flexibility.

Addressing Modes (total 13)

Immediate
Zero page
Absolute
Accumulator
Implied
Zero page X or Y (Indexed) (Z Page X, Z Page Y)
Absolute X or Y (Indexed) (ABS.X, ABS.Y)
Indirect Y Indexed   (IND).Y
Indexed X Indirect   (IND).X

6502

Relative
Indirect Absolute (used only with the JMP instruction)

Fig. M17a Architecture of the **6502**

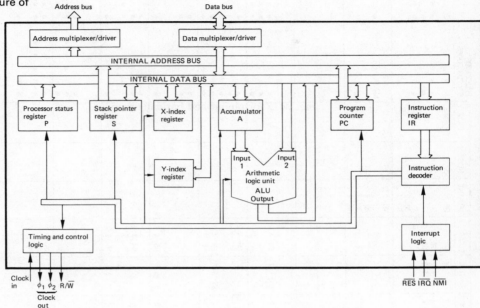

Fig. M17b Pinout of the **6502**

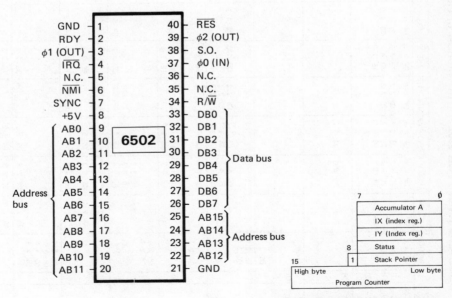

N.C. = NOT CONNECTED

Fig. M18 Register set of the **6502**

6502

OP CODE AND TIMING FOR 6502

(n = number of clock cycles   # = number of bytes per instruction)

MNEMONIC	IMPLIED OP n #	ACCUM OP n #	ABSOLUTE OP n #	ZERO PAGE OP n #	IMMEDIATE OP n #	ABS. X OP n #	ABS. Y OP n #	(IND,X) OP n #	(IND),Y OP n #	Z. PAGE, X OP n #	RELATIVE OP n #	INDIRECT OP n #	Z. PAGE, Y OP n #	STATUS N V B D I Z C
ADC			6D 4 3	65 3 2	69 2 2	7D 4 3	79 4 3	61 6 2	71 5 2	75 4 2				N V · · · Z C
AND			2D 4 3	25 3 2	29 2 2	3D 4 3	39 4 3	21 6 2	31 5 2	35 4 2				N · · · · Z ·
ASL		0A 2 1	0E 6 3	06 5 2		1E 7 3				16 6 2				N · · · · Z C
BCC (1)											90 2 2			
BCS (1)											B0 2 2			
BEQ (2)											F0 2 2			
BIT			2C 4 3	24 3 2										M7 M6 · · · Z ·
BMI (2)											30 2 2			
BNE (2)											D0 2 2			
BPL (2)											10 2 2			
BRK	00 7 1													· · 1 · 1 · ·
BVC (2)											50 2 2			
BVS (2)											70 2 2			
CLC	18 2 1													· · · · · · 0
CLD	D8 2 1													· · · 0 · · ·
CLI	58 2 1													· · · · 0 · ·
CLV	B8 2 1													· 0 · · · · ·
CMP			CD 4 3	C5 3 2	C9 2 2	DD 4 3	D9 4 3	C1 6 2	D1 5 2	D5 4 2				N · · · · Z C
CPX			EC 4 3	E4 3 2	E0 2 2									N · · · · Z C
CPY			CC 4 3	C4 3 2	C0 2 2									N · · · · Z C
DEC			CE 6 3	C6 5 2		DE 7 3				D6 6 2				N · · · · Z ·
DEX	CA 2 1													N · · · · Z ·
DEY	88 2 1													N · · · · Z ·
EOR			4D 4 3	45 3 2	49 2 2	5D 4 3	59 4 3	41 6 2	51 5 2	55 4 2				N · · · · Z ·
INC			EE 6 3	E6 5 2		FE 7 3				F6 6 2				N · · · · Z ·
INX	E8 2 1													N · · · · Z ·
INY	C8 2 1													N · · · · Z ·
JMP			4C 3 3									6C 5 3		
JSR			20 6 3											
LDA (1)			AD 4 3	A5 3 2	A9 2 2	BD 4 3	B9 4 3	A1 6 2	B1 5 2	B5 4 2				N · · · · Z ·
LDX (1)			AE 4 3	A6 3 2	A2 2 2		BE 4 3						B6 4 2	N · · · · Z ·
LDY (1)			AC 4 3	A4 3 2	A0 2 2	BC 4 3				B4 4 2				N · · · · Z ·
LSR		4A 2 1	4E 6 3	46 5 2		5E 7 3				56 6 2				0 · · · · Z C
NOP	EA 2 1													
ORA			0D 4 3	05 3 2	09 2 2	1D 4 3	19 4 3	01 6 2	11 5 2	15 4 2				N · · · · Z ·
PHA	48 3 1													
PHP	08 3 1													
PLA	68 4 1													N · · · · Z ·
PLP	28 4 1													(restored)
ROL		2A 2 1	2E 6 3	26 5 2		3E 7 3				36 6 2				N · · · · Z C
ROR		6A 2 1	6E 6 3	66 5 2		7E 7 3				76 6 2				N · · · · Z C
RTI	40 6 1													(restored)
RTS	60 6 1													
SBC			ED 4 3	E5 3 2	E9 2 2	FD 4 3	F9 4 3	E1 6 2	F1 5 2	F5 4 2				N V · · · Z C
SEC	38 2 1													· · · · · · 1
SED	F8 2 1													· · · 1 · · ·
SEI	78 2 1													· · · · 1 · ·
STA			8D 4 3	85 2		9D 5 3	99 5 3	81 6 2	91 6 2	95 4 2				
STX			8E 4 3	86 2									96 4 2	
STY			8C 4 3	84 2						94 4 2				
TAX	AA 2 1													N · · · · Z ·
TAY	A8 2 1													N · · · · Z ·
TSX	BA 2 1													N · · · · Z ·
TXA	8A 2 1													N · · · · Z ·
TXS	9A 2 1													
TYA	98 2 1													N · · · · Z ·

(1) Add 1 to n if crossing page boundary   (2) Add 2 to n if branch within page; Add 3 to n if branch within another page

(1) Add 1 to n if crossing page boundary   (2) Add 2 to n if branch within page; Add 3 to n if branch within another page

6502

ADC	Add with carry
AND	Logical AND
ASL	Arithmetic shift left
BCC	Branch if carry clear
BCS	Branch if carry set
BEQ	Branch if result = 0
BIT	Test bit
BMI	Branch if minus
BNE	Branch if not equal to 0
BPL	Branch if plus
BRK	Break
BVC	Branch if overflow clear
BVS	Branch if overflow set
CLC	Clear carry
CLD	Clear decimal flag
CLI	Clear interrupt disable
CLV	Clear overflow
CMP	Compare to accumulator
CPX	Compare to X
CPY	Compare to Y
DEC	Decrement memory
DEX	Decrement X
DEY	Decrement Y
EOR	Exclusive OR
INC	Increment memory
INX	Increment X
INY	Increment Y
JMP	Jump

JSR	Jump to subroutine
LDA	Load accumulator
LDX	Load X
LDY	Load Y
LSR	Logical shift right
NOP	No operation
ORA	Logical OR
PHA	Push A
PHP	Push P status
PLA	Pull A
PLP	Pull P status
ROL	Rotate left
ROR	Rotate right
RTI	Return from interrupt
RTS	Return from subroutine
SBC	Subtract with carry
SEC	Set carry
SED	Set decimal
SEI	Set interrupt disable
STA	Store accumulator
STX	Store X
STY	Store Y
TAX	Transfer A to X
TAY	Transfer A to Y
TSX	Transfer SP to X
TXA	Transfer X to A
TXS	Transfer X to SP
TYA	Transfer Y to A

6502

IMMEDIATE ADDRESSING same as 6800.

Example
LDA #$F6   Load Acc with hex. number F6

ZERO PAGE ADDRESSING (similar to Direct in 6800) uses 2-byte instructions, with the second byte specifying the address within the range $0000 to $00FF.

Example
AND $8F   AND the contents of address $008F with the accumulator
             (result left in accumulator)

ABSOLUTE MODE requires the full address to be specified in the instruction, with the low byte preceding the high bytes.

Example

                                              Hex. code
LDX $3F20   Load X reg. from $3F20   AE 203F

INDEXED ADDRESSING   The address is formed by adding an offset given in the instruction to the contents of one of the index registers (X or Y). There are several indexed modes available.

ZERO PAGE X or Y   The address will be on zero page and will be formed by adding the single byte offset given in the instruction to the contents of the specified index register.

Examples
LDX #$30   X register holds hex. number 30
LDA $4F,X   Load accumulator indexed

The effective address is

$004F + $0030 = $007F

Note that for this addressing mode the Y index register can only be specified when using instructions operating on the X register (LDX and STX).

ABSOLUTE X or Y   In this mode the offset will be two bytes and the effective address will be given by adding the offset to the specified index register.

Example
LDY #$60   Y register holds hex. number $60
STA $1020,Y Store accumulator indexed

The effective address is

$1020 + $0060 = $1080

INDIRECT Y INDEXED   The effective address is obtained from a location on page zero (the offset) pointed at by the instruction address register. The offset (2 bytes) is then added to the contents of the Y register to give the effective address.

Example
LDY #$30   Y register holds hex. number $30
LDA ($6F)   Y load accumulator (IND).Y

6502

The address $006F will contain the offset (suppose this is $2050). The effective address is then: $2050 + $30 = $2080

INDEXED X INDIRECT   The effective address will be contained in an address on zero page pointed to by the sum of the X register and the offset specified in the instruction.

Example
LDX   #$50   X register holds hex. number $50
LDA   ($10,X)   Load accumulator indexed indirect

Address on zero page which holds the effective address:

$0010 + $0050 = $0060

Control Signals
RESET   Active low input used for reset or start-up. When pulled low, the processor loads the contents of $FFFC and $FFFD (reset vector) into the program counter. The contents of the address loaded into the PC must be the first instruction of the user's restart routine.
R/W̄   An output used to signal the direction of data movement.
RDȲ   Ready. An input, active low, that can be used by DMA controllers and dynamic RAM circuits to force the processor to wait for a number of machine cycles. Note that the address and data bus are not tri-stated—this function has to be carried out by external hardware.
SYNC   An output used to identify the FETCH cycle of an instruction.
SO   An active low input which sets the overflow flag in the status register.

I/O Addressing   I/O is memory mapped.

Interrupt Facilities (total 2)
a)   **N̄M̄Ī**   (non-maskable interrupt)
An active low input, which when activated by an external device causes an immediate interrupt. The processor completes the current instruction and then pushes the contents of the PC and the Flag register onto the stack. The PC is then loaded with an address taken from the NMI vector ($FFFA and $FFFB).
b)   **ĪR̄Q̄**   (interrupt request)
The usual interrupt input for peripheral service routines. This interrupt can be masked out by setting the I-bit in the Flag register (instruction SEI). If the mask bit is clear (instruction CLI), a negative edge on ĪR̄Q̄ will initiate the interrupt. The processor completes the current instruction, pushes the contents of the PC and Flag registers onto the stack, and loads the PC from the ĪR̄Q̄ vector ($FFFE and $FFFF). If the contents of other internal registers have to be saved, the first instructions of the interrupt service routine must be push instructions.

Benchmarks 1 MHz clock assumed
1. Transfer from memory to memory (absolute addressing)   8 μsec
2. Output accumulator to port   4 μsec
3. Transfer register to accumulator   2 μsec
4. ĪR̄Q̄ to start of interrupt service routine (assuming current instruction completed)   5 μsec

6502

Sample Program (see page 124)
Flowchart: *fig. M20*

	ASSEMBLY LANGUAGE			MACHINE CODE		
				Address	Code	(hex.)
	LDX	#$00	Clear X reg.	1000	A2	00
NEXT	LDA	$50,X	Load data	1002	B5	50
	INX		Increment X reg.	1004	E8	
	CMP	#$03	= EOT?	1005	C9	03
	BNE	NEXT	Branch	1007	D0	F9
	STX	$3000	Store result	1009	8E	00 30
	BRK		Stop	100C	00	

Support Chips (various)
VIA 6522   RIOT 6532   ACIA 6551

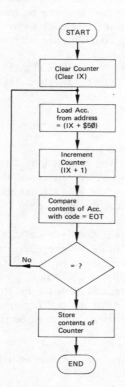

Fig. M20 Flowchart for **6502** program to find the length of a list of ASCII code

START

Clear Counter
(Clear IX)

Load Acc.
from address
= (IX + $50)

Increment
Counter
(IX + 1)

Compare
contents of Acc.
with code = EOT

No   = ?

Store
contents of
Counter

END

65C02

This is a CMOS version of the 6502 developed by Rockwell to provide enhanced performance at low power. The 65C02 processor is downward software compatible with the 6502 with twelve additional instructions and two new addressing modes. The 65C02 also executes instructions faster than the basic 6502.

65C02 features
Power supply +5 V (requires only 4 mA/MHz)
Clock 2 MHz from an external ϕ_0 clock generator (3 MHz and 4 MHz versions available).
16-bit address bus ⎫
 8-bit data bus ⎬ Dedicated lines
Fig. M21a for pinout diagram.

Fig. M21a Pinout of the 65C02

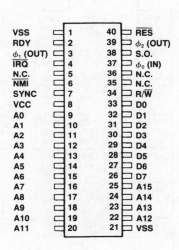

VSS	1	40	RES
RDY	2	39	ϕ_2 (OUT)
ϕ_1 (OUT)	3	38	S.O.
IRQ	4	37	ϕ_0 (IN)
N.C.	5	36	N.C.
NMI	6	35	N.C.
SYNC	7	34	R/W̄
VCC	8	33	D0
A0	9	32	D1
A1	10	31	D2
A2	11	30	D3
A3	12	29	D4
A4	13	28	D5
A5	14	27	D6
A6	15	26	D7
A7	16	25	A15
A8	17	24	A14
A9	18	23	A13
A10	19	22	A12
A11	20	21	VSS

Registers Same set as 6502.

Instruction Set (*fig. M21b*)
Same set as 6502 with 12 additional instructions which are:

BBR Branch on Bit Reset
BBS Branch on Bit Set
BRA Branch Always
PHX Push X register on stack
PHY Push Y register on stack
PLX Pull X register from stack
PLY Pull Y register from stack
RMB Reset Memory Bit
SMB Set Memory Bit
STZ Store Zero
TRB Test and Reset Bits
TSB Test and Set Bits

65C02

Fig. M21b Instruction set of the **65C02**

MSD\LSD	0	1	2	3	4	5	6	7	8	9	A	B	C	D	E	F
0	BRK Implied 1 7	ORA (IND, X) 2 6			TSB ZP 2 5	ORA ZP 2 3	ASL ZP 2 5	RMB0 ZP 2 5	PHP Implied 1 3	ORA IMM 2 2	ASL Accum 1 2		TSB ABS 3 6	ORA ABS 3 4	ASL ABS 3 6	BBR0 ZP 3 5**
1	BPL Relative 2 2**	ORA (IND), Y 2 5*	ORA (IND) 2 5		TRB ZP 2 5	ORA ZP, X 2 4	ASL ZP, X 2 6	RMB1 ZP 2 5	CLC Implied 1 2	ORA ABS, Y 3 4*	INC Accum 1 2		TRB ABS 3 6	ORA ABS, X 3 4*	ASL ABS, X 3 7	BBR1 ZP 3 5**
2	JSR Absolute 3 6	AND (IND, X) 2 6			BIT ZP 2 3	AND ZP 2 3	ROL ZP 2 5	RMB2 ZP 2 5	PLP Implied 1 4	AND IMM 2 2	ROL Accum 1 2		BIT ABS 3 4	AND ABS 3 4	ROL ABS 3 6	BBR2 ZP 3 5**
3	BMI Relative 2 2**	AND (IND), Y 2 5*	AND (IND) 2 5		BIT ZP, X 2 4	AND ZP, X 2 4	ROL ZP, X 2 6	RMB3 ZP 2 5	SEC Implied 1 2	AND ABS, Y 3 4*	DEC Accum 1 2		BIT ABS, X 3 4*	AND ABS, X 3 4*	ROL ABS, X 3 7	BBR3 ZP 3 5**
4	RTI Implied 1 6	EOR (IND, X) 2 6				EOR ZP 2 3	LSR ZP 2 5	RMB4 ZP 2 5	PHA Implied 1 3	EOR IMM 2 2	LSR Accum 1 2		JMP ABS 3 3	EOR ABS 3 4	LSR ABS 3 6	BBR4 ZP 3 5**
5	BVC Relative 2 2**	EOR (IND), Y 2 5*	EOR (IND) 2 5			EOR ZP, X 2 4	LSR ZP, X 2 6	RMB5 ZP 2 5	CLI Implied 1 2	EOR ABS, Y 3 4*	PHY Implied 1 3			EOR ABS, X 3 4*	LSR ABS, X 3 7	BBR5 ZP 3 5**
6	RTS Implied 1 6	ADC (IND, X) 2 6†			STZ ZP 2 3	ADC ZP 2 3†	ROR ZP 2 5	RMB6 ZP 2 5	PLA Implied 1 4	ADC IMM 2 2†	ROR Accum 1 2		JMP Indirect 3 5	ADC ABS 3 4†	ROR ABS 3 6	BBR6 ZP 3 5**
7	BVS Relative 2 2**	ADC (IND), Y 2 5†	ADC (IND) 2 5†		STZ ZP, X 2 4	ADC ZP, X 2 4†	ROR ZP, X 2 6	RMB7 ZP 2 5	SEI Implied 1 2	ADC ABS, Y 3 4*†	PLY Implied 1 4		JMP (IND), X 3 6	ADC ABS, X 3 4*†	ROR ABS, X 3 7	BBR7 ZP 3 5**
8	BRA Relative 2 3*	STA (IND, X) 2 6			STY ZP 2 3	STA ZP 2 3	STX ZP 2 3	SMB0 ZP 2 5	DEY Implied 1 2	BIT IMM 2 2	TXA Implied 1 2		STY ABS 3 4	STA ABS 3 4	STX ABS 3 4	BBS0 ZP 3 5**
9	BCC Relative 2 2**	STA (IND), Y 2 6	STA (IND) 2 5		STY ZP, X 2 4	STA ZP, X 2 4	STX ZP, Y 2 4	SMB1 ZP 2 5	TYA Implied 1 2	STA ABS, Y 3 5	TXS Implied 1 2		STZ ABS 3 4	STA ABS, X 3 5	STZ ABS, X 3 5	BBS1 ZP 3 5**
A	LDY IMM 2 2	LDA (IND, X) 2 6	LDX IMM 2 2		LDY ZP 2 3	LDA ZP 2 3	LDX ZP 2 3	SMB2 ZP 2 5	TAY Implied 1 2	LDA IMM 2 2	TAX Implied 1 2		LDY ABS 3 4	LDA ABS 3 4	LDX ABS 3 4	BBS2 ZP 3 5**
B	BCS Relative 2 2**	LDA (IND), Y 2 5*	LDA (IND) 2 5		LDY ZP, X 2 4	LDA ZP, X 2 4	LDX ZP, Y 2 4	SMB3 ZP 2 5	CLV Implied 1 2	LDA ABS, Y 3 4*	TSX Implied 1 2		LDY ABS, X 3 4*	LDA ABS, X 3 4*	LDX ABS, Y 3 4*	BBS3 ZP 3 5**
C	CPY IMM 2 2	CMP (IND, X) 2 6			CPY ZP 2 3	CMP ZP 2 3	DEC ZP 2 5	SMB4 ZP 2 5	INY Implied 1 2	CMP IMM 2 2	DEX Implied 1 2		CPY ABS 3 4	CMP ABS 3 4	DEC ABS 3 6	BBS4 ZP 3 5**
D	BNE Relative 2 2**	CMP (IND), Y 2 5*	CMP (IND) 2 5			CMP ZP, X 2 4	DEC ZP, X 2 6	SMB5 ZP 2 5	CLD Implied 1 2	CMP ABS, Y 3 4*	PHX Implied 1 3			CMP ABS, X 3 4*	DEC ABS, X 3 7	BBS5 ZP 3 5**
E	CPX IMM 2 2	SBC (IND, X) 2 6†			CPX ZP 2 3	SBC ZP 2 3†	INC ZP 2 5	SMB6 ZP 2 5	INX Implied 1 2	SBC IMM 2 2†	NOP Implied 1 2		CPX ABS 3 4	SBC ABS 3 4†	INC ABS 3 6	BBS6 ZP 3 5**
F	BEQ Relative 2 2**	SBC (IND), Y 2 5*†	SBC (IND) 2 5†			SBC ZP, X 2 4†	INC ZP, X 2 6	SMB7 ZP 2 5	SED Implied 1 2	SBC ABS, Y 3 4*†	PLX Implied 1 4			SBC ABS, X 3 4*†	INC ABS, X 3 7	BBS7 ZP 3 5**

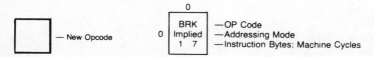

□ — New Opcode

0
BRK Implied 1 7

—OP Code
—Addressing Mode
—Instruction Bytes: Machine Cycles

† Add 1 to N if in decimal mode.
* Add 1 to N if page boundary is crossed.
** Add 1 to N if branch occurs to same page;
Add 2 to N if branch occurs to different page.

65C02

Addressing Modes (total 13)

Accumulator	
Immediate	Implied
Absolute	Relative
Zero page	Indexed Indirect (X)
Indexed zero page (X, Y)	Indirect Indexed (Y)
Indexed Absolute (X, Y)	Absolute Indirect
*Indexed Absolute Indirect (X)	*Indirect (IND, X)

The two addressing modes marked * are additional to those used in the 6502.
INDEXED ABSOLUTE INDIRECT   The contents of the 2nd and 3rd bytes of the instruction are added to the contents of the X register. The 16-bit word is a memory address which contains the effective address for the instruction.

Example
AND   ($32ØØ,X)   AND memory with accumulator (op-code 21 32 ØØ)

Assume that X register holds $5Ø, then the effective address (the one whose contents are to be ANDed with the accumulator) will be pointed at by address $325Ø (*fig. M22*).

Fig. M22 Indexed absolute indirect mode for the 65C02

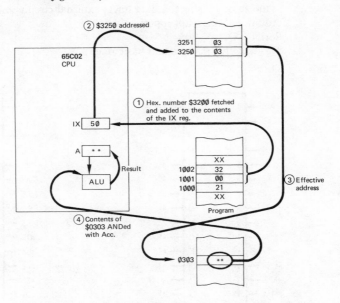

INDIRECT   In this mode the 2nd byte of the instruction will be a zero page address. The effective address is then contained in this zero page address.

Example
AND   (5Ø)   AND memory with accumulator (op-code 325Ø)

The effective address (the one whose contents are to be ANDed with the accumulator) will be pointed at by address $ØØ5Ø.

For all other points concerning the 65C02 consult the notes on the 6502.

8080/8085

The 8080 was developed by Intel as an enhanced version of their 8008 device. It differs from the 6800 and 6502 in a number of important respects.

a) It is a more register-oriented processor with a bank of 6 general-purpose 8-bit registers which can be used for temporary data storage or act as memory pointers.

b) The 8-bit data bus is multiplexed with control and timing signals.

c) Isolated I/O is used with special IN/OUT instructions.

8080 features

Power supply $+5$ V, -5 V and $+12$ V.

Clock 2 MHz supplied by external circuit (8224) (also a high-speed version at 3 MHz).

16-bit address bus.

8-bit data bus [external chip must be provided to demultiplex data and control signals (8228)].

8085 features

Single $+5$ V supply.

Clock 3.125 MHz on chip (high-speed version at 5 MHz).

16-bit address bus with the lower 8 bits ($A_\emptyset$ to A7) multiplexed with and sharing the same pins as the data lines; external circuits must be used.

Additional interrupt inputs.

Serial I/O.

Fig. M23 for pinouts and basic diagrams.

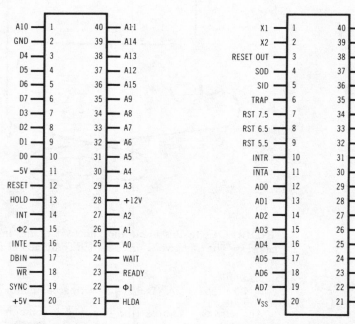

Fig. M23*a* Pinout for the 8080

Fig. M23*b* Pinout for the 8085

8080/8085

Registers 8080/8085 (*fig. M23d*)

One 8-bit Accumulator—the A register.

Six 8-bit general-purpose registers B, C, D, E, H, L.

These can be combined, i.e. BC, DE and HL pairs, to hold 16-bit words, either for 16-bit operations or as memory pointers. The HL pair is most often used.

16-bit Stack Pointer (SP).

16-bit Program Counter (PC).

Flag Register: Processor Status Word (PSW).

Flags S   Sign
         Z   Zero
         A   Auxiliary carry (from bit 3 to bit 4)
         P   Parity
         C   Carry

An interrupt flag (I) exists but is not included in the status register.

Fig. M23c Minimum system set-up [8080]

Fig. M23d Register set of 8080/8085

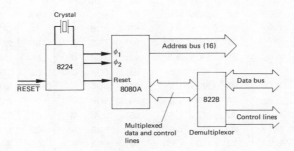

Accum. A (8)	F (5) Processor status Word	
B (8)	C	(8)
D (8)	E	(8)
H (8)	L	(8)
STACK POINTER (16)		
PROGRAM COUNTER (16)		

Instruction Set (*Fig. M24*)

The 8080 has 78 basic instructions used to move data between registers, between memory and registers, and between registers and I/O.

The 8085 has two additional instructions, RIM and SIM, which are used to control the additional interrupt features.

Addressing Modes (total 4)

Immediate
Direct
Register
Register Indirect

8080/8085

OP CODE	MNEMONIC	OP CODE	MNEMONIC	OP CODE	MNEMONIC	OP CODE	MNEMONIC	OP CODE	MNEMONIC	OP CODE	MNEMONIC	OP CODE	MNEMONIC
00	NOP	2B	DCX H	56	MOV D,M	81	ADD C	AC	XRA H	D7	RST 2		
01	LX1 B,D16	2C	INR L	57	MOV D,A	82	ADD D	AD	XRA L	D8	RC		
02	STAX B	2D	DCR L	58	MOV E,B	83	ADD E	AE	XRA M	D9	—		
03	INX B	2E	MVI L,D8	59	MOV E,C	84	ADD H	AF	XRA A	DA	JC Adr		
04	INR B	2F	CMA	5A	MOV E,D	85	ADD L	B0	ORA B	DB	IN D8		
05	DCR B	30	SIM	5B	MOV E,E	86	ADD M	B1	ORA C	DC	CC Adr		
06	MVI B,D8	31	LXI SPD16	5C	MOV E,H	87	ADD A	B2	ORA D	DD	—		
07	RLC	32	STA Adr	5D	MOV E,L	88	ADC B	B3	ORA E	DE	SBI D8		
08	—	33	INX SP	5E	MOV E,M	89	ADC C	B4	ORA H	DF	RST 3		
09	DAD B	34	INR M	5F	MOV E,A	8A	ADC D	B5	ORA L	E0	RPO		
0A	LDAX B	35	DCR M	60	MOV H,B	8B	ADC E	B6	ORA M	E1	POP H		
0B	DCX B	36	MVI M,D8	61	MOV H,C	8C	ADC H	B7	ORA A	E2	JPO Adr		
0C	INR C	37	STC	62	MOV H,D	8D	ADC L	B8	CMP B	E3	XTHL		
0D	DCR C	38	——	63	MOV H,E	8E	ADC M	B9	CMP C	E4	CPO Adr		
0E	MVI C,D8	39	DAD SP	64	MOV H,H	8F	ADC A	BA	CMP D	E5	PUSH H		
0F	RRC	3A	LDA Adr	65	MOV H,L	8G	SUB B	BB	CMP E	E6	ANI D8		
10	——	3B	DCX SP	66	MOV H,M	91	SUB C	BC	CMP H	E7	RST 4		
11	LXI D,D16	3C	INR A	67	MOV H,A	92	SUB D	BD	CMP L	E8	RPE		
12	STAX D	3D	DCR A	68	MOV L,B	93	SUB E	BE	CMP M	E9	PCHL		
13	INX D	3E	MVI A,D8	69	MOV L,C	94	SUB H	BF	CMP A	EA	JPE Adr		
14	INR D	3F	CMC	6A	MOV L,D	95	SUB L	C0	RNZ	EB	XCHG		
15	DCR D	40	MOV B,B	6B	MOV L,E	96	SUB M	C1	POP B	EC	CPE Adr		
16	MVI D,D8	41	MOV B,C	6C	MOV L,H	97	SUB A	C2	JNZ Adr	ED	——		
17	RAL	42	MOV B,D	6D	MOV L,L	98	SBB B	C3	JMP Adr	EE	ERI D8		
18	——	43	MOV B,E	6E	MOV L,M	99	SBB C	C4	CNZ Adr	EF	RST 5		
19	DAD D	44	MOV B,H	6F	MOV L,A	9A	SBB D	C5	PUSH B	F0	RP		
1A	LDAX D	45	MOV B,L	70	MOV M,B	9B	SBB E	C6	ADI D8	F1	POP PSW		
1B	DCX D	46	MOV B,M	71	MOV M,C	9C	SBB H	C7	RST 0	F2	JP Adr		
1C	INR E	47	MOV B,A	72	MOV M,D	9D	SBB L	C8	RZ	F3	DI		
1D	DRC E	48	MOV C,B	73	MOV M,E	9E	SBB M	C9	RET Adr	F4	CP Adr		
1E	MVI E,D8	49	MOV C,C	74	MOV M,H	9F	SBB A	CA	JZ	F5	PUSH PSW		
1F	RAR	4A	MOV C,D	75	MOV M,L	A0	ANA B	CB	——	F6	ORI D8		
20	RIM	4B	MOV C,E	76	HLT	A1	ANA C	CC	CZ Adr	F7	RST 6		
21	LXI H,D16	4C	MOV C,H	77	MOV M,A	A2	ANA D	CD	CALL Adr	F8	RM		
22	SHLD Adr	4D	MOV C,L	78	MOV A,B	A3	ANA E	CE	ACI D8	F9	SPHL		
23	INX H	4E	MOV C,M	79	MOV A,C	A4	ANA H	CF	RST 1	FA	JM Adr		
24	INR H	4F	MOV C,A	7A	MOV A,D	A5	ANA L	D0	RNC	FB	E1		
25	DCR H	50	MOV D,B	7B	MOV A,E	A6	ANA M	D1	POP D	FC	CM Adr		
26	MVI H,D8	51	MOV D,C	7C	MOV A,H	A7	ANA A	D2	JNC Adr	FD	——		
27	DAA	52	MOV D,D	7D	MOV A,L	A8	XRA B	D3	OUT D8	FE	CPI D8		
28	——	53	MOV D,E	7E	MOV A,M	A9	XRA C	D4	CNC Adr	FF	RST 7		
29	DAD H	54	MOV D,H	7F	MOV A,A	AA	XRA D	D5	PUSH D				
2A	LHLD Adr	55	MOV D,L	80	ADD B	AB	XRA E	D6	SUI D8				

D8 = constant, or logical/arithmetic expression that evaluates to an 8-bit data quantity. D16 = constant, or logical/arithmetic expression that evaluates to a 16-bit data quantity. Adr = 16-bit address.

8080/8085

Mnemonic	Instruction Code D_7 D_6 D_5 D_4 D_3 D_2 D_1 D_0	Operations Description
MOVE, LOAD, AND STORE		
MOV r1 r2	0 1 D D D S S S	Move register to register
MOV M.r	0 1 1 1 0 S S S	Move register to memory
MOV r.M	0 1 D D D 1 1 0	Move memory to register
MVI r	0 0 D D D 1 1 0	Move immediate register
MVI M	0 0 1 1 0 1 1 0	Move immediate memory
LXI B	0 0 0 0 0 0 0 1	Load immediate register Pair B & C
LXI D	0 0 0 1 0 0 0 1	Load immediate register Pair D & E
LXI H	0 0 1 0 0 0 0 1	Load immediate register Pair H & L
STAX B	0 0 0 0 0 0 1 0	Store A indirect
STAX D	0 0 0 1 0 0 1 0	Store A indirect
LDAX B	0 0 0 0 1 0 1 0	Load A indirect
LDAX D	0 0 0 1 1 0 1 0	Load A indirect
STA	0 0 1 1 0 0 1 0	Store A direct
LDA	0 0 1 1 1 0 1 0	Load A direct
SHLD	0 0 1 0 0 0 1 0	Store H & L direct
LHLD	0 0 1 0 1 0 1 0	Load H & L direct
XCHG	1 1 1 0 1 0 1 1	Exchange D & E, H & L Registers
STACK OPS		
PUSH B	1 1 0 0 0 1 0 1	Push register Pair B & C on stack
PUSH D	1 1 0 1 0 1 0 1	Push register Pair D & E on stack
PUSH H	1 1 1 0 0 1 0 1	Push register Pair H & L on stack
PUSH PSW	1 1 1 1 0 1 0 1	Push A and Flags on stack
POP B	1 1 0 0 0 0 0 1	Pop register Pair B & C of stack
POP D	1 1 0 1 0 0 0 1	Pop register Pair D & E off stack
POP H	1 1 1 0 0 0 0 1	Pop register Pair H & L of stack
POP PSW	1 1 1 1 0 0 0 1	Pop A and Flags off stack
XTHL	1 1 1 0 0 0 1 1	Exchange top of stack, H & L
SPHL	1 1 1 1 1 0 0 1	H & L to stack pointer
LXI SP	0 0 1 1 0 0 0 1	Load immediate stack pointer
INX SP	0 0 1 1 0 0 1 1	Increment stack pointer
DCX SP	0 0 1 1 1 0 1 1	Decrement stack pointer
JUMP		
JMP	1 1 0 0 0 0 1 1	Jump unconditional
JC	1 1 0 1 1 0 1 0	Jump on carry
JNC	1 1 0 1 0 0 1 0	Jump on no carry
JZ	1 1 0 0 1 0 1 0	Jump on zero
JNZ	1 1 0 0 0 0 1 0	Jump on no zero
JP	1 1 1 1 0 0 1 0	Jump on positive
JM	1 1 1 1 1 0 1 0	Jump on minus
JPE	1 1 1 0 1 0 1 0	Jump on parity even
JPO	1 1 1 0 0 0 1 0	Jump on parity odd
PCHL	1 1 1 0 1 0 0 1	H & L to program counter
CALL		
CALL	1 1 0 0 1 1 0 1	Call unconditional
CC	1 1 0 1 1 1 0 0	Call on carry
CNC	1 1 0 1 0 1 0 0	Call on no carry

Mnemonic	Instruction Code D_7 D_6 D_5 D_4 D_3 D_2 D_1 D_0	Operations Description
CZ	1 1 0 0 1 1 0 0	Call on zero
CNZ	1 1 0 0 0 1 0 0	Call on no zero
CP	1 1 1 1 0 1 0 0	Call on positive
CM	1 1 1 1 1 1 0 0	Call on minus
CPE	1 1 1 0 1 1 0 0	Call on parity even
CPO	1 1 1 0 0 1 0 0	Call on parity odd
RETURN		
RET	1 1 0 0 1 0 0 1	Return
RC	1 1 0 1 1 0 0 0	Return on carry
RNC	1 1 0 1 0 0 0 0	Return on no carry
RZ	1 1 0 0 1 0 0 0	Return on zero
RNZ	1 1 0 0 0 0 0 0	Return on no zero
RP	1 1 1 1 0 0 0 0	Return on positive
RM	1 1 1 1 1 0 0 0	Return on minus
RPE	1 1 1 0 1 0 0 0	Return on parity even
RPO	1 1 1 0 0 0 0 0	Return on parity odd
RESTART		
RST	1 1 A A A 1 1 1	Restart
INPUT/OUTPUT		
IN	1 1 0 1 1 0 1 1	Input
OUT	1 1 0 1 0 0 1 1	Output
INCREMENT AND DECREMENT		
INR r	0 0 D D D 1 0 0	Increment register
DCR r	0 0 D D D 1 0 1	Decrement register
INR M	0 0 1 1 0 1 0 0	Increment memory
DCR M	0 0 1 1 0 1 0 1	Decrement memory
INX B	0 0 0 0 0 0 1 1	Increment B & C registers
INX D	0 0 0 1 0 0 1 1	Increment D & E registers
INX H	0 0 1 0 0 0 1 1	Increment H & L registers
DCX B	0 0 0 0 1 0 1 1	Decrement B & C
DCX D	0 0 0 1 1 0 1 1	Decrement D & E
DCX H	0 0 1 0 1 0 1 1	Decrement H & L
ADD		
ADD r	1 0 0 0 0 S S S	Add register to A
ADC r	1 0 0 0 1 S S S	Add register to A with carry
ADD M	1 0 C 0 0 1 1 0	Add memory to A
ADC M	1 0 0 0 1 1 1 0	Add memory to A with carry
ADI	1 1 0 0 0 1 1 0	Add immediate to A
ACI	1 1 0 0 1 1 1 0	Add immediate to A with carry
DAD B	0 0 0 0 1 0 0 1	Add B & C to H & L
DAD D	0 0 0 1 1 0 0 1	Add D & E to H & L
DAD H	0 0 1 0 1 0 0 1	Add H & L to H & L
DAD SP	0 0 1 1 1 0 0 1	Add stack pointer to H & L
SUBTRACT		
SUB r	1 0 0 1 0 S S S	Subtract register from A
SBB r	1 0 0 1 1 S S S	Subtract register from A with borrow
SUB M	1 0 0 1 0 1 1 0	Subtract memory from A
SBB M	1 0 0 1 1 1 1 0	Subtract memory from A with borrow
SUI	1 1 0 1 0 1 1 0	Subtract immediate from A
SBI	1 1 0 1 1 1 1 0	Subtract immediate from A with borrow

8080/8085

IMMEDIATE   The instruction contains the data.

Example
MVI   A,Ø1H   Load Acc. immediate with ØØ1

DIRECT   A memory address is specified as part of the instruction.

Example
STA   Ø12ØH   Store Acc. at address ØØ12Ø

REGISTER   A register or register pair is specified in the instruction.

Example
INX   H   Increment H and L registers
MOV   C,A   Transfer contents of A into register C

REGISTER INDIRECT   The instruction specifies a register pair where the address for the operation is given. The register pair is used as a memory pointer.

Example
MVI   B,Ø2H⎫   Load B,C pair with
MVI   C,ØØH⎭   Ø2ØØ hex.
LDA X   B   Load Acc. from address contained in B,C pair

Control Signals [8080]
The data lines are multiplexed with control signals as follows:
DØ (INTA) D1 (WO) D2 (STACK) D3 (HLTA) D4 (OUT) D5 (MI) D6 (INP) D7 (MEMR)
INTA   Interrupt Acknowledge. Pulled high when an interrupt is accepted.
WO   Write output. Low to indicate a memory write operation.
STACK   Pulled high to indicate that a stack address is on the address bus.
HLTA   Halt Acknowledge. Pulled high when processor has executed a Halt instruction.
OUT   High to indicate that an output address is on the low-order address lines ($A_Ø$ to A_7).
MI   Goes high to indicate an op-code fetch cycle.
INP   Input address. High to indicate that an input address is on the low-order address lines ($A_Ø$ to A_7).
MEMR   Memory Read. High to indicate a read operation.

Other control signals
SYNC   A processor output that goes high to indicate the first clock cycle of each machine cycle.
DBIN   Data Bus In. Active high processor output for a read operation.
WR   Write. Goes low to indicate memory write or output.
RESET   Active high input for restart. User reset routine must begin at ØØØØ.
INT   Interrupt ⎫ see Interrupts
INTE   Interrupt Enable⎭
READY   Active low input. Used by external devices to temporarily delay a read or write operation. When low, the processor inserts wait states until the READY is returned high.

8080/8085

WAIT Active high input. Used to indicate that the processor is inserting wait states in response to a ready input.

HOLD Active high input that forces the processor to halt at the end of its current machine cycle and to put its address and data bus lines into a high impedance state. This allows external devices to take control of the bus.

Control Signals [8085]

ALE Address Latch Enable. An output which is taken high during the first T-clock cycle to indicate that a valid address is an $A_{\emptyset}$ to A_7 (see I/O Addressing).

$\overline{\text{RD}}$ Read. Active low.

$\overline{\text{WR}}$ Write. Active low.

IO/$\overline{\text{M}}$ Input/output or memory. An output signal that indicates an input/output or memory operation.

$\overline{\text{RESET IN}}$ Active low input for restart. User routine must start at $8\emptyset\emptyset\emptyset$.

$\overline{\text{RESET OUT}}$ Active low output which can be used to reset peripheral chips and devices.

TRAP An active high non-maskable interrupt.

RSTX.5 Fixed vector interrupt lines—see Interrupts.

INTR Interrupt Request.

$\overline{\text{INTA}}$ Interrupt Acknowledge.

READY same as 8080

HOLD same as 8080

HLDA Hold Acknowledge

SID Serial Input Data. A software-controlled serial input data line.

When RIM (Read Interrupt Masks) instruction is executed, the bit of data present at SID input is loaded into bit 7 of the accumulator.

SOD Serial Output Data. Softward-controlled output using the SIM (Set Interrupt Masks) instruction is executed. Bit 7 of the accumulator will be output at SOD when SIM is used. (See *fig. M25*.)

Fig. M25 Interface to convert the TTL type signals SOD and SID into a 20 mA loop

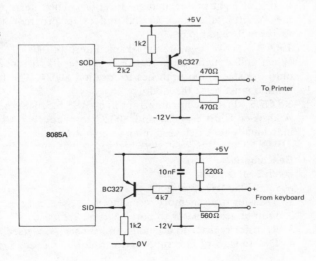

8080/8085

I/O Addressing

Two methods   *a*) Memory mapped.

                 b) Isolated I/O, using the IN and OUT instructions.

During the execution of an IN or OUT instruction, the processor outputs a control signal [INP or OUT for the 8080; IO/$\overline{\text{M}}$ for the 8085] that signals the presence of an I/O address on the lower-order address lines ($A_0 \rightarrow A_7$). In this way fast access to 512 ports can be provided. (See *fig. M26*.)

Fig. M26 Principle of isolated I/O in the 8080/8085

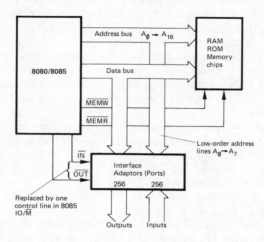

Interrupt Facilities

INT   Active high, maskable interrupt [8080]

When pulled high by an external device, and assuming that the I-bistable is set (EI instruction), the processor completes the current instruction, and then expects the next instruction to be provided externally. This is often RST (restart) which automatically pushes the PC content onto the stack and then causes a jump to one of eight preset memory locations. The interrupt service routine must pull the PC from the stack at the end of its program and must also stack other registers if required.

TRAP   Active high, non-maskable interrupt [8085]

When pulled high, the processor completes its current instruction, pushes the PC onto the stack, and branches to location 0024. The first instruction of the user routine must be at this address.

RSTX.5   Fixed vector interrupt lines RST 5.5, RST 6.5, RST 7.5 [8085]

Addresses $003C$, 0034 and $002C$ respectively. All three are maskable, and individually set or cleared in an interrupt register.

Benchmarks

8080: 2 MHz clock

8085: 3.125 MHz (2nd figures)

1. Transfer from memory to memory   8 μsec; 5.12 μsec
2. Output accumulator to port   5 μsec; 3.2 μsec
3. Transfer register to accumulator   3 μsec; 1.28 μsec
4. INT to start of interrupt service routine   6 μsec; 5 μsec

8080/8085

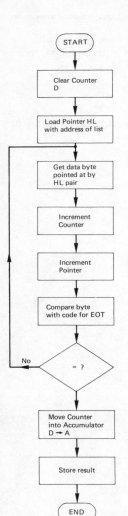

START

Clear Counter
D

Load Pointer HL
with address of list

Get data byte
pointed at by
HL pair

Increment
Counter

Increment
Pointer

Compare byte
with code for EOT

= ?   No

Move Counter
into Accumulator
D → A

Store result

END

Fig. M27 Flowchart for
8080/8085 program to
find the length of a list of
ASCII code

Sample Program (see page 124)

Flowchart: *fig. M27*

Note In most 8080/8085 systems, the low-order addresses on zero page will hold the monitor. However, the address of the list in this case is still assumed to be $0050.

	ASSEMBLY LANGUAGE			MACHINE CODE Address	Code	(hex.)
	MVI	D,$00	Clear counter	1000	16	00
	MVI	H,$00 ⎫	Load HL pair	1002	26	00
	MVI	L,$50 ⎬	with List address	1004	2E	50
NEXT	MOV	A,M	Load data	1006	7E	
	INR	D	Increment counter	1007	14	
	INX	H	Increment HL pair	1008	23	
	CPI	$03	= EOT?	1009	FE	03
	JNZ	NEXT	Branch back	100B	C2	06 10
	MOV	A,D	Load counter into A	100E	7A	
	STA	$3000	Store result	100F	32	00 30
	JMP	MON	Return	1010	C3	00 00

Support Chips

A wide range which includes:

8224 clock generator

8228 system controller (8080 bus)

8212 8-bit I/O port

8251 serial I/O interface.

8255A programmable parallel I/O.

Z80

Designed as an enhanced 8080 with which it is nominally code-compatible, the Z80 however has an extended register set, a much enlarged instruction set, more addressing modes, and a dedicated bus system.

Z80 features

Single +5 V power supply.

Clock frequency 2.5 MHz supplied by external clock generator (Z80A runs at 4 MHz).

16-bit address bus⎫
 8-bit data bus ⎬ Dedicated lines

Fig. M28 for pinout and basic diagram.

Fig. M28a Pinout for the Z80

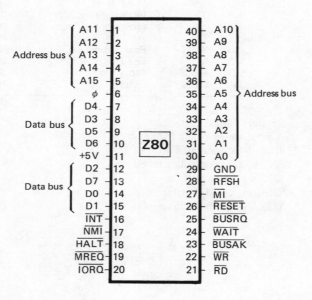

Register Set (*fig. M28c*)

8-bit registers—two banks of 8 general-purpose registers:

AF	AF′
BC	BC′
DE	DE′
HL	HL′

The A register is the primary accumulator. The registers can be used to store data or in pairs (BC, DE, HL) as memory pointers holding 16-bit addresses. The HL is commonly used for this. A programmer has access to the main register set but two instructions EX and EXX allow transfers between banks:

EX	AF	AF′
EXX	BC	BC′
	DE	DE′
	HL	HL′

Z80

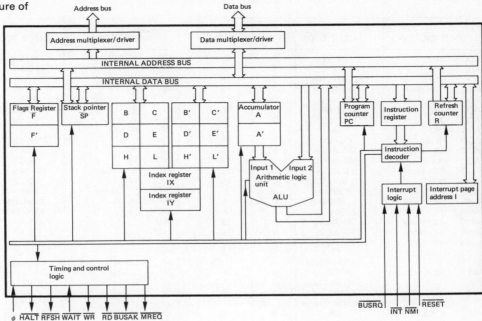

This will allow fast interrupt since any registers used in the main program can be saved simply by switching to the alternative set.

Two 16-bit index registers IX, IY are used as memory pointers in the Indexed Addressing mode.

16-bit Program Counter (PC).

16-bit Stack Pointer (SP).

I register: used for Mode 3 interrupts.

R register: refresh address for dynamic RAM.

Flag Register (processor status).

MSB	S	Sign
	Z	Zero
	*	Not used
	H	Half-carry
	*	Not used
	P/V	Parity/overflow
	N	Subtract
	C	Carry

The I bit (Interrupt mask) is a separate bistable.

Fig. M28c Register set of
the **Z80**

A	F	A′	F′
B	C	B′	C′
D	E	D′	E′
H	L	H′	L′
I (interrupts)		Flags	
IXH		IXL	
IYH		IYL	
SPH		SPL	
PCH		PCL	

153

Z80

INSTRUCTION		OBJECT CODE	BYTES	CLOCK PERIODS
ADC	data	CE yy	2	7
ADC	(HL)	8E	1	7
ADC	HL,rp	ED 01xx1010	2	15
ADC	(IX+disp)	DD 8E yy	3	19
ADC	(IY+disp)	FD 8E yy	3	19
ADC	reg	10001xxx	1	4
ADD	data	C6 yy	2	7
ADD	(HL)	86	1	7
ADD	HL,rp	00xx1001	1	11
ADD	(IX+disp)	DD 86 yy	3	19
ADD	IX,pp	DD 00xx1001	2	15
ADD	(IY+disp)	FD 88 yy	3	19
ADD	IY,rr	FD 00xx1001	2	15
ADD	reg	10000xxx	1	4
AND	data	E6 yy	2	7
AND	(HL)	A6	1	7
AND	(IX+disp)	DD A6 yy	3	19
AND	(IY+disp)	FD A6 yy	3	19
AND	reg	10100xxx	1	4
BIT	b,(HL)	CB 01bbb110	2	12
BIT	b,(IX+disp)	DD CB yy 01bbb110	4	20
BIT	b,(IY+disp)	FD CB yy 01bbb110	4	20
BIT	b,reg	CB 01bbbxxx	2	9
CALL	label	CD ppqq	3	17
CALL	C,label	DC ppqq	3	10/17
CALL	M,label	FC ppqq	3	10/17
CALL	NC,label	D4 ppqq	3	10/17
CALL	NZ,label	C4 ppqq	3	10/17
CALL	P,label	F4 ppqq	3	10/17
CALL	PE,label	EC ppqq	3	10/17
CALL	PO,label	E4 ppqq	3	10/17
CALL	Z,label	CC ppqq	3	10/17
CCF		3F	1	4
CP	data	FE yy	2	7
CP	(HL)	BE	1	7
CP	(IX+disp)	DD BE yy	3	19
CP	(IY+disp)	FD BE yy	3	19
CP	reg	10111xxx	1	4
CPD		ED A9	2	16
CPDR		ED B9	2	21/16*
CPI		ED A1	2	16
CPIR		ED B1	2	21/16*
CPL		2F	1	4
DAA		27	1	4
DEC	(HL)	35	1	11
DEC	IX	DD 2B	2	10
DEC	(IX+disp)	DD 35 yy	3	23
DEC	IY	FD 2B	2	10
DEC	(IY+disp)	FD 35 yy	3	23
DEC	rp	00xx1011	1	6
DEC	reg	00xxx101	1	4
DI		F3	1	4
DJNZ	disp	10 yy	2	8/13
EI		FB	1	4
EX	AF,AF	08	1	4
EX	DE,HL	EB	1	4
EX	(SP),HL	E3	1	19
EX	(SP),IX	DD E3	2	23

INSTRUCTION		OBJECT CODE	BYTES	CLOCK PERIODS
EX	(SP),IY	FD E3	2	23
EXX		D9	1	4
HALT		76	1	4
IM	0	ED 46	2	8
IM	1	ED 56	2	8
IM	2	ED 5E	2	8
IN	A,port	DB yy	2	10
IN	reg,(C)	ED 01ddd000	2	11
INC	(HL)	34	1	11
INC	IX	DD 23	2	10
INC	(IX+disp)	DD 34 yy	3	23
INC	IY	FD 23	2	10
INC	(IY+disp)	FD 34 yy	3	23
INC	rp	00xx0011	1	6
INC	reg	00xxx100	1	4
IND		ED AA	2	15
INDR		ED BA	2	20/15
INI		ED A2	2	15
INIR		ED B2	2	20/15
JP	label	C3 ppqq	3	10
JP	C,label	DA ppqq	3	10
JP	(HL)	E9	1	4
JP	(IX)	DD E9	2	8
JP	(IY)	FD E9	2	8
JP	M,label	FA ppqq	3	10
JP	NC,label	D2 ppqq	3	10
JP	NZ,label	C2 ppqq	3	10
JP	P,label	F2 ppqq	3	10
JP	PE,label	EA ppqq	3	10
JP	PO,label	E2 ppqq	3	10
JP	Z,label	CA ppqq	3	10
JR	C,disp	38 yy	2	7/12
JR	disp	18 yy	2	12
JR	NC,disp	30 yy	2	7/12
JR	NZ,disp	20 yy	2	7/12
JR	Z,disp	28 yy	2	7/12
LD	A,(addr)	3A ppqq	3	13
LD	A,(BC)	0A	1	7
LD	A,(DE)	1A	1	7
LD	A,I	ED 57	2	9
LD	A,R	ED 5F	2	9
LD	(addr),A	32 ppqq	3	13
LD	(addr),BC	ED 43 ppqq	4	20
LD	(addr),DE	ED 53 ppqq	4	20
LD	(addr),HL	22 ppqq	3	16
LD	(addr),IX	DD 22 ppqq	4	20
LD	(addr),IY	FD 22 ppqq	4	20
LD	(addr),SP	ED 73 ppqq	4	20
LD	(BC),A	02	1	7
LD	(DE),A	12	1	7
LD	HL,(addr)	2A ppqq	3	16
LD	(HL),data	36 yy	2	10
LD	(HL),reg	01110sss	1	7
LD	I,A	ED 47	2	9
LD	IX,(addr)	DD 2A ppqq	4	20
LD	IX,data 16	DD 21 yyyy	4	14
LD	(IX+disp),data	DD 36 yy yy	4	19
LD	(IX+disp),reg	DD 01110sss yy	3	19
LD	IY,(addr)	FD 2A ppqq	4	20
LD	IY,data 16	FD 21 yyyy	4	14

INSTRUCTION		OBJECT CODE	BYTES	CLOCK PERIODS
LD	(IY+disp),data	FD 36 yyyy	4	19
LD	(IY+disp),reg	FD 01110sss yy	3	19
LD	R,A	ED 4F	2	9
LD	reg,data	00ddd110 yy	2	7
LD	reg,(HL)	01ddd110	1	7
LD	reg,(IX+disp)	DD 01ddd110 yy	3	19
LD	reg,(IY+disp)	FD 01dddd110 yy	3	19
LD	reg,reg	01dddsss	1	4
LD	rp,(addr)	ED 01xx1011 ppqq	4	20
LD	rp,data16	00xx0001 yyyy	3	10
LD	SP,HL	F9	1	6
LD	SP,IX	DD F9	2	10
LD	SP,IY	FD F9	2	10
LDD		ED A8	2	16
LDDR		ED B8	2	21/16*
LDI		ED A0	2	16
LDIR		ED B0	2	21/16*
NEG		ED 44	2	8
NOP		00	1	4
OR	data	F6 yy	2	7
OR	(HL)	B6	1	7
OR	(IX+disp)	DD B6 yy	3	19
OR	(IY+disp)	FD B6 yy	3	19
OR	reg	10110xxx	1	4
OTDR		ED B8	2	20/15*
OTIR		ED B3	2	20/15*
OUT	(C),reg	ED 01sss001	2	12
OUT	port,A	D3 yy	2	11
OUTD		ED AB	2	15
OUTI		ED A3	2	15
POP	IX	DD E1	2	14
POP	IY	FD E1	2	14
POP	pr	11xx0001	1	10
PUSH	IX	DD E5	2	15
PUSH	IY	FD E5	2	15
PUSH	pr	11xx0101	1	11
RES	b,(HL)	CB 10bbb110	2	15
RES	b,(IX+disp)	DD CB yy 10bbb110	4	23
RES	b,(IY+disp)	FD CB yy 10bbb110	4	23
RES	b,reg	CB 10bbbxxx	2	8
RET		C9	1	10
RET	C	D8	1	5/11
RET	M	F8	1	5/11
RET	NC	D0	1	5/11
RET	NZ	C0	1	5/11
RET	P	F0	1	5/11
RET	PE	E8	1	5/11
RET	PO	E0	1	5/11
RET	Z	C8	1	5/11
RETI		ED 4D	2	14

INSTRUCTION		OBJECT CODE	BYTES	CLOCK PERIODS
RETN		ED 45	2	14
RL	(HL)	CB 16	2	15
RL	(IX+disp)	DD CB yy 16	4	23
RL	(IY+disp)	FD CB yy 16	4	23
RL	reg	CB 00010xxx	2	8
RLA		17	1	4
RLC	(HL)	CB 06	2	15
RLC	(IX+disp)	DD CB yy 06	4	23
RLC	(IY+disp)	FD CB yy 06	4	23
RLC	reg	CB 00000xxx	2	8
RLCA		07	1	4
RLD		ED 6F	2	18
RR	(HL)	CB 1E	2	15
RR	(IX+disp)	DD CB yy 1E	4	23
RR	(IY+disp)	FD CB yy 1E	4	23
RR	reg	CB 00011xxx	2	8
RRA		1F	1	4
RRC	(HL)	CB 0E	2	15
RRC	(IX+disp)	DD CB yy 0E	4	23
RRC	(IY+disp)	FD CB yy 0E	4	23
RRC	reg	CB 00001xxx	2	8
RRCA		0F	1	4
RRD		ED 67	2	18
RST	n	11xxx111	1	11
SBC	data	DE yy	2	7
SBC	(HL)	9E	1	7
SBC	HL,rp	ED 01xx0010	2	15
SBC	(IX+disp)	DD 9E yy	3	19
SBC	(IY+disp)	FD 9E yy	3	19
SBC	reg	10011xxx	1	4
SCF		37	1	4
SET	b,(HL)	CB 11bbb110	2	15
SET	b,(IX+disp)	DD CB yy 11bbb110	4	23
SET	b,(IY+disp)	FD CB yy 11bbb110	4	23
SET	b,reg	CB 11bbbxxx	2	8
SLA	(HL)	CB 26	2	15
SLA	(IX+disp)	DD CB yy 26	4	23
SLA	(IY+disp)	FD CB yy 26	4	23
SLA	reg	CB 00100xxx	2	8
SRA	(HL)	CB 2E	2	15
SRA	(IX+disp)	DD CB yy 2E	4	23
SRA	(IY+disp)	FD CB yy 2E	4	23
SRA	reg	CB 00101xxx	2	8
SRL	(HL)	CB 3E	2	15
SRL	(IX+disp)	DD CB yy 3E	4	23
SRL	(IY+disp)	FD CB yy 3E	4	23
SRL	reg	CB 00111xxx	2	8
SUB	data	D6 yy	2	7
SUB	(HL)	96	1	7
SUB	(IX+disp)	DD 96 yy	3	19
SUB	(IY+disp)	FD 96 yy	3	19
SUB	reg	10010xxx	1	4
XOR	data	EE yy	2	7
XOR	(HL)	AE	1	7
XOR	(IX+disp)	DD AE yy	3	19
XOR	(IY+disp)	FD AE yy	3	19
XOR	reg	10101xxx	1	4

* Execution time shown is for one iteration.

x	represents an optional binary digit.
bbb	represents optional binary digits identifying a bit location in a register or memory byte. (000 = LSB, 111 = MSB)
ddd	represents optional binary digits identifying a destination register.
	111 = A 000 = B 001 = C 010 = D 011 = E 100 = H 101 = L
sss	represents optional binary digits identifying a source register—same coding as ddd.
ppqq	represents a four hexadecimal digit memory address.
yy	represents two hexadecimal data digits.
yyyy	represents four hexadecimal data digits.

When two possible execution times are shown (i.e., 5/11), it indicates that the number of clock periods depends on condition flags.

Z80

Instruction Set (fig. M29)

158 basic instructions which include additional instructions over the 8080/8085 such as: 16-bit arithmetic operations; block move; exchange and group; and bit set, reset and test. Some instructions are 4 bytes. The Z80 has the largest, and considered by some, the most flexible instruction set of all 8-bit processors.

Addressing Modes (total 10)

Immediate
Immediate Extended
Implied
Extended
Indexed
Register Indirect
Register
Modified Page Zero
Relative
Bit

IMMEDIATE EXTENDED is similar to immediate except that the operand is a 2-byte number rather than single byte.

IMPLIED   The location is one of the internal registers which is named in the op-code.

Example
INC H   Increment H register (hex. code 24)

EXTENDED   The address is specified in the instruction as a 2-byte number; low byte first, high byte last.

Example
LDA ($Ø834)   Load A from address $Ø834 (hex. code 3A 34Ø8)

INDEXED   A single-byte offset specified in the instruction is added to the contents of one of the index register (IX or IY) to give the effective address.

Example
LD IX, $2Ø5Ø   Set IX reg. to point to address $2Ø5Ø
LD A, (IX + Ø3)   Load A from pointed address +Ø3

REGISTER INDIRECT   The address is given by the contents of a specified register pair. The HL pair is used by most instructions in this mode, but some instructions use the BC or DE pairs.

Example
LD HL, $Ø33F   Point HL pair to address $Ø33F
LD A, (HL)   Load A from address held by HL pair

REGISTER   The operand is located in a specified register.
LD A, H   Load A from register H

MODIFIED ZERO   Used with the RST (Restart) instruction where the location of the next instruction that is to be executed is in a page zero address.

RELATIVE ADDRESSING   Used with conditional jump instructions where the second byte of the instruction is a twos complement offset that allows a

Z80

relative jump to +127 or −128 locations from the content of the program counter.

BIT ADDRESSING This mode is used in combination with one of the other modes to carry out bit set, test and reset on a particular bit in any general-purpose register or memory location.

Control Signals

RFSH Active low output used for refresh of dynamic RAM.

M1 Machine Cycle 1. Active low output used to indicate that the current operation is an op-code fetch.

RESET Used for start-up. When pulled low, the program counter is loaded with ∅∅∅∅. The user reset routine must begin at ∅∅∅∅.

BUSRQ Bus Request. An input which allows external devices to take over control of the bus lines. When pulled low, the processor completes the current instruction and then disconnects itself by tri-stating the address, data, and control bus lines.

BUSAK Bus Acknowledge. An output signal taken low to indicate that the processor has responded to a $\overline{BUSRQ}$ input and that the bus lines are available.

WAIT An input used by I/O or slow memory chips to allow more time for a read or write operation. When pulled low by an external device, the processor inserts wait states into the system clock.

WR Write. An output taken low when a memory write or output operation is required.

RD Read. An output taken low when a memory read or input operation is required.

IORQ I/O Request. An output (low) which indicates that an I/O operation is about to take place and that the address on the address bus is a valid I/O port not a memory location. Usually ORed with $\overline{RD}$ and $\overline{WR}$ signals to give control of I/O direction.

MREQ Memory Request. An output (low) which indicates that a memory read or write operation is about to occur and that the address on the address bus is a valid memory address and not an I/O port. ORed with $\overline{RD}$ and $\overline{WR}$ signals to give control of memory data transfer direction.

HALT An output which signals that the processor has executed a halt instruction and is waiting for an interrupt request.

NMI Interrupt input.

INT Interrupt input.

I/O Addressing

Two methods a) Memory mapped.
$\qquad\qquad$ b) Isolated I/O, using IN and OUT instructions.
When an I/O operation is required, the processor takes the $\overline{IORQ}$ (I/O Request) line low to indicate that a valid I/O port address is on the lower 8 bits of the address bus ($A_∅$ to A_7). Thus, fast access to 512 ports can be provided.

Interrupt Facilities (total 2)

a) **NMI** Non-maskable interrupt
An input which, when pulled low by an external source, forces an immediate interrupt. The processor completes the current instruction, pushes the content of the PC onto the stack, and executes a restart to address 8∅∅66. The first instruction of the user $\overline{NMI}$ routine must be at this address.

Z80

b) $\overline{\text{INT}}$ Interrupt request used by peripherals

This interrupt is maskable by the I bit. When $\overline{\text{INT}}$ is taken low by a peripheral, the processor first completes the current instruction and then checks the state of the I bit. If the I bit is set, the interrupt is accepted, and the processor responds in one of three software-determined modes:

1) *Mode* 0   An op-code (RST) must be placed on the data bus by the interrupting device. The RST instruction is most often used in this mode since it automatically pushes the PC onto the stack and then causes a jump to a predetermined location that will contain the start of the interrupt service routine.

2) *Mode* 1   The processor automatically saves the contents of PC on the stack and executes a restart to $0038. The first instruction of the service routine must be at this address.

3) Mode 2   The processor automatically saves the contents of the PC on the stack and then the user must supply part of the address of the first instruction of the interrupt service routine via the data bus. The interrupt vector (the full address) is formed when the contents of the I register are loaded into the high byte of the PC and the user byte is loaded into the low byte of the PC. The user must have previously set the required value of the high byte into the I register.

Mode 1 is automatically selected by a system reset. The other modes can be selected by software with IM (Interrupt Mode) instruction. The interrupt mask bit is enabled with EI and disabled with DI instructions.

Benchmarks

4 MHz clock assumed.
1. Transfer from memory to memory   6.4 μsec
2. Output accumulator to port   4.8 μsec
3. Transfer from register to accumulator   1.6 μsec
4. INT to start of interrupt service routine (depends on mode)   6 μsec typ.

Program Example (see page 124)

Flowchart: *fig. M30*
Note   The operating system will normally be on zero page but in this case the list is still assumed to start at $0050.

| | ASSEMBLY LANGUAGE | | MACHINE CODE | | |
			Address	Code	(hex.)
	LD HL, 0	Clear counter	1000	21	0000
	LD IX, $0050	Point X reg. at list	1003	DD	21 50 00
NEXT	LD A, (IX + 0)	Load data	1007	DD	7E 00
	INC IX	Increment pointer	100A	DD	23
	INC HL	Increment	100C	23	
	CP $03		100D	FE	03
	JR NZ, NEXT		100F	20	F6
	LD A, L		1011	67	
	LD ($3000), A		1012	32	00 30
	HALT		1015	76	

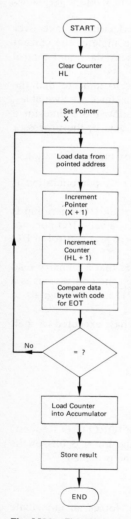

Fig. M30 Flowchart for **Z80** program to find the length of a list of ASCII code

START

Clear Counter HL

Set Pointer X

Load data from pointed address

Increment Pointer (X + 1)

Increment Counter (HL + 1)

Compare data byte with code for EOT

= ?   No

Load Counter into Accumulator

Store result

END

Z80

An alternative program using one of the block search instructions could be:

ASSEMBLY LANGUAGE		MACHINE CODE	
		Address	Code
LD A, $03	Load A with $03	1000	3E 03
LD HL, $0050	Load HL pair	1002	21 50 00
LD BC, 0	Clear counter	1005	01 00 00
CPIR	(see note below)	1008	ED B1
XOR A	⎫ Load count value	100A	CF
SUB C	⎭ into A	100B	91
LD ($3000), A	Store result	100C	32 00 30
HALT		100F	76

The instruction CPIR compares the content of the address pointed at by the HL pair with the content of A; then increments HL; decrements BC; and then decrements PC by 2 (to repeat) if the comparison is not equal.

Support Chips These include:
Z80 PIO Two 8-bit I/O parallel port interfaces.
Z80 CTC Counter timer circuit.
Z80 DMA Direct memory access controller.
Z80 SIO Serial I/O controller.
Z80 DART Dual asynchronous receiver/transmitter.

6809

Developed by Motorola as a much-enhanced 6800-type processor. The 6809, although based on the architecture and instruction set of the 6800, has additional registers, more powerful addressing modes, an extended instruction set, a fast interrupt request input, and an on-chip clock generator. The 6809 will interface with the entire range of 6800 chips.

6809 features

Single ±5 V supply.

Built-in clock circuit, basic frequency 1 MHz.

A direct page register; allows direct addressing mode to be used to any page in memory.

8-bit data bus (bidirectional)⎫
16-bit address bus ⎬ Dedicated lines

A fast interrupt input $\overline{\text{FIRQ}}$.

Faster versions (1.5 MHz and 2 MHz) are available. The addressing range (basic 64 K bytes) can be extended to 2 M bytes by using an additional chip (6829).

Pin out and basic diagrams: *fig. M31.*

Register Set (*fig. M31c*)

Two 8-bit Accumulators: AccA, AccB.

These can be combined to give one 16-bit Accumulator: AccD.

Direct Page Register (DPR) for instructions using the direct addressing mode. The DPR holds the most significant byte of the operand address and the instruction (2 bytes only) gives the address within the page. On reset, the DPR defaults to ØØ (zero page) and must be set up for other pages by the user. An accumulator is loaded with the required value (page number) and this is then transferred to the DPR.

16-bit Program Counter (PC).

Two 16-bit Index Registers (IX and IY).

Two 16-bit Stack Pointers

a) System SP: used for interrupts and subroutines (S).

b) User SP: for temporary storage purposes and is controlled exclusively by the programmer (U).

Condition Code Register (CCR): Status flags.

MSB	E	Entire: used by the processor to determine which registers have been stacked during an interrupt
	F	Mask bit for Fast Interrupt Request
	H	Half-carry
	I	Mask bit for Interrupt Request
	S	Sign: set when result is negative
	V	Overflow
	C	Carry from bit 7 to bit 8

Instruction Set (*fig. M32*)

Similar to the 6800 and upward-compatible with all the 6800 processors at source code level. The number of basic instructions is only 59 but because of the greatly enhanced addressing modes the total number of available op-codes is 1464.

6809

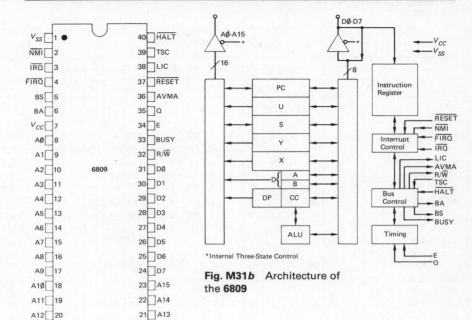

Fig. M31b Architecture of the **6809**

V_{SS}	1	40	$\overline{\text{HALT}}$
$\overline{\text{NMI}}$	2	39	TSC
$\overline{\text{IRQ}}$	3	38	LIC
$\overline{\text{FIRQ}}$	4	37	$\overline{\text{RESET}}$
BS	5	36	AVMA
BA	6	35	Q
V_{CC}	7	34	E
A0	8	33	BUSY
A1	9	32	R/$\overline{\text{W}}$
A2	10	31	D0
A3	11	30	D1
A4	12	29	D2
A5	13	28	D3
A6	14	27	D4
A7	15	26	D5
A8	16	25	D6
A9	17	24	D7
A10	18	23	A15
A11	19	22	A14
A12	20	21	A13

6809

*Internal Three-State Control

Fig. M31c Register set of the **6809**

Acc A (8)	Acc B (8)
Acc D	
Status CCR	DPR
PCH	PCL
IXH	IXL
IYH	IYL
SPH (S)	SPL (S)
USPH (U)	USPL (U)

Addressing Modes
8 basic modes but this increases to 13 when all variations are taken into consideration.

Inherent
Register
Immediate
Direct
Extended and Extended Indirect
Indexed   Zero offset
           Constant offset
           Accumulator offset
           Auto Increment/Decrement
Indexed Indirect
Relative
   Short/long relative branching
   Program counter relative

6809

Fig. M32 Instruction set of the **6809**

INSTRUCTION / FORMS		INHERENT OP	~	#	DIRECT OP	~	#	EXTENDED OP	~	#	IMMEDIATE OP	~	#	INDEXED[1] OP	~	#	RELATIVE OP	~[5]	#	DESCRIPTION	H (5)	N (3)	Z (2)	V (1)	C (0)
ABX		3A	3	1																B + X → X (UNSIGNED)	•	•	•	•	•
ADC	ADCA				99	4	2	B9	5	3	89	2	2	A9	4+	2+				A + M + C → A	↕	↕	↕	↕	↕
	ADCB				D9	4	2	F9	5	3	C9	2	2	E9	4+	2+				B + M + C → B	↕	↕	↕	↕	↕
ADD	ADDA				9B	4	2	BB	5	3	8B	2	2	AB	4+	2+				A + M → A	↕	↕	↕	↕	↕
	ADDB				DB	4	2	FB	5	3	CB	2	2	EB	4+	2+				B + M → B	↕	↕	↕	↕	↕
	ADDD				D3	6	2	F3	7	3	C3	4	3	E3	6+	2+				D + M:M + 1 → D	↕	↕	↕	↕	↕
AND	ANDA				94	4	2	B4	5	3	84	2	2	A4	4+	2+				A · M → A	•	↕	↕	0	•
	ANDB				D4	4	2	F4	5	3	C4	2	2	E4	4+	2+				B · M → B	•	↕	↕	0	•
	ANDCC										1C	3	2							CC · IMM → CC					1
ASL	ASLA	48	2	1																A ⎱ C ← b7…b0 ← 0	8	↕	↕	↕	↕
	ASLB	58	2	1																B ⎰ (c b1 b0)	8	↕	↕	↕	↕
	ASL				08	6	2	78	7	3				68	6+	2+				M	8	↕	↕	↕	↕
ASR	ASRA	47	2	1																A ⎱ b7…b0 → C	8	↕	↕	•	↕
	ASRB	57	2	1																B ⎰ (b7 b0 c)	8	↕	↕	•	↕
	ASR				07	6	2	77	7	3				67	6+	2+				M	8	↕	↕	•	↕
BCC	BCC																24	3	2	Branch C = 0	•	•	•	•	•
	LBCC																10 24	5(6)	4	Long Branch C = 0	•	•	•	•	•
BCS	BCS																25	3	2	Branch C = 1	•	•	•	•	•
	LBCS																10 25	5(6)	4	Long Branch C = 1	•	•	•	•	•
BEQ	BEQ																27	3	2	Branch Z = 0	•	•	•	•	•
	LBEQ																10 27	5(6)	4	Long Branch Z = 0	•	•	•	•	•
BGE	BGE																2C	3	2	Branch > Zero	•	•	•	•	•
	LBGE																10 2C	5(6)	4	Long Branch > Zero	•	•	•	•	•
BGT	BGT																2E	3	2	Branch > Zero	•	•	•	•	•
	LBGT																10 2E	5(6)	4	Long Branch > Zero	•	•	•	•	•
BHI	BHI																22	3	2	Branch Higher	•	•	•	•	•
	LBHI																10 22	5(6)	4	Long Branch Higher	•	•	•	•	•
BHS	BHS																24	3	2	Branch Higher or Same	•	•	•	•	•
	LBHS																10 24	5(6)	4	Long Branch Higher or Same	•	•	•	•	•
BIT	BITA				95	4	2	B5	5	3	85	2	2	A5	4+	2+				Bit Test A (M · A)	•	↕	↕	0	•
	BITB				D5	4	2	F5	5	3	C5	2	2	E5	4+	2+				Bit Test B (M · B)	•	↕	↕	0	•
BLE	BLE																2F	3	2	Branch ≤ Zero	•	•	•	•	•
	LBLE																10 2F	5(6)	4	Long Branch ≤ Zero	•	•	•	•	•

INSTRUCTION/ FORMS		INHERENT OP	~	#	DIRECT OP	~	#	EXTENDED OP	~	#	IMMEDIATE OP	~	#	INDEXED[1] OP	~	#	RELATIVE OP	~[5]	#	DESCRIPTION	5 H	3 N	2 Z	1 V	0 C
BLO	BLO																25	3	2	Branch Lower	•	•	•	•	•
	LBLO																10 25	5(6)	4	Long Branch Lower	•	•	•	•	•
BLS	BLS																23	3	2	Branch Lower or Same	•	•	•	•	•
	LBLS																10 23	5(6)	4	Long Branch Lower or Same	•	•	•	•	•
BLT	BLT																2D	3	2	Branch < Zero	•	•	•	•	•
	LBLT																10 2D	5(6)	4	Long Branch < Zero	•	•	•	•	•
BMI	BMI																2B	3	2	Branch Minus	•	•	•	•	•
	LBMI																10 2B	5(6)	4	Long Branch Minus	•	•	•	•	•
BNE	BNE																26	3	2	Branch $Z \neq 0$	•	•	•	•	•
	LBNE																10 26	5(6)	4	Long Branch $Z \neq 0$	•	•	•	•	•
BPL	BPL																2A	3	2	Branch Plus	•	•	•	•	•
	LBPL																10 2A	5(6)	4	Long Branch Plus	•	•	•	•	•
BRA	BRA																20	3	2	Branch Always	•	•	•	•	•
	LBRA																16	5	3	Long Branch Always	•	•	•	•	•
BRN	BRN																21	3	2	Branch Never	•	•	•	•	•
	LBRN																10 21	5	4	Long Branch Never	•	•	•	•	•
BSR	BSR																8D	7	2	Branch to Subroutine	•	•	•	•	•
	LBSR																17	9	3	Long Branch to Subroutine	•	•	•	•	•
BVC	BVC																28	3	2	Branch $V = 0$	•	•	•	•	•
	LBVC																10 28	5(6)	4	Long Branch $V = 0$	•	•	•	•	•
BVS	BVS																29	3	2	Branch $V = 1$	•	•	•	•	•
	LBVS																10 29	5(6)	4	Long Branch $V = 1$	•	•	•	•	•
CLR	CLRA	4F	2	1																$0 \rightarrow A$	•	0	1	0	0
	CLRB	5F	2	1																$0 \rightarrow B$	•	0	1	0	0
	CLR				0F	6	2	7F	7	3				6F	6+	2+				$0 \rightarrow M$	•	0	1	0	0
CMP	CMPA				91	4	2	B1	5	3	81	2	2	A1	4+	2+				Compare M from A	8	↕	↕	↕	↕
	CMPB				D1	4	2	F1	4	3	C1	2	1	E1	4+	2+				Compare M from B	8	↕	↕	↕	↕
	CMPD				10 93	7	3	10 B3	8	4	10 83	5	4	10 A3	7+	3+				Compare M:M E 1 from D	•	↕	↕	↕	↕
	CMPS				11 9C	7	3	11 BC	8	4	11 8C	5	4	11 AC	7+	3+				Compare M:M + 1 from S	•	↕	↕	↕	↕
	CMPU				11 93	7	3	11 B3	8	4	11 83	5	4	11 A3	7+	3+				Compare M:M + 1 from U	•	↕	↕	↕	↕
	CMPX				9C	6	2	BC	7	3	8C	4	3	AC	6+	2+				Compare M:M + 1 from X	•	↕	↕	↕	↕
	CMPY				10 9C	7	3	10 BC	8	4	10 8C	5	4	10 AC	7+	3+				Compare M:M + 1 from Y	•	↕	↕	↕	↕

INSTRUCTION/FORMS		INHERENT			DIRECT			EXTENDED			IMMEDIATE			INDEXED[1]			RELATIVE			DESCRIPTION	5 H	3 N	2 Z	1 V	0 C
		OP	~	#	OP	~	#	OP	~	#	OP	~	#	OP	~	#	OP	~[5]	#						
COM	COMA	43	2	1																A →A	•	↕	↕	0	1
	COMB	53	2	1																B →B	•	↕	↕	0	1
	COM				03	6	2	73	7	3				63	6+	2+				M →M	•	↕	↕	0	1
CWAI		3C	20	2																CC IMM →CC Wait for Interrupt					1
DAA		19	2	1																Decimal Adjust A	•	↕	↕	0	↕
DEC	DECA	4A	2	1																A - 1 →A	•	↕	↕	↕	•
	DECB	5A	2	1																B - 1 →B	•	↕	↕	↕	•
	DEC				0A	6	2	7A	7	3				6A	6+	2+				M - 1 →M	•	↕	↕	↕	•
EOR	EORA				98	4	2	B8	5	3	88	2	2	A8	4+	2+				A M →A	•	↕	↕	0	•
	EORB				D8	4	2	F8	5	3	C8	2	2	E8	4+	2+				B M →B	•	↕	↕	0	•
EXG	R1, R2	1E	7	2																R1 R2[2]	•	•	•	•	•
INC	INCA	4C	2	1																A + 1 →A	•	↕	↕	↕	•
	INCB	5C	2	1																B + 1 →B	•	↕	↕	↕	•
	INC				0C	6	2	7C	7	3				6C	6+	2+				M + 1 →M	•	↕	↕	↕	•
JMP					0E	3	2	7E	4	3				6E	3+	2+				EA[3] →PC	•	•	•	•	•
JSR					9D	7	2	BD	8	3				AD	7+	2+				Jump to Subroutine	•	•	•	•	•
LD	LDA				96	4	2	B6	5	3	86	2	2	A6	4+	2+				M →A	•	↕	↕	0	•
	LDB				D6	4	2	F6	5	3	C6	2	2	E6	4+	2+				M →B	•	↕	↕	0	•
	LDD				DC	5	2	FC	6	3	CC	3	3	EC	5+	2+				M:M + 1 →D	•	↕	↕	0	•
	LDS				10 DE	6	3	10 FE	7	4	10 CE	4	4	10 EE	6+	3+				M:M + 1 →S	•	↕	↕	0	•
	LDU				DE	5	2	FE	6	3	CE	3	3	EE	5+	2+				M:M + 1 →U	•	↕	↕	0	•
	LDX				9E	5	2	BE	6	3	8E	3	3	AE	5+	2+				M:M + 1 →X	•	↕	↕	0	•
	LDY				10 9E	6	3	10 BE	7	4	10 8E	4	4	10 AE	6+	3+				M:M + 1 →Y	•	↕	↕	0	•
LEA	LEAS													32	4+	2+				EA[3] →S	•	•	•	•	•
	LEAU													33	4+	2+				EA[3] →U	•	•	•	•	•
	LEAX													30	4+	2+				EA[3] →X	•	•	↕	•	•
	LEAY													31	4+	2+				EA[3] →Y	•	•	↕	•	•
LSL	LSLA	48	2	1																A ⎫ B ⎬ M ⎭ C b7 b0	•	↕	↕	↕	↕
	LSLB	58	2	1																	•	↕	↕	↕	↕
	LSL				08	6	2	78	7	3				68	6+	2+					•	↕	↕	↕	↕
LSR	LSRA	44	2	1																A ⎫ B ⎬ M ⎭ b7 b0 c	•	0	↕	•	↕
	LSRB	54	2	1																	•	0	↕	•	↕
	LSR				04	6	2	74	7	3				64	6+	2+					•	0	↕	•	↕
MUL		3D	11	1																A x B →D (Unsigned)	•	•	↕	•	9
NEG	NEGA	40	2	1																Ā + 1 →A	8	↕	↕	↕	↕
	NEGB	50	2	1																B̄ + 1 →B	8	↕	↕	↕	↕
	NEG				00	6	2	70	7	3				60	6+	2+				M̄ + 1 →M	8	↕	↕	↕	↕
NOP		12	2	1																No Operation	•	•	•	•	•
OR	ORA				9A	4	2	BA	5	3	8A	2	2	AA	4+	2+				A v M →A	•	↕	↕	0	•
	ORB				DA	4	2	FA	5	3	CA	2	2	EA	4+	2+				B v M →B	•	↕	↕	0	•
	ORCC										1A	3	2							CC v IMM →CC					7
PSH	PSHS	34	5+[4]	2																Push Registers on S Stack	•	•	•	•	•
	PSHU	36	5+[4]	2																Push Registers on U Stack	•	•	•	•	•

6809

INSTRUCTION/ FORMS		INHERENT			DIRECT			EXTENDED			IMMEDIATE			INDEXED[1]			RELATIVE			DESCRIPTION	5 H	3 N	2 Z	1 V	0 C
		OP	~	#	OP	~	#	OP	~	#	OP	~	#	OP	~	#	OP	~[5]	#						
PUL	PULS	35	5	2																Pull Registers from S Stack	•	•	•	•	•
	PULU	37	5	2																Pull Registers from U Stack	•	•	•	•	•
ROL	ROLA	49	2	1																A	•	↕	↕	↕	↕
	ROLB	59	2	1																B	•	↕	↕	↕	↕
	ROL				09	6	2	79	7	3				69	6+	2+				M c b7 ← b0	•	↕	↕	↕	↕
ROR	RORA	46	2	1																A	•	↕	↕	↕	↕
	RORB	56	2	1																B	•	↕	↕	↕	↕
	ROR				06	6	2	76	7	3				66	6+	2+				M c b7 → b0	•	↕	↕	↕	↕
RT1		3B	6/15	1																Return from Interrupt					7
RTS		39	5	1																Return from Subroutine	•	•	•	•	•
SBC	SBCA				92	4	2	B2	5	3	82	2	2	A2	4+	2+				A – M – C → A	8	↕	↕	↕	↕
	SBCB				D2	4	2	F2	5	3	C2	2	2	E2	4+	2+				B – M – C → B	8	↕	↕	↕	↕
SEX		1D	2	1																Sign Extend B into A	•	↕	↕	0	•
ST	STA				97	4	2	B2	5	3				A7	4+	2+				A → M	•	↕	↕	0	•
	STB				D7	4	2	F7	5	3				E7	4+	2+				B → M	•	↕	↕	0	•
	STD				DD	5	2	FD	6	3				ED	5+	2+				D → M:M + 1	•	↕	↕	0	•
	STS				10 DF	6	3	10 FF	7	4				10 EF	6+	3+				S → M:M + 1	•	↕	↕	0	•
	STU				DF	5	2	FF	6	3				EF	5+	2+				U → M:M + 1	•	↕	↕	0	•
	STX				9F	5	2	BF	6	3				AF	5+	2+				X → M:M + 1	•	↕	↕	0	•
	STY				10 9F	6	3	10 BF	7	4				10 AF	6+	3+				Y → M:M + 1	•	↕	↕	0	•
SUB	SUBA				90	4	2	B0	5	3	80	2	2	A0	4+	2+				A – M → A	8	↕	↕	↕	↕
	SUBB				D0	4	2	F0	5	3	C0	2	2	E0	4+	2+				B – M → B	8	↕	↕	↕	↕
	SUBD				93	6	2	B3	7	3	83	4	3	A3	6+	2+				D – M:M + 1 → D	•	↕	↕	↕	↕
SW1	SW1[6]	3F	19	1																Software Interrupt 1	•	•	•	•	•
	SW12[6]	10 3F	20	2																Software Interrupt 2	•	•	•	•	•
	SW13[6]	11 3F	20	2																Software Interrupt 3	•	•	•	•	•
SYNC		13	≥2	1																Synchronize to Interrupt	•	•	•	•	•
TFR	R1, R2	1F	7	2																R1 → R2[2]	•	•	•	•	•
TST	TSTA	4D	2	1																Test A	•	↕	↕	0	•
	TSTB	5D	2	1																Test B	•	↕	↕	0	•
	TST				0D	6	2	7D	7	3				6D	6+	2+				Test M	•	↕	↕	0	•

6809

INHERENT   The op-code contains the address which will be one of the processor registers.

Examples
DAA   Decimal Adjust Acc
CLR B   Clear AccB

REGISTER   A form of inherent (implied) addressing used for transfers, exchanges and push/pull instructions. A post-byte is required to specify the registers being used

Examples
TFR   A,DP   Transfer AccA into the direct page register
EXG   X,Y   Exchange data in index X and Y

IMMEDIATE   The data to be operated on follows immediately after the op-code.

Example
ADD A   #$08   Add the hex. value 08 immediately to AccA

EXTENDED   The full address of the operand is specified in the instruction.

Example
LDA $22F0   Load AccA from address $22F0

DIRECT   Used for direct page addressing which is automatically on zero page unless the DP has been previously set up. Only two bytes needed.

Example
LDA $39   Load AccA from address 0039 (DP assumed to hold 00)

Otherwise, to set up DP use

LDA   #$50 ⎫
TFR   A,DP ⎭ set DP to $50 (page $50_{16})

Then   STB $80   Store AccB at $5080

EXTENDED INDIRECT is a special case of Indexed addressing. In this mode, the two bytes following the "post-byte" of an indexed instruction contain the address of the data.

Example
ADD A   [$30FD]   Add to AccA the data found at the address pointed at
                              by address $30FD

This mode is illustrated in *fig. M33*.

INDEXED   There are several variations, and these different indexed modes are specified in the instruction by the "Post-byte". This post-byte follows the op-code and precedes any offset or address that has to be specified. *Fig. M34* shows the Post-byte Register bit assignment together with a table of assembly mnemonics required for the various Indexed modes. These are

a) ZERO OFFSET: the address of the operand is specified in a selected register: X, Y, U or S.

6809

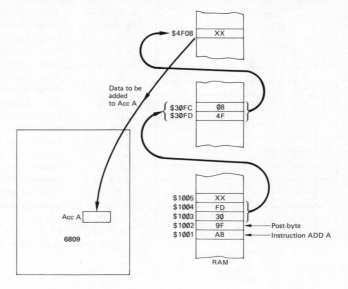

b) CONSTANT OFFSET from a specified register (R).

The address of the operand is the sum of the twos complement offset given in the instruction and the contents of the selected register X, Y, U or S. The offset can be 5, 8 or 16 bits. A 5-bit offset is given as part of the post-byte, whereas the 8 and 16-bit offsets must be one byte and two bytes respectively immediately following the post-byte.

c) ACCUMULATOR OFFSET from Register (R).

The address is the sum of a twos complement offset contained in the A, B or D accumulator and the content of the selected register X, Y, U or S.

d) AUTO-INCREMENT/AUTO-DECREMENT register (R).

Similar to zero offset with the added facility of automatic increment or decrement of the specified register X, Y, U or S. Increments/decrements can be 1 or 2 with the magnitude specified in the post-byte.

e) INDEXED INDIRECT

Except for the modes using increment/decrement by one and 5-bit offset, all the indexed modes may have a specified level of indirection added. With indirect addressing, the effective address is contained at the location specified by the contents of the indexing register plus any offset.

Example   LDA   [,X]

RELATIVE   The destination address of a branch instruction is the sum of an 8-bit or 16-bit offset (specified with the instruction) and the content of the program counter.

Short relative branching: 1 byte offset (range −128 to +127)

Long relative branching: 2 byte offset (range −32768 to +32767)

If the branch is true, then the PC is loaded with the calculated address and program execution continues from that address.

Fig. M34 Post-byte register assignment in the 6809

7	6	5	4	3	2	1	0	Indexed Addressing Mode
\< Post-Byte Register Bit \>								
0	R	R	d	d	d	d	d	EA = ,R + 5 Bit Offset
1	R	R	0	0	0	0	0	,R +
1	R	R	i	0	0	0	1	,R + +
1	R	R	0	0	0	1	0	, – R
1	R	R	i	0	0	1	1	, – – R
1	R	R	i	0	1	0	0	EA = ,R + 0 Offset
1	R	R	i	0	1	0	1	EA = ,R + ACCB Offset
1	R	R	i	0	1	1	0	EA = ,R + ACCA Offset
1	R	R	i	1	0	0	0	EA = ,R + 8 Bit Offset
1	R	R	i	1	0	0	1	EA = ,R + 16 Bit Offset
1	R	R	i	1	0	1	1	EA = ,R + D Offset
1	x	x	i	1	1	0	0	EA = ,PC + 8 Bit Offset
1	x	x	i	1	1	0	1	EA = ,PC + 16 Bit Offset
1	R	R	i	1	1	1	1	EA = [,Address]

Addressing Mode Field

Indirect Field
(Sign bit when $b_7 = 0$)

Register Field: RR

x = Don't Care
d = Offset Bit
i = { 0 = Not Indirect
1 = Indirect

00 = X
01 = Y
10 = U
11 = S

Ø, R	Indexed with zero offset
[Ø, R]	Indexed with zero offset (indirect)
,R +	Auto increment by 1
,R + +	Auto increment by 2
[,R + +]	Auto increment by 2 (indirect)
, –R	Auto decrement by 1
, – – R	Auto decrement by 2
[, – – R]	Auto decrement by 2 (indirect)
n, p	Indexed with signed n as offset (5, 8, 16 bits)
[n, p]	Indexed with signed n as offset (indirect)
A, R	Indexed with ACCA as offset
[A, R]	Indexed with ACCA as offset (indirect)
B, R	Indexed with ACCB as offset
[B, R]	Indexed with ACCB as offset (indirect)
D, R	Indexed with ACCD as offset
[D, R]	Indexed with ACCD as offset (indirect)

R = X, Y, U or S
P = PC, X, Y, U or S
Square brackets indicate: indirect

Type	Forms	Non Indirect				Indirect			
		Assembler Form	Postbyte OP Code	+~	+#	Assembler Form	Postbyte OP Code	+~	+#
Constant Offset From R	No Offset	R	1RR00100	0	0	[,R]	1RR10100	3	0
(2's Complement Offsets)	5 Bit Offset	n, R	0RRnnnnn	1	0	defaults to 8-bit			
	8 Bit Offset	n, R	1RR01000	1	1	[n, R]	1RR11000	4	1
	16 Bit Offset	n, R	1RR01001	4	2	[n, R]	1RR11001	7	2
Accumulator Offset From R	A Register Offset	A, R	1RR00110	1	0	[A, R]	1RR10110	4	0
(2's Complement Offsets)	B Register Offset	B, R	1RR00101	1	0	[B, R]	1RR10101	4	0
	D Register Offset	D, R	1RR01011	4	0	[D, R]	1RR11011	7	0
Auto Increment/Decrement R	Increment By 1	,R +	1RR00000	2	0	not allowed			
	Increment By 2	,R + +	1RR00001	3	0	[,R + +]	1RR10001	6	0
	Decrement By 1	, – R	1RR00010	2	0	not allowed			
	Decrement By 2	, – – R	1RR00011	3	0	[, – – R]	1RR10011	6	0
Constant Offset From PC	8 Bit Offset	n, PCR	1xx01100	1	1	[n, PCR]	1xx11100	4	1
(2's Complement Offsets)	16 Bit Offset	n, PCR	1xx01101	5	2	[n, PCR]	1xx11101	8	2
Extended Indirect	16 Bit Address	–	–	–	–	[n]	10011111	5	2

R = X, Y, U or S
x = Don't Care

RR:
00 = X
01 = Y
10 = U
11 = S

$+~$ and $+#$ indicate the number of additional cycles and bytes respectively for the particular indexing variation.

6809

Example

BEQ   LOOP1   Branch if equal to zero to the address of Loop 1 (single byte offset required)

or

LBEQ   LOOP2   Long branch if equal to zero (double byte offset required)

Program Counter Relative allows the use of the PC as a pointer with 8-bit or 16-bit offsets. The offset is added to the PC contents and the sum is then the address of the operand.

Control Signals

R/W̄   Read/Write. Indicates direction of data transfer on data bus.

RESET   Reset. Active low input used for restart. PC is loaded from locations $FFFE and $FFFF. The contents of the address pointed to by $FFFE and $FFFF must be the first instruction of the user restart routine.

HALT   A low-level input which, when pulled low by an external device, will cause the processor to stop running and to tri-state its bus lines. The BA output is driven high to indicate that the buses are in a high impedance state. BS is also driven high to give the bus grant signal.

BA, BS   Bus Available; Bus Status.

BA	BS	CPU state
Ø	Ø	Normal (running)
Ø	1	Interrupt or RESET Acknowledge.
1	Ø	SYNC Acknowledge.
1	1	HALT or Bus Grant.

N̄M̄Ī   Non-maskable Interrupt ⎫

F̄ĪR̄Q̄   Fast Interrupt Request ⎬ see Interrupt Facilities

ĪR̄Q̄   Interrupt Request ⎭

M̄R̄D̄Ȳ   Memory Ready. An active low input which can be used by external devices (slow memory) to stretch the E clock signal. The E signal, which stays high until the M̄R̄D̄Ȳ input goes high, may be stretched to a maximum of 10 μsec.

D̄M̄Ā/B̄R̄Ē Q̄   Direct Memory Access/Bus Request. An active low input which can be used by external devices to gain control of the buses. When pulled low, this input forces the processor to stretch the internal clock (10 μsec max) while still maintaining the external E and Q clock signals. The processor effectively disconnects itself from the address and data buses and the R/W̄ line, thereby allowing external devices to carry out refresh or DMA operations.

I/O Addressing

Input/Output is memory mapped.

Interrupt Facilities (total 3)

a) **N̄M̄Ī**   Non-maskable Interrupt. Used for events such as power failure or other fault condition. It causes an immediate interrupt to the processor. If a negative edge is detected on this input, the current instruction will be completed; processor status (contents of all internal registers except system stack pointer) is

6809

saved on the stack and the program counter will be loaded with the address contained in the NMI pointer (pointer address = $FFFC and $FFFD).

b) **FIRQ** Fast Interrupt Request. An active low input which can be masked out by the F bit in the condition code register. If the F bit is clear (∅), the interrupt is accepted. The processor finishes its current instruction and then pushes only the PC and CCR onto the stack. It then sets the F and I flags to prevent other interrupts and reloads the PC from the FIRQ vector ($FFF6 and $FFF7). The first instruction for the FIRQ user routine must be at the address pointed to by the FIRQ vector. Note that if other registers have to be saved then the next instructions in the user routine must be push instructions. The F bit can be set or cleared using ORCC and AND CC instructions.

c) **IRQ** Interrupt Request. Maskable by the I flag in the CCR. If the I bit is clear (∅), IRQ (active low) will be accepted by the processor. The current instruction will be completed, status (contents of all registers except system SP) will be saved, the E and I flags will be set to prevent further interrupts, and the PC will be reloaded from the IRQ vector ($FFF8 and $FFF9). The contents of the location pointed to by the IRQ vector must be the first instruction of the user interrupt service routine. The I flag can be set or cleared using ORCC and AND CC instructions.

Benchmarks   4 MHz crystal assumed
                              1 MHz clock
1. Transfer from memory to memory (extended addressing mode)   10 μsec
2. Output accumulator to port 5 μsec
3. Transfer register to accumulator (D)   7 μsec (16-bit exchange)
4. IRQ to start of interrupt service routine (assuming current instruction completed):
         FIRQ 4 μsec   IRQ 10 μsec

Sample Program (see page 124)
Flowchart: *fig. M35*

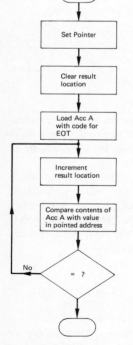

Fig. M35 Flowchart for **6809** program to find the length of a list of ASCII code

ASSEMBLY LANGUAGE			MACHINE CODE Address	Code	(hex.)
LDX	#$0050	Set pointer	1000	8E	00 50
CLR	$3000	Clear counter	1003	7F	30 00
LDA	#$03	Load A with value = EOT	1006	86	03
NEXT INC	$3000	Increment counter	1008	7C	30 00
CMP A	,X +	Compare and increment	100B	A1	80
BNE	NEXT	Branch back	100D	26	F9
SWI		Stop	100F	3F	

Support Chips

All the range of support chips designed for use with the 6800 family can be used.

16-Bit Microprocessors
(fig. M36)

Apart from the most obvious difference between a 16-bit processor and an 8-bit type, that is the use of a *16-bit wide data bus*, the 16-bit machines are more than just simple extensions of 8-bit designs. Naturally there will be common features such as a register set that contains a program counter, working registers, address pointers (index registers), and a stack pointer, and there will be recognisable instructions and addressing modes. But a 16-bit machine will have a much more complex architecture with many more registers, an enhanced instruction set, and a wider variety of addressing modes.

TYPE	PACKAGE	CLOCK	ADDRESSING	
68000	64 pin	External 8 MHz (10 MHz and 12 MHz available)	23 address lines giving an addressing range of 8 M bytes.	8 general-purpose 32-bit registers. Any can be used as an accumulator. 7 32-bit address registers. User SP, system SP and 16-bit status register. 23-bit program counter. (fig. M38)
Z8001 **Z8002**	48 pin 40 pin	External 4 MHz	Address lines A_0–A_{15} multiplexed with data. External demultiplexing required. Segmented addressing giving an addressing range of 8 M bytes. (Z8002 limited to 64 K bytes.)	8 general-purpose 16-bit registers which may be used in pairs for 32-bit operations. All except R_0 can be used as address pointers. Normal and system SPs. PC (one for segment, one for offset). Status register. (fig. M39)
8086	40 pin	External 5 MHz (8 MHz and 10 MHz available)	20 address lines. Address lines A_0–A_{15} multiplexed with data. Simple memory management on chip. Segmented addressing giving an addressing range of 1 M bytes.	Enhancement of the 8080 set. 4 16-bit general-purpose registers AX, BX, CX, DX. AX is primary accumulator. BX base address register. SP, PC, SR, index registers (2) plus 4 segment registers. (fig. M37)

Fig. M36 Short-form data for three 16-bit microprocessors

These features give the 16-bit machines facilities that allow easy creation of multi-user systems and easier support of structured high-level languages.

Three commonly used 16-bit microprocessor families are:

Intel 8086   Motorola 68000   Zilog Z8000

Briefly the main features of these processors are as follows.

1   Intel 8086 (fig. M37)

This 40-pin package is a design intended to be upward-compatible from the 8080 series; therefore software developed for the 8080/8085 processors should also run on the 8086. Upward compatibility is not provided in the other types of 16-bit machines.

Address lines A_0–A_{15} are multiplexed with data lines, and external latches are required if standard memory chips are to be used. The actual 20-bit address, giving an addressing range of 1 M bytes, is formed using a segmented addressing scheme. The effective address is made up using a 16-bit segment address and a 16-bit offset. The base addresses are held in the following registers.

GND	1	40	V_CC
AD14	2	39	AD15
AD13	3	38	A16/S3
AD12	4	37	A17/S4
AD11	5	36	A18/S5
AD10	6	35	A19/S6
AD9	7	34	$\overline{BHE}$/S7
AD8	8	33	MN/$\overline{MX}$
AD7	9	32	$\overline{RD}$
AD6	10	31	HOLD ($\overline{RQ}/\overline{GT0}$)
AD5	11	30	HLDA ($\overline{RQ}/\overline{GT1}$)
AD4	12	29	$\overline{WR}$ ($\overline{LOCK}$)
AD3	13	28	M/$\overline{IO}$ ($\overline{S2}$)
AD2	14	27	DT/$\overline{R}$ ($\overline{S1}$)
AD1	15	26	$\overline{DEN}$ ($\overline{S0}$)
AD0	16	25	ALE (QS0)
NMI	17	24	$\overline{INTA}$ (QS1)
INTR	18	23	$\overline{TEST}$
CLK	19	22	READY
GND	20	21	RESET

7	AH	0	7	AL	0
7	BH	0	7	BL	0
7	CH	0	7	CL	0
7	DH	0	7	DL	0
15	SP				0
15	BP				0
15	SI				0
15	DI				0
15	Status				0
15	IP				0
15	CS				0
15	DS				0
15	SS				0
15	ES				0

Fig. M37b Register set of the **8086**

CS	Code Segment
DS	Data Segment
SS	Stack Segment
ES	Extra Segment

Contents of all these registers, when required, are shifted 4 places left and then added to the appropriate offset to give the full 20-bit address.

The content of one of these registers gives the segment of memory used and the offset gives the location within that segment. For example, suppose the op-code of an instruction is to be fetched. The contents of the instruction pointer (used as program counter) will be combined with the contents of the code segment to produce the full 20-bit address. Suppose the code segment holds $A256 and the instruction pointer $0053. The address is formed by shifting the code segment content four places to the left and then adding the offset held in the instruction pointer:

A256Ø +
ØØ53
─────
A25B3   Effective 20-bit address

The rest of the register set is similar to the 8080: a bank of four 16-bit general-purpose registers (AX, BX, CX, DX) with AX normally used as the primary accumulator. BX can be used as an address register, CX as a loop counter, and DX provides the addresses of I/O devices. These registers can also be treated as a bank of eight 8-bit registers.

Other registers include a 16-bit status register (ST) and four 16-bit pointers. These are the Instruction Pointer (PC), Base Address Pointer (BP), Source Index Pointer (SI), and Destination Index Pointer (DI).

The 8086 has 108 basic instructions, which include string handling, and a wide range of addressing modes.

The 8086 can be used with many of the support chips designed for the 8080/8085 series and in addition there are several support chips specially designed for the 8086.

D4	1	64	D5
D3	2	63	D6
D2	3	62	D7
D1	4	61	D8
D0	5	60	D9
$\overline{AS}$	6	59	D10
$\overline{UDS}$	7	58	D11
$\overline{LDS}$	8	57	D12
R/$\overline{W}$	9	56	D13
$\overline{DTACK}$	10	55	D14
$\overline{BG}$	11	54	D15
$\overline{BGACK}$	12	53	GND
$\overline{BR}$	13	52	A23
V_{CC}	14	51	A22
CLK	15	50	A21
GND	16	49	V_{CC}
$\overline{HALT}$	17	48	A20
$\overline{RESET}$	18	47	A19
$\overline{VMA}$	19	46	A18
E	20	45	A17
$\overline{VPA}$	21	44	A16
$\overline{BERR}$	22	43	A15
$\overline{IPL2}$	23	42	A14
$\overline{IPL1}$	24	41	A13
$\overline{IPL0}$	25	40	A12
FC2	26	39	A11
FC1	27	38	A10
FC0	28	37	A9
A1	29	36	A8
A2	30	35	A7
A3	31	34	A6
A4	32	33	A5

Fig. M38a Pinout for the **68000**

2 Motorola 68000 (*fig. M38*)

This features 32-bit wide internal registers and a dedicated 23-bit address bus giving a basic addressing range of 8 M bytes. These dedicated address pins dictate the 64-pin package. The processor is not code-compatible with the 6800/6802/6809 but it can be used with the wide range of 6800 support chips.

The processor operates in either a *User* or *Supervisory State*. In the user state, for all normal functions, most instructions can be executed except those that change the state of the machine. The supervisor state is for system control. These separate operational states make the design and support of multi-user systems relatively straightforward.

The register set includes eight 32-bit general-purpose registers $D_\emptyset$–D_7 and any of these can be used as an accumulator. Data can be handled as packed BCD, bytes (8-bit), words (16-bit), and long-words (32-bit).

Eight other 32-bit registers (address registers) can function as base address registers and pointers. Registers A_7 and A_7' contain two separate 32-bit user and system stack pointers.

To complete the set there is a 32-bit program counter (23-bits used) and a 16-bit status register.

Interrupt priority is provided at seven levels with interrupt vectors located in the supervisor memory space. Address areas in memory are allocated to either user (program and data) or supervisor (program and data), which are indicated by the code on the $FC_\emptyset$, FC_1 and FC_2 status lines. When an interrupt is accepted, the processor switches into the supervisor state and the system stack pointer is then used.

The instruction set contains 56 basic instructions but the 14 possible addressing modes give a combined number of over one thousand executable instructions. The speed of execution for certain multiplication and division is increased by the use of extra hardware in the ALU.

In addition to working with the full range of 6800/6802/6809 support chips the 68000 has several specially dedicated devices:

68120	Intelligent peripheral controller
68230	Parallel interface with timer
68450	D.M.A. controller
68451	Memory management unit
68341	Floating point mathematics ROM

31	16	15	8	7	0	Bit
31	16	15	8	7	0	Data Register 0
31	16	15	8	7	0	Data Register 1
31	16	15	8	7	0	Data Register 2
31	16	15	8	7	0	Data Register 3
31	16	15	8	7	0	Data Register 4
31	16	15	8	7	0	Data Register 5
31	16	15	8	7	0	Data Register 6
31	16	15	8	7	0	Data Register 7
31	16	15			0	Address Register 0
31	16	15			0	Address Register 1
31	16	15			0	Address Register 2
31	16	15			0	Address Register 3
31	16	15			0	Address Register 4
31	16	15			0	Address Register 5
31	16	15			0	Address Register 6
31	16	15			0	U or S Stack Pointer
31	16	15			0	Program Counter
	23	15	Sys 8	7 Usr	0	Status Register

Fig. M38b Register set of the **68000**

3 Z8001/2 (fig. M39)

The Z8001 is a 48-pin 16-bit processor with a 23-bit-wide address bus. The lower-order address lines are multiplexed with the 16 data lines and external logic may be required to demultiplex address information from data. The addressing range is 8 M bytes, but since a segmented addressing scheme is used, memory can be divided into areas for system and user, and into separate data and program areas. These areas are all defined by status control lines output from the processor. The Z8002, in a 40-pin package, is limited to an addressing range of 64 K bytes. It does not use segmented addressing.

A bank of 16 general-purpose 16-bit registers is provided (R_0 to R_{15}). Any of the registers R_0 to R_{13} can be used as an accumulator and the first eight registers R_0 to R_7 may also be used as pairs of 8-bit registers. 32-bit operations and in some cases 64-bit can be carried out by combining certain registers.

Two stack pointers (user and system) are included with R_{14} giving the memory segment number and the offset being obtained from R_{15}.

The program counter is also two registers, one for the segment address the other giving the offset.

The register set includes a 16-bit status register, two registers used as pointers to a program status area for interrupt servicing, and a register for refresh of dynamic memories.

The instruction set has 110 basic types and there are several addressing modes.

The Z8000 family is backed by a number of support devices:

Z8010 Memory management unit
Z8030 Serial communications controller
Z8036 Parallel I/O with counter/timer
Z8034 Universal peripheral controller

AD0	1	48	AD8
AD9	2	47	SN6
AD10	3	46	SN5
AD11	4	45	AD7
AD12	5	44	AD6
AD13	6	43	AD4
$\overline{\text{STOP}}$	7	42	SN4
$\overline{\text{MI}}$	8	41	AD5
AD15	9	40	AD3
AD14	10	39	AD2
+5V	11	38	AD1
$\overline{\text{VI}}$	12	37	SN2
$\overline{\text{NVI}}$	13	36	GND
$\overline{\text{SEGT}}$	14	35	CLOCK
$\overline{\text{NMI}}$	15	34	$\overline{\text{AS}}$
$\overline{\text{RESET}}$	16	33	RESERVED
$\overline{\text{M0}}$	17	32	B/$\overline{\text{W}}$
$\overline{\text{MREQ}}$	18	31	N/$\overline{\text{S}}$
$\overline{\text{DS}}$	19	30	R/$\overline{\text{W}}$
ST3	20	29	$\overline{\text{BUSAK}}$
ST2	21	28	$\overline{\text{WAIT}}$
ST1	22	27	$\overline{\text{BUSRQ}}$
ST0	23	26	SN0
SN3	24	25	SN1

(A) The Z8001 pinout.

AD9	1	40	AD0
AD10	2	39	AD8
AD11	3	38	AD7
AD12	4	37	AD6
AD13	5	36	AD4
$\overline{\text{STOP}}$	6	35	AD5
$\overline{\text{MI}}$	7	34	AD3
AD15	8	33	AD2
AD14	9	32	AD1
+5V	10	31	GND
VI	11	30	CLOCK
$\overline{\text{NVI}}$	12	29	$\overline{\text{AS}}$
$\overline{\text{NMI}}$	13	28	RESERVED
$\overline{\text{RESET}}$	14	27	B/$\overline{\text{W}}$
$\overline{\text{M0}}$	15	26	N/$\overline{\text{S}}$
$\overline{\text{MREQ}}$	16	25	R/$\overline{\text{W}}$
$\overline{\text{DS}}$	17	24	$\overline{\text{BUSAK}}$
ST3	18	23	$\overline{\text{WAIT}}$
ST2	19	22	$\overline{\text{BUSRQ}}$
ST1	20	21	ST0

(B) The Z8002 pinout.

Fig. M39a Pinout for the **Z8001** and **Z8002**

R0	7	RH0	0	7 RL0 0	
R1	7	RH1	0	7 RL1 0	
R2	7	RH2	0	7 RL2 0	
R3	7	RH3	0	7 RL3 0	
R4	7	RH4	0	7 RL4 0	
R5	7	RH5	0	7 RL5 0	
R6	7	RH6	0	7 RL6 0	
R7	7	RH7	0	7 RL7 0	
R8	15				0
R9	15				0
R10	15				0
R11	15				0
R12	15				0
R13	15				0
R14	15 N/S SP Seg				0
R15	15 N/S SP PC				0
FCW	15 FCW				0
SEG	15 PC Segment				0
PC	15 PC Offset				0
SEG	15 PSAP Segment				0
PSA	15 PSAP				0
RES	15 Refresh Counter				0

Fig. M39b Register set of the **Z8001**

Mnemonic Code

Mnemonic, which means literally memory-evoking, is a way of writing assembly language where the instructions are given easy-to-remember codes: for example

LD for Load

ST for Store

MOV for Move   and so on

All processors have their own unique set of mnemonics covering the instruction set used.

● ASSEMBLER   ● ASSEMBLY LANGUAGE

Modem

An acronym for a *mo*dulator/*dem*odulator device, which is used in the transmission of serial data for data links in excess of 20 m.

Logic signals in serial format are applied to the modem and modulate a carrier wave so that a.c. audio signals are transmitted over the line. The modem receiving these audio signals then demodulates the carrier and outputs the original digital logic (*fig. M40*).

Fig. M40   Principle of the modem

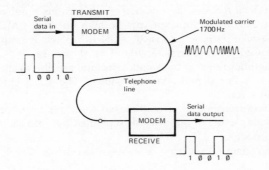

Three basic techniques can be used for the modulation of the carrier:

Frequency modulation

Amplitude modulation

Phase modulation

The first, using FSK (frequency shift keying), is the most popular method with the carrier frequency often at 1700 Hz modulated by ±500 Hz by the two logical levels.

● SERIAL INTERFACE ADAPTOR

Monitor Program

This is a program used to supervise and control the operation of a computer system. It is normally held in ROM or PROM so that it is available on power-up. In this way it initialises the system when power is first switched on and provides control so that user programs can be loaded and run. Debugging facilities are also usually included in the monitor, allowing memory and register contents to be examined and/or modified and program trace, breakpoints and single-step features to be carried out.

● FIRMWARE   ● RESET/RESTART

MOS

A metal oxide silicon field effect transistor, a device operated by the controlling voltage applied between its gate and source. A positive voltage (for an n channel type) sets up a conducting path between source and drain allowing drain current to flow. The enhancement-mode MOSFET, which can be readily made to operate as a switch, is used extensively in microchips and logic (CMOS). Since there is an insulating oxide layer between the gate and the main body of the device, it has a very high input resistance resulting in low power operation.

● FIELD EFFECT TRANSISTOR   ● CMOS

A data transfer instruction, with the mnemonic MOV, that is used in some processors (8080/8085 range) for storing, loading and transferring data:

a) from register to register

b) from memory to register/register to memory.

Examples

MVI A	Move immediate data to register A
MOV B,A	Move content of register A into register B
MOV A,M	Move content of memory address into register A
MOV M,A	Move content of register A to memory

● INSTRUCTION   ● MICROPROCESSOR [8080/8085]

Multiplexor

A multiplexor (time division type) is an electronic circuit that performs the function of a fast rotary switch. It connects several information channels, *one at a time*, to a common line. The use of a multiplexor in a data acquisition system enables several sources of information to be sent along the common line and therefore reduces the number of connections required in any particular application. Analog multiplexors can be built up using CMOS or JFET analog switches or special-purpose i.c.s such as the LF 13508. A simple example of a multiplexor followed by a sample-and-hold is shown in *fig. M41*. Digital multiplexors, sometimes referred to as **data selectors,** are also available in i.c. form. In *fig. M42* a 4-to-1 line digital system is shown. The select channel address can be driven from a counter.

Data transmitted in multiplexed form has to be decoded at the receiver by a demultiplexor, in other words separated out into the correct sequence of channel information.

● INTERFACE CIRCUITS   ● SAMPLE-AND-HOLD

Fig. M41   Multiplexor

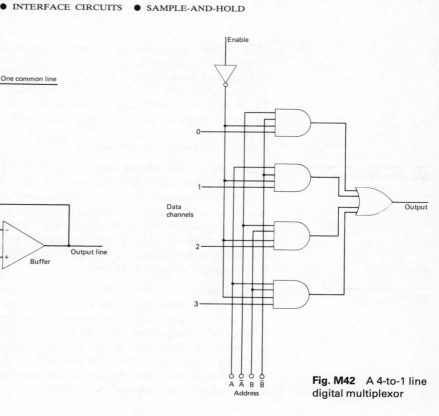

Fig. M42   A 4-to-1 line digital multiplexor

Multiprocessor/Multiprocessing

A system connection where two or more microprocessors share a common memory and carry out independent or related programming tasks.

One use of multiprocessing is in interfacing a slow peripheral device using a second processor to control the data transfers from the peripheral to the main memory (*Fig. M43*). The second processor (2) accepts data from the peripheral and stores it in block form in the temporary memory. This process may take several seconds but does not interfere with the running of the main program in processor (1). When a complete block of data has been transferred from the peripheral, processor (2) puts out a DMA request to processor (1). When this is granted, processor (2) transfers, at a fast rate, the data block from the temporary memory to the main memory. This sort of arrangement can save valuable programming time for processor (1).

● DIRECT MEMORY ACCESS

Fig. M43 Arrangement for one form of multiprocessing

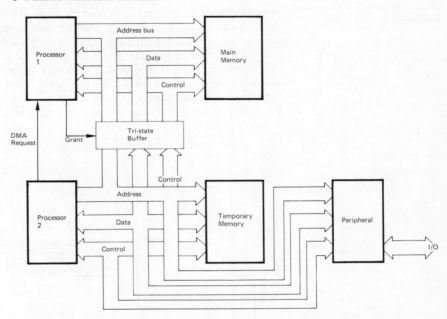

NAND Gate

Inputs   Output

A logic gate that gives a logic ∅ output only when all its inputs are simultaneously at logic 1 (*fig. N1*). This is the AND-NOT function and for a three-input gate is represented by the Boolean expression:

$$F = \overline{A \cdot B \cdot C}$$

The truth table is shown in the margin.

BS   **Fig. N1**

INPUTS			OUTPUT
C	B	A	F
∅	∅	∅	1
∅	∅	1	1
∅	1	∅	1
∅	1	1	1
1	∅	∅	1
1	∅	1	1
1	1	∅	1
1	1	1	∅

Note that, if any input is ∅, then the output of the NAND gate is 1.

The NAND function can be achieved in a microcomputer system by using the AND instruction followed by the COMPLEMENT instruction:

AccA holds $35

∅	∅	1	1	∅	1	∅	1

AND A #$0F   Result

∅	∅	∅	∅	∅	1	∅	1

COM A (1s complement)

1	1	1	1	1	∅	1	∅

● AND INSTRUCTION   ● BOOLEAN ALGEBRA

Negate

An instruction that carries out the operation of converting a binary number held in a register or memory location into its twos complement form.

$$\emptyset\emptyset - r \rightarrow r \quad \text{and} \quad \emptyset\emptyset - m \rightarrow m$$

Suppose register A holds the number $\emptyset9$; the value held following the instruction NEG A would be $F7$.

● TWOS COMPLEMENT

Negative Bit (N)

A flag contained in the status or condition code register of a processor which is used to indicate when the result of an operation is negative: that is, when the MSB of the result is logic 1. For this reason, the N flag is often called the sign flag (S).

● SIGN BIT

Nesting

A term used in programming to describe those situations where a routine, called in a main program, itself calls yet another routine and so on. This occurs for both subroutine calls and multiple interrupts. *Fig. N2* shows a typical situation where sub. 1 is called from the main program and, in the middle of the execution of the sub. 1 routine, sub. 2 is called. The return addresses are saved in an orderly queue on the stack and are pulled in reverse order so that sub. 1 is completed before the main program is re-entered.

● DELAY ● INTERRUPT ● STACK AND STACK POINTER ● SUBROUTINE

Fig. N2 Nested subroutines

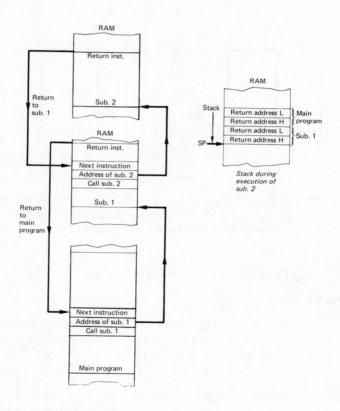

Nibble

A term used to describe a four-bit binary word.

● WORD

NMOS

MOS (metal oxide silicon) technology using n-channel enhancement-mode devices. One of the most popular technologies for microprocessors and memory ICs.
● CMOS   ● FIELD EFFECT TRANSISTOR   ● MOS

Non-volatile

A characteristic of a memory which does not lose its stored data pattern when power is switched off. All types of read only memory (ROM) are therefore non-volatile.
● MEMORIES

No Operation (NOP)

An instruction which does nothing except cause the program counter to increment. This dummy instruction can be useful in creating short time delays and in filling in spaces in programs where other instructions, data, or addresses can be inserted at a later date.
● DELAY   ● DUMMY INSTRUCTION

NOR Gate

A logic circuit that gives a logic Ø at its output when any one of its inputs, or a combination of inputs, is a logic 1 (*fig. N3*). The Boolean function for NOR is:

$$F = \overline{A + B + C} \qquad \text{which is the OR-NOT function}$$

For a three-input gate the truth table is:

INPUTS			OUTPUT
C	B	A	F
Ø	Ø	Ø	1
Ø	Ø	1	Ø
Ø	1	Ø	Ø
Ø	1	1	Ø
1	Ø	Ø	Ø
1	Ø	1	Ø
1	1	Ø	Ø
1	1	1	Ø

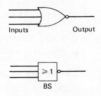

Fig. N3   NOR gate

The NOR function can be executed in a microcomputer by following the OR instruction with the COMPLEMENT instruction.
● BOOLEAN ALGEBRA   ● OR INSTRUCTION

NOT Gate (NOT Instruction)

An invertor which gives an output that is the logical complement of its input (*fig. N4*).

The Boolean function is $F = \bar{A}$

Its truth table is:

A	F
Ø	1
1	Ø

The COMPLEMENT instruction is used in a microprocessor to perform the NOT function on each bit of a register or memory location. For example,

[6800/6802]   COM   A   Complement AccA
[Z80]   CPL   Complement Acc

Fig. N4   NOT gate

Object Code

The name given to the hexadecimal program code (machine code) which results when a source program such as mnemonic code is assembled or when a high-level language program is compiled. (*Fig. O1.*)

● ASSEMBLER ● ASSEMBLY LANGUAGE ● COMPILER

Fig. O1 The place of object code

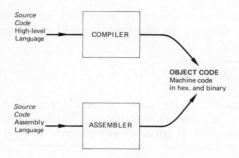

Octal Numbers

These are numbers to base 8, with symbols 0 to 7 to represent the value in each column. Thus the octal number 672_8 is

$$(6 \times 8^2) + (7 \times 8) + (2 \times 1) = 442_{10}$$

Conversion from octal to binary and vice versa is very straightforward; each digit is converted in turn.

Thus $672_8 = 110111010_2$
and $011101100_2 = 354_8$

For this reason, coding of some computers is carried out using octal numbers.

● BINARY AND BINARY CODED DECIMAL ● HEXADECIMAL NUMBERS

Offset

The offset is that part of an instruction, contained in the operand field, which is added to the value held in an addressing register to give the effective address for the instruction. Offsets are used in the following addressing modes:

Indexed (either specified in the instruction or held in the indexed register [6502])

Base relative

Relative (used with conditional branch instructions)

A typical example using 6800/6802 code is:

LDX   #$1500   Point X Reg. at $1500
LDA $50,X   Load Acc indexed with offset = $50

Here the offset $50 is added to the content of the X register to give an effective address of $1550. AccA would be loaded from that address (*fig. O2*).

In 8-bit machines, offsets are usually limited to a value of either $+255_{10}$ places, or approximately ±128 places for branch instructions.

● INDEX REGISTER AND INDEXED ADDRESSING ● RELATIVE ADDRESSING

Op-code

Every instruction within the program of a microprocessor consists of two parts: the operation code (op-code) and the operand. The *op-code* is that part which defines the basic operation of the instruction.

Thus in these instructions the op-code is as shown:

a)   LDX $4F20   Load Index Reg. from $4F20
      Op-code Operand
b)   STA $0085   Store Acc. at $85
      Op-code Operand

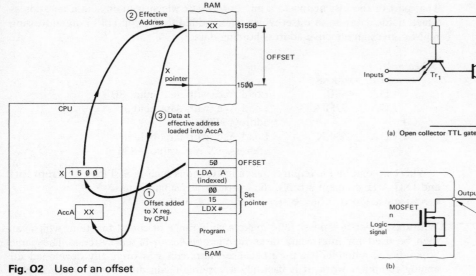

Fig. O2 Use of an offset

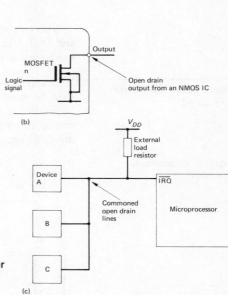

(a) Open collector TTL gate

(b)

Fig. O3 Open collector (open drain) and its application

(c)

Some instructions, those which are single byte and use the implied addressing mode, are completely specified by the op-code. For example,

INX   Increment X register

CLC   Clear carry

● ASSEMBLY LANGUAGE   ● INSTRUCTION

Open Collector (Open Drain)

A description of the output arrangement from certain logic gates and i.c.s where the device driving the output pin has no internal load (*fig. O3*). The advantage of this type of output is that several such gates or lines can be connected together to give what is called a wired-or connection. A common load resistor is provided so that, when any one line is taken low, the common point also goes low. A good example in a microprocessor system is the interrupt request line input. Because of pin limitations, only one $\overline{IRQ}$ input can be provided to the microprocessor. Thus, peripherals and chips requiring a connection to the $\overline{IRQ}$ input must be all connected together. When any of the peripherals signals that it requires attention, the $\overline{IRQ}$ line is pulled low and the interrupt service routine can be carried out. The first task of this routine will be to scan the devices to see which requires attention.

● INTERRUPT   ● POLLING   ● WIRED LOGIC

Operand

That part of the instruction to a microprocessor which contains data, an address which holds data, or an offset which when added to the content of an addressing register gives an effective address holding data.

Example

OP-CODE	OPERAND	
LDA	#$3B	Load Acc. with hex. num. 3B
LDA	$2F0A	Load Acc. with data held at address 2F0A
LDA	$30,X	Load Acc. with data held at address = X reg. value +$30

Where no operand is required, as in instructions such as SEI (Set Interrupt Bit) and INC A (Increment AccA), the instruction is single byte.

● ASSEMBLY LANGUAGE ● INSTRUCTION ● OP-CODE

Operational Amplifier (Op-amp)

With this device it is possible to make a wide range of circuit functions which can then be used for interfacing tasks in microprocessor-based systems. The name "operational amplifier" is used because the circuit was originally developed for analog computer work; it is basically a very-high-gain differential direct-coupled amplifier circuit (*fig. O4*).

Fig. O4 Operational amplifier

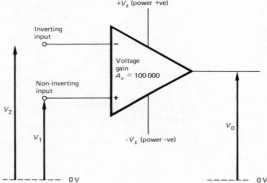

The voltage gain, a multiplying factor, is usually 100 000 or more. The output voltage level is then determined by this voltage gain times the *difference* in input voltage between the inverting and non-inverting pins. This can be expressed using a formula:

$$V_o = A_v(V_1 - V_2)$$

Thus if $V_1 = V_2$ then $V_o = 0$

In practice a small offset will be present. Only a very small "differential" between the input voltages is required to give a large output voltage.

For example, if $V_1 = +0.1$ mV and $V_2 = 0$, then

$$V_o = 100\,000 \times (0.1\,\text{mV}) = +10\,\text{V}$$

Similarly if $V_1 = +0.1$ mV and $V_2 = 0.2$ mV, then

$$V_o = 100\,000 \times (0.1\,\text{mV} - 0.2\,\text{mV}) = -10\,\text{V}$$

Since the amplifier circuit is directly coupled, in other words there are no coupling capacitors in the circuit, it will respond to d.c. levels at its inputs as well as varying signals.

However, an op-amp will have an upper frequency limit and the parameter which is concerned with the speed response of the device is called *slew-rate*. This is measured in volts per microsecond, and is the speed with which the output can change when a sudden step-like input is applied. The faster the speed, the better will the op-amp be able to follow high frequency input signals. Slew-rate can vary from as low as $0.4\,\text{V}/\mu\text{sec}$ (type 301 A) to $35\,\text{V}/\mu\text{sec}$ (type 531) or higher. High speed is really essential in comparator applications.

Offset, which has been previously mentioned, is caused by small differences in the properties of the input components inside the IC. It is defined as the input voltage that would have to be applied between the two input pins to adjust the output to exactly zero volts. In many applications the tiny offset does not cause problems and where it does most op-amps are provided with pins to which a potentiometer can be connected to give what is called *offset null facility*.

We shall concentrate on applications of the op-amp which are particularly useful in interfacing and this should then show how the devices can be used, and also more about the way in which they operate.

Fig. O5 Op-amp used as a buffer (unity gain voltage follower)

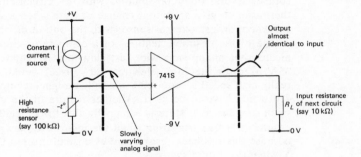

In *fig. O5*, an op-amp is wired up as a **unity gain voltage follower** to act as a buffer between a relatively high resistance sensor and the load presented by some circuit. The output of the op-amp is connected directly back to its inverting input, and the signal from the sensor is connected to the non-inverting input. This connection method gives not only near unity voltage gain but also very high input resistance and low output resistance. Because of the very high differential gain (100 000), only a tiny difference in levels will exist between the two input pins of the op-amp.

Suppose the output level is $+2\,\text{V}$, then from the basic formula:

$$V_o = A_v(V_1 - V_2)$$

we get $\quad (V_1 - V_2) = V_o/A_v = \dfrac{2}{100\,000} = 0.02\,\text{mV}$

Therefore the difference between V_1, the signal input, and V_o (the same connection as V_2) is very small. In other words, the output "follows" the input. The high input resistance also results because of the feedback from output to inverting input. R_{in} is very high for the reason that only a tiny input current is necessary to provide the small "difference" voltage between the op-amp input pins to set up the required output. This high resistance input means that there will be hardly any distortion of the signal from the sensor. In addition, the low output resistance of the op-amp is able to supply the current required by R_L.

Another common application of op-amps is as a **comparator** (see *fig. O6*). In this example the non-inverting terminal is held at a fixed voltage ($+6\,\text{V}$) and, while the light beam is falling onto the ORP12 (a light-dependent resistor), the

183

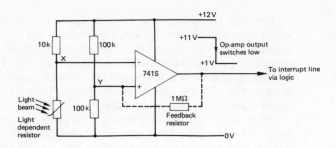

voltage on the inverting input will be lower, at say 1 V. The op-amp output will therefore be driven into positive saturation and will be at about +11 V. If the light beam is broken, the LDR resistance rises, and the voltage at point X will then exceed that at point Y. This will cause the op-amp output to switch rapidly to its negative saturation level at about +1 V. This change of state can be used, after shaping by a logic gate, as the interrupt for a micro system. There are, of course, several other possibilities with this circuit since the sensor could be a thermistor to give an output change of state when a set value of temperature is exceeded, or a smoke/gas sensor with the output driving an alarm.

One of the desirable features of a comparator circuit is high speed, and this means that an op-amp with fast slew-rate is required. The 531 (slew-rate of 35 V/μsec) or the 741S (slew-rate 20 V/μsec) would be suitable choices; but if really high speed is required a specially designed comparator IC such as a 311 or 710 would have to be used. Another feature of the circuit is the inclusion of a small amount of hysteresis set up by the 1 MΩ feedback resistor. This should ensure jitter-free triggering when the input level has just crossed the trip point, because this feedback resistor causes a small drop in the reference level at point Y when the output switches.

Fig. O7 Non-inverting amplifier

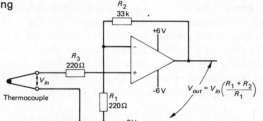

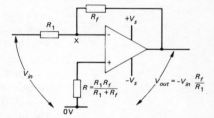

Fig. O8 Inverting amplifier

The circuit in *fig. O7* shows an op-amp used as a **linear non-inverting amplifier** to increase the small signal obtained from a thermocouple. The thermocouple gives an output voltage of about 40 μV/°C which, with the values given, would be increased by a factor of 150. In the non-inverting amplifier, a portion of the output signal is fed back to the inverting terminal to oppose the input. This negative feedback arrangement gives a stable fixed value of voltage gain that depends on the values of R_1 and R_2:

$$\text{Voltage gain } A_v = \frac{R_1 + R_2}{R_1}$$

The **inverting amplifier** configuration (*fig. O8*), the opposite to the previous example, again has the negative feedback connected from output to the inverting terminal but the input is applied via a resistor R_1 to the same point. Because of the very high internal gain of the op-amp, the common point of R_1 and R_f hardly changes at all, even when the output is a few volts. For this reason point X is often referred to as a "virtual earth" point. The gain of the arrangement is fixed by the resistor values to R_f/R_1.

The circuit can be extended to make a summing amplifier, and this in turn can be used as the basis of a simple **4-bit digital-to-analog convertor.** Each of the input resistors is weighted in value in a binary sequence, i.e. R, 2R, 4R and 8R, and the digital word to be converted is used to operate electronic switches which connect either a fixed reference voltage ($+5\,V$) or zero volts to the input resistors. For example, suppose the digital word to be converted is Ø11Ø. Switches 2 and 3 (*fig. O9*) will operate to connect the reference voltage to resistors R_2 and R_3 giving an analog output voltage of

$$V_o = \frac{R_f}{R_1} V_{\text{ref}}(0 + \tfrac{1}{2} + \tfrac{1}{4} + 0) = 3.75 \text{ V}$$

Fig. O9 DAC using inverting summer

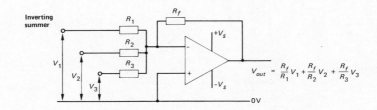

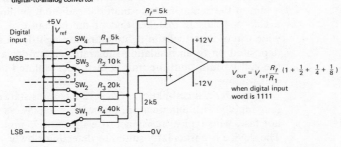

The DAC shown is a simple low-cost type which can only be used for relatively low accuracy and in situations where there are only a few bits to be converted. Otherwise the resistor values become unwieldy (to convert an 8-bit word the largest resistor would have to be $640\,k\Omega$) and fairly large errors can occur.

● COMPARATOR ● DIGITAL-TO-ANALOG CONVERTOR ● INTERFACE CIRCUITS ● SENSOR

Opto-device

The general name of **opto-electronics** is given to the wide variety of devices used to detect light (photo-sensitive) and to generate and radiate light (photo-emissive). This term for our purposes covers:

Photoconductive cells (light-dependent resistors)

Photodiodes and phototransistors

Photovoltaic cells (silicon solar cells)

Slotted opto-switches

Reflective opto-switches

Light-emitting diodes.

Typical light levels

LIGHT SOURCE	ILLUMINATION IN LUX (LUMEN/SQ. METRE)
Bright sunlight	25 000
Fluorescent lights	500
60 W lamp at 1 m	50
Moonlight	0.1

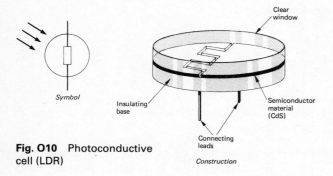

Fig. O10 Photoconductive cell (LDR)

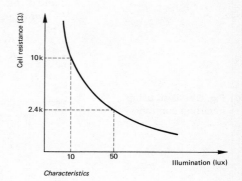

1 Photoconductive cells (*fig. O10*) The resistance of these devices falls as the amount of light incident on a cell increases. For this reason they are often called light-dependent resistors (LDR). The most commonly used types are made from a film of the semiconductor material cadmium sulphide. The spectral response of a CdS cell closely matches that of the human eye, which is one reason for the wide use of these cells in lightmeters and light-level detectors. The film of CdS is deposited on to an insulating substrate, electrodes are added to the two ends of the cell pattern, and the unit is then encapsulated in epoxy resin leaving a clear end window.

In the dark, a cell like the ORP 12 has a resistance of nearly 10^7 ohms but this falls rapidly with illumination, following a log law as shown. The response time is not fast, with typical resistance rise times of 75 msec and fall times of 350 msec. The device is particularly suited to detecting slowly varying light levels, as smoke detectors and in lighting controllers. The change in resistance with light from the cell can be converted into a voltage by supplying the cell with a constant current or by using a bridge arrangement.

2 Photodiodes and Phototransistors (*fig. O11*) These are much faster-operating devices than the LDR with rise times of a few microseconds or even nanoseconds in some cases. The photodiode, usually silicon, has a small glass window that allows light to fall on the pn junction. This light creates hole-electron pairs at the junction and therefore induces current in the diode. Normally, the diode is operated with reverse bias so that its dark current is very low (typically a few tens of nanoamps with a reverse bias of 20 V). Then, as the incident light is increased, the output current will rise in proportion and this relationship is very linear. Typical sensitivity is about $1\,\mu A/mW/cm^2$. A circuit arrangement for detecting light levels and allowing the output to be strobed via a micro is shown in *fig. O12*. The op-amp is a MOSFET type 3130 which has a very high input resistance ($1.5 \times 10^{12}\,\Omega$). With the resistor values shown, the output is 1 V per 10 nA of diode current.

The phototransistor uses the same principle as the photodiode, but because it is an amplifier the device is even more sensitive. Light falling on the base of the

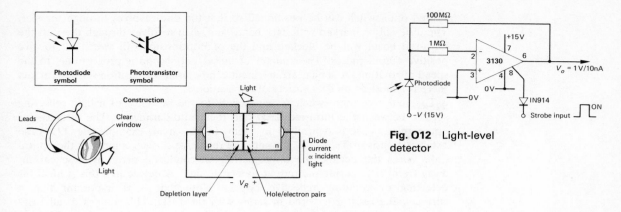

Fig. O11 Photodiode and phototransistor

Fig. O12 Light-level detector

transistor via the glass window sets up a base current and this is amplified to appear as a large collector current.

3 Photovoltaic cells These silicon devices, sometimes called *solar cells*, generate an e.m.f. between the output terminals proportional to the incident light. Again it is basically a pn junction, but one of the regions is very thin so that light can pass without too much energy loss. This light causes hole-electron pairs to be generated at the junction. Because one region is thin this rapidly saturates and a voltage is set up. The cell can, of course, be used in the photoconductive mode with current output instead of voltage.

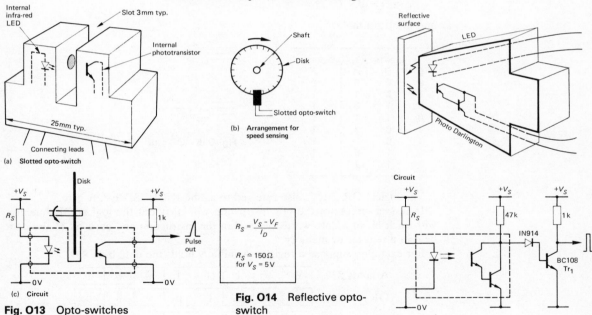

Fig. O13 Opto-switches

Fig. O14 Reflective opto-switch

4 Opto-switches (*fig. O13*) These sensors, which provide an ON/OFF type of indication, are particularly useful for limit detection, batch counting, position sensing, and level indication. The units are constructed using an infra-red emitting diode and a silicon phototransistor in one moulded package. The optical link in the first type (*fig. O14*) is across a slot, and the beam can be interrupted to give a positive output pulse from the phototransistor. Suppose the speed of rotation of a shaft is required. A disk can be fitted to the shaft as shown and the

187

slotted opto-switch can be positioned so that the disc revolves through the slot. The disk will be marked with dark bands and, as it revolves through the slot, the infra-red beam will be blocked and the phototransistor will switch off to give positive output pulses. The number of pulses per second is proportional to the speed of rotation. A similar arrangement can be used for position sensing; in fact there is almost an endless variety of applications.

The reflective opto-switch responds only to the presence of a light-reflecting surface between the infra-red LED and the photo-darlington. The distance for optimum response is typically 4 to 5 mm. In the circuit example (*fig. O14*) the external transistor Tr_1 will be on until the reflective surface completes the optical link. When this occurs, the photo-darlington conducts, diverting base current away from Tr_1, causing the output to switch high. A device like this is ideal for detecting or counting reflective targets. Note that it is important that a correct-value resistor is wired in series with the LED. This applies to all LED devices and the resistor should be chosen so that the diode current is set to about 20 mA (absolute maximum is usually 40 mA). If the supply is +5 V then R_S is about 150 Ω. Watch also that the reverse voltage rating (2 V) of the LED is not exceeded. This can happen if the supply is accidentally reversed.

● LIGHT-EMITTING DIODE   ● SENSOR

OR Gate (OR Function)

The logic OR gate (symbol *fig. O15*) will give a logic 1 output if one or any combination of its inputs is at logic 1. In Boolean Algebra the function is (for a three input OR gate):

$$F = A + B + C$$

and the truth table:

INPUTS			OUTPUT
C	B	A	F
0	0	0	0
0	0	1	1
0	1	0	1
0	1	1	1
1	0	0	1
1	0	1	1
1	1	0	1
1	1	1	1

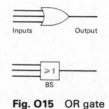

Fig. O15   OR gate

The logical OR gate is also referred to as the INCLUSIVE-OR gate.

In a microprocessor the OR instruction will carry out the logical OR function with each bit of a data word specified in the instruction and each bit of the data held in a register or memory.

For example, suppose a register A initially holds the data byte $39.

A holds $39	0	0	1	1	1	0	0	1
OR A #$80	1	0	0	0	0	0	0	0
Result placed in A	1	0	1	1	1	0	0	1

This is a copy of the original word except that the MSB has been set to 1. The OR instruction can be used as a bit setting instruction.

● GATE   ● LOGICAL INSTRUCTIONS AND LOGICAL OPERATIONS

Origin

A "directive" used in an Assembler which allows the programmer to specify the start address of an assembler language program.

● ASSEMBLER

OUT Instruction	An instruction used in 8080/Z80 processors where the I/O ports are not memory mapped.

● IN/OUT INSTRUCTION

Overflow

In twos complement representation, the sign bit effectively reduces the number of bits (for an 8-bit machine) to 7. These 7 bits are used to give the magnitude of the number. For example,

$$+25_{10} = \emptyset\emptyset\emptyset11\emptyset\emptyset1$$
$$-25_{10} = 111\emptyset\emptyset111$$

magnitude

sign bit (1 for negative numbers)

The range is from -128 to $+127$.

When twos complement arithmetic operations are performed, the carry or *overflow* will occur between bits 6 and 7. The V-flag is used in the Condition Code (status) register to indicate when this occurs.

● SIGN BIT ● TWOS COMPLEMENT ● V-FLAG

Page

In order to ease the programmer's task the full memory area of a microcomputer is divided up into convenient sized chunks, called *pages* (*fig. P1*). In microprocessor-based systems a common page size is 256 bytes (although 1 K and 2 K page sizes can also be used), and this will give:

Page zero (∅∅)   from $∅∅∅∅$ to $∅∅FF$
Page one (∅1)   from $∅1∅∅$ to $∅1FF$
Page two (∅2)   from $∅2∅∅$ to $∅2FF$

If page zero is specified in an instruction, the leading zeros, which constitute the most significant byte, are not required and in this way Page Zero Addressing (6502) or Direct Addressing (6800) saves one byte of code per instruction for a program that uses this page. Some instruction examples are:

LDX $7∅   Load X reg. from address $∅∅7∅
STA $8F   Store Acc. at address $∅∅8F

● MEMORY MAP ● PAGE REGISTER

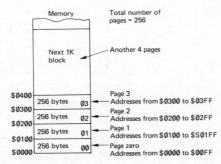

Fig. P1 Memory pages in a system

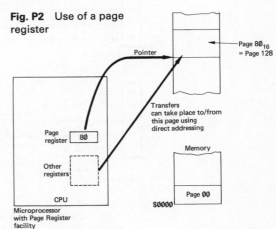

Fig. P2 Use of a page register

Page Register	A register provided in some microprocessors (e.g. 6809) that can be programmed to point to one particular page in memory (*fig. P2*). This allows page addressing with the direct mode to be used within the specified page, thus saving one byte per instruction.

● DIRECT ADDRESSING ● MICROPROCESSOR [6809]

An abbreviation for Peripheral (or Parallel) Interface Adaptor and Parallel Input/Output interface (*fig. P3*). These ICs contain programmable I/O ports with control and handshake lines and allow easy interfacing between a microprocessor system and peripherals that send or receive data in parallel form.

● PERIPHERAL INTERFACE ADAPTOR

Fig. P3 General view of interface adaptor

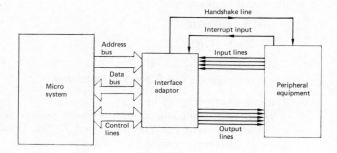

Parameter

A term used in programming to describe any value used in a routine which may vary depending on other conditions. When the parameter is required, its value is passed to the routine before execution. For example, the same time delay subroutine structure can be used to produce different time delays by passing a multiplier (the parameter) to the routine every time it is called, the multiplier varying in value depending upon other external conditions.

● DELAY

Parity

Parity is a simple and effective method of error detection and error indication and consists of adding one or more bits to a system word that is being transmitted (*fig. P4*). If interference causes the loss of some data bit(s), a parity checker at the receiver can be used to indicate this loss.

Fig. P4 Principle of error detection using parity

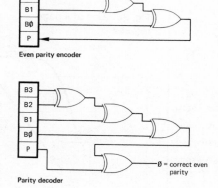

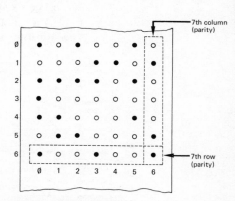

Fig. P5 Double parity checking system (odd parity shown)

In the most simple system the extra bit, called the *parity bit*, is added so that the transmitted word contains either an even number of 1s (even parity) or an odd number of 1s (odd parity). Before transmission each word is examined by a parity generator which calculates whether a Ø or 1 is to be placed in the parity bit. Following transmission, the parity checking circuit examines the transmitted word to see if the correct parity still exists. If there has been an error this can be indicated by a flag and if necessary the data word can be retransmitted.

This type of scheme can only detect the presence of single or odd errors in a word. More complicated schemes such as double parity checking can be used for data checking on magnetic tape for example. In this system both vertical and horizontal parity bits are generated during the store operation, and then in any subsequent read operations parity in both rows and columns (see *fig. P5*) can be checked. Single errors can be detected and corrected, and double errors can be detected.

● ACIA ● SERIAL DATA FORMAT

Peripheral Interface Adaptor (PIA)

This type of IC is provided as a support chip for microprocessor families so that fairly easy interfacing can be arranged between the processor and external peripherals that send and receive data in parallel form. A typical example is the MC 6821 PIA which is a device provided for interfacing the entire range of 6800 microprocessors. A simplified view of the device is shown in *fig. P6*. It contains two independent interface circuits (A and B) which are identical in most respects except that the B side has a higher drive capability.

Fig. P6 PIA: simplified block diagram of the MC 6821

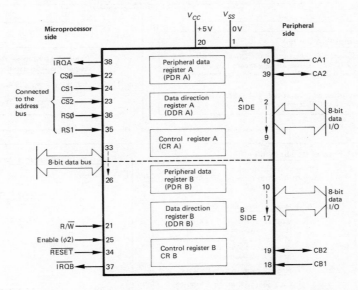

Various control lines from the microprocessor to the PIA are necessary:

ENABLE Connected to the ϕ_2 clock line, this is the only timing signal supplied to the PIA.

R/$\overline{\text{W}}$ Controls whether data is read from (logic 1) or written to (logic $\emptyset$).

$\overline{\text{RESET}}$ Used to reset all the internal PIA registers, in other words to clear all registers to zero. This input is usually connected to the reset line of the microprocessor and is therefore active during a reset or power-up condition.

Interrupt Request ($\overline{\text{IRQA}}$ and $\overline{\text{IRQB}}$) These are outputs from the PIA which are active low to interrupt the microprocessor either directly or through interrupt priority circuits. These outputs are "open drain" type which allows all interrupt request lines to be tied together in a wired-or arrangement.

Each $\overline{\text{IRQ}}$ line from the PIA has two internal flags (these are in the control register, see *fig. P7*) which can cause the interrupt request line to go low. These flags are associated with a particular peripheral interrupt line (CA1, CA2, CB1, CB2). The various methods by which the interrupts may be set up and accepted are shown in *fig. P7*. The interrupt flags are cleared when the microprocessor executes a read peripheral data register operation.

Determine Active CA1 (CB1) Transition for Setting Interrupt Flag IRQA(B)1 — (bit b7)

b1 = 0 : IRQA(B)1 set by high-to-low transition on CA1 (CB1).

b1 = 1 : IRQA(B)1 set by low-to-high transition on CA1 (CB1).

CA1 (CB1) Interrupt Request Enable/Disable

b0 = 0 : Disables IRQA(B) MPU Interrupt by CA1 (CB1) active transition.[1]

b0 = 1 : Enable IRQA(B) MPU Interrupt by CA1 (CB1) active transition.

1. IRQA(B) will occur on next (MPU generated) positive transition of b0 if CA1 (CB1) active transition occurred while interrupt was disabled.

IRQA(B) 1 Interrupt Flag (bit b7)

Goes high on active transition of CA1 (CB1); Automatically cleared by MPU Read of Output Register A(B). May also be cleared by hardware Reset.

b7	b6	b5	b4	b3	b2	b1	bϕ
IRQA(B)1 Flag	IRQA(B)2 Flag	CA2(CB2) Control			DDR Access	CA1(CB1) Control	

IRQA(B)2 Interrupt Flag (bit b6)

CA2 (CB2) Established as Input (b5 = 0): Goes high on active transition of CA2 (CB2); Automatically cleared by MPU Read of Output Register A(B). May also be cleared by hardware Reset.

CA2 (CB2) Established as Output (b5 = 1): IRQA(B)2 = 0, not affected by CA2 (CB2) transitions.

Determines Whether Data Direction Register Or Output Register is Addressed

b2 = 0 : Data Direction Register selected.

b2 = 1 : Output Register selected.

CA2 (CB2) Established as Output by b5 = 1

b5	b4	b3	(Note that operation of CA2 and CB2 output functions are not identical)
1	0		

► CA2

b3 = 0 : **Read Strobe With CA1 Restore**

CA2 goes low on first high-to-low E transition following an MPU Read of Output Register A; returned high by next active CA1 transition.

b3 = 1 : **Read Strobe with E Restore**

CA2 goes low on first high-to-low E transition following an MPU Read of Output Register A; returned high by next high-to-low E transition.

► CB2

b3 = 0 : **Write Strobe With CB1 Restore**

CB2 goes on low on first low-to-high E transition following an MPU Write into Output Register B; returned high by the next active CB1 transition.

b3 = 1 : **Write Strobe With E Restore**

CB2 goes low on first low-to-high E transition following an MPU Write into Output Register B; returned high by the next low-to-high E transition.

b5	b4	b3	
1	1		

► Set/Reset CA2 (CB2)

CA2 (CB2) goes low as MPU writes b3 = 0 into Control Register.

CA2 (CB2) goes high as MPU writes b3 = 1 into Control Register.

CA2 (CB2) Established as Input by b5 = 0

b5	b4	b3	
0			

► CA2 (CB2) Interrupt Request Enable/Disable

b3 = 0 : Disables IRQA(B) MPU Interrupt by CA2 (CB2) active transition.[1]

b3 = 1 : Enables IRQA(B) MPU Interrupt by CA2 (CB2) active transition.

1. IRQA(B) will occur on next (MPU generated) positive transition of b3 if CA2 (CB2) active transition occurred while interrupt was disabled.

► Determines Active CA2 (CB2) Transition for Setting Interrupt Flag IRQA(B)2 — (bit b6)

b4 = 0 : IRQA(B)2 set by high-to-low transition on CA2 (CB2).

b4 = 1 : IRQA(B)2 set by low-to-high transition on CA2 (CB2).

Before considering the peripheral interface lines, we shall look at the arrangement of the internal registers. Since the A and B sides are identical, the description of operation applies to both sides.

The data lines connected internally to the Peripheral Data Register (PDR) can each be made to act as an input from, or an output to, the peripheral device. The programming to make the lines either inputs or outputs is achieved during initialisation by setting the bits in the Data Direction Register (DDR). This register performs as it is named: that is to say, a logic 1 in a bit of the DDR causes the corresponding bit in the PDR to be an output, and a logic Ø forces it to be an input. This is shown in *fig. P8* where the word loaded into the DDR is $0F. This makes bØ to b3 in the PDR outputs and b4 to b7 inputs. If the DDR was cleared to zeros, all lines to the PDR would be inputs, while if the word loaded was $FF all PDR data lines would be outputs.

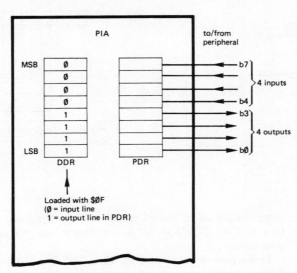

Fig. P8 Setting the state of the peripheral data register

The control register in the PIA has important functions, for during initialisation the programmer will load the control register, and the control word then sets the way in which the PIA is to operate; in other words, how it is to handle interrupts and in its handshaking. The control register has 8 bits which are used as shown in *fig. P9*. Bits bØ and b1 are used to control the CA1 line; bØ can be used to mask CA1, because if bØ is cleared the IRQ line is masked. Bit 1 provides edge control; if b1 = Ø the interrupt flag b7 responds to the negative (high-to-low) edge of a signal on CA1, whereas if b1 = 1 the IRQ flag is set by the positive (low-to-high) edge.

The next bit (b2) in the CR is used to set the addressing for either the Data Direction Register or the Peripheral Data Register. This is necessary because the PDR and DDR share the same address as far as the micro is concerned. If b2 = Ø, the DDR is accessed during addressing and, if b2 = 1, the PDR is accessed during addressing. This is explained more fully in the paragraph on addressing the PIA but essentially the method used during initialisation is, first, to clear the control register (b2 = Ø) and, then when the DDR is to be loaded with the word that sets up either inputs to the PDR, the common external address for PDR/DDR is selected but internally the data word is routed to the DDR.

Bits 3, 4 and 5 are used to provide CA2 (CB2) control; b5 defines CA2 as an input or output. If b5 = Ø, the CA2 (CB2) is set as an interrupt input. Under

193

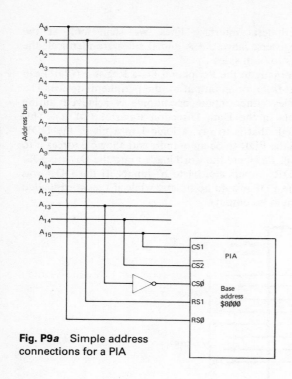

Fig. P9a Simple address connections for a PIA

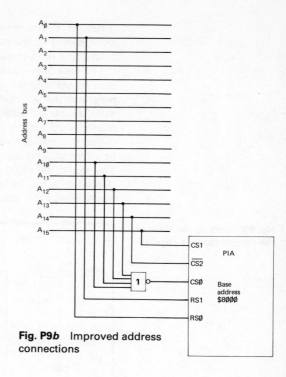

Fig. P9b Improved address connections

these conditions b3 and b4 are used for masking and edge control respectively. If b5 = 1, CA2 (CB2) is set as an output and b3 and b4 define the mode of operation.

Three chip select lines CSØ, CS1, and $\overline{CS2}$ together with register select lines RSØ and RS1 are used for addressing. These have to be connected to the appropriate lines of the address bus to determine exactly where in memory the PIA is located. Four locations are required for a PIA. Suppose the base address is $8000, then a table showing the various locations is as follows:

	Address	PIA Register	Comments
Base address	{8000	Peripheral data register	A side (bit 2 of CRA 1)
	{8000	Data direction register	A side (bit 2 of CRA Ø)
	8001	Control register	A side
	8002	Peripheral data register	B side (bit 2 of CRB 1)
	8002	Data direction register	B side (bit 2 of CRB Ø)
	8003	Control register	B side

The register select lines RSØ and RS1 are used as follows:

RS1	RSØ	Register selected in PIA
Ø	Ø	PDR/DDR A side
Ø	1	CR A
1	Ø	PDR/DDR B side
1	1	CR B

Therefore, for a PIA base address of $8000, the minimum connections required are (*fig. P9a*):

A_{15} to CS1
A_{14} to $\overline{CS2}$
A_{13} via an invertor to CS$\emptyset$
A_1 to RS1
$A_\emptyset$ to RS$\emptyset$

Then, when address $8000 is put on the address bus by the micro, CS1 = 1, $\overline{CS2} = \emptyset$, CS$\emptyset$ = 1, RS1 = $\emptyset$, and RS$\emptyset$ = $\emptyset$. However this simple method of connection has a drawback because of the unconnected address lines (A_2 through to A_{12}). This results in a large area of memory overwrite. In other words, the PIA would occupy a memory area from $8000 up to $9FFC. In a control system set up where only a small amount of program space is required, this overwrite may not be important, but in other situations where memory space is limited it cannot be tolerated. The solution is to use some form of address decoding. In *fig. P9b*, a four-input NOR gate is used to decode address lines A_{10}, A_{11}, A_{12} and A_{13} to connect to the CS$\emptyset$ pin on the PIA. The area of memory overwrite is then reduced substantially for the PIA now occupies from $8000 up to $83FC. By decoding all address lines there will be no overwrite at all.

The method by which the PIA is set up or configured to suit a particular system requirement is called *initialisation*. A flowchart showing the steps for initialisation is given in *fig. P10*.

Suppose the PIA is connected on the B side to an 8-bit DAC and to a switch input on the A side and that whenever the switch is operated a simple program outputs full-scale voltage for 1 sec, then $\frac{1}{2}$ full-scale for 1 sec. (See *fig. P11*.)

Fig. P10 Initialisation for the PIA

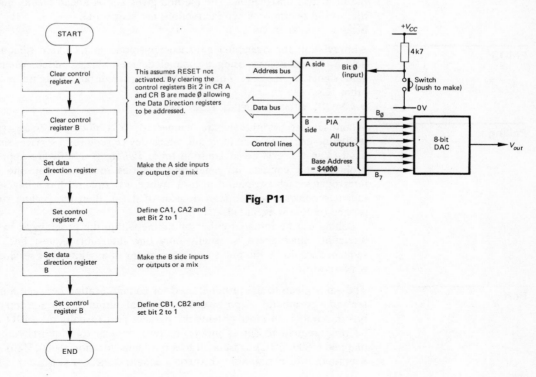

Fig. P11

195

The initialisation routine in assembly language is:

```
CLR      $4001      Clear CRA
CLR      $4003      Clear CRB
CLR      $4000      Set A side all inputs
LDA A    #$FF
STA A    $4002      Set B side all outputs
LDA A    #$04       Control word
STA A    $4001      Set CRA
STA A    $4003      Set CRB
CLR      $4002      Clear port B
```

and the routine for scanning the switch and outputting the required values is:

```
LOOP  LDA A  $4000      Get switch input
      BIT  A  #$01      Test for Ø in bit 1
      BNE    LOOP       Branch back if not Ø
      LDA A  #$FF       = Max. value
      STA A  $4002      Output value
      JSR    WAIT       Wait 1 sec
      LDA A  #$80       = half full scale
      STA A  $4002      Output value
      JSR    WAIT       Wait 1 sec
      CLR    $4002      Output zero
      BRA    LOOP       Read switch again
```

Pipelining

A technique used in some processors to improve the speed at which instructions are fetched and executed. Basically the method forces the fetch of the next instruction to begin before the current instruction execution is completed. To achieve this a *pipeline register* is used which holds the result of the previous microinstruction, a portion of the current microinstruction, and information on the next microinstruction. The method gives a look-ahead facility and speeds up the overall operation when instructions are sequential.

● MICROINSTRUCTION

PMOS

Abbreviation for p-channel enhancement-mode metal oxide silicon field effect device. A technology using p-channel devices which conduct when a negative gate signal is applied. These MOSFETS are used to create memories and other ICs.

● CMOS   ● FIELD EFFECT TRANSISTOR

Polling

When several peripherals are connected to a microprocessor system, some technique has to be used to decide which device requires a service, since only one device can be serviced at any one time. *Polling* is a software approach to this problem and consists of generating a series of signals (or one signal) that interrogates each peripheral in turn. When a peripheral has a flag set indicating that it requires a service (i.e. transfer of data), then the polling stops and the service routine is executed.

Polling can be initiated either by timing within the program or by an external interrupt. Since there is usually only one interrupt request line, the polling sequence would be the first set of instructions in any interrupt service routine.

● INTERRUPT

Port

The name given to the terminal used for communication between a microcomputer and a peripheral. A port can be one serial output line or a group of 8 or more bits in parallel. In most systems the parallel port (usually on a PIO or PIA) can be programmed to act as inputs, outputs or a mixture. Ports can be memory mapped (6800, 6502) or isolated to a particular location (8080, Z80).

● PERIPHERAL INTERFACE ADAPTOR   ● SERIAL INTERFACE ADAPTOR

Microprocessors are often used to control, via a suitable interface, the power applied to a load. There are several techniques available. Some sort of power interface is essential so that the relatively small output power (milliwatts) available from the micro port can be boosted to provide the necessary drive to the load. If the load is connected to a high voltage supply (the mains for example), then isolation techniques should be used to prevent the possibility of damage to the sensitive microprocessor and interface chips. One common method for achieving effective isolation is to use an opto-coupler or opto-isolator. Electrical isolation of 4 kV or higher is possible. *Fig. P12* shows a typical circuit arrangement.

Fig. P12 Typical circuit arrangement to isolate a.c. mains from the micro port

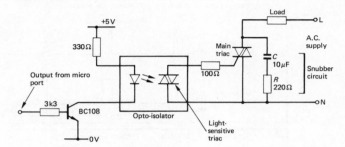

1 Control in an ON/OFF switching situation is relatively straightforward (*fig. P13*). The interface will consist of an electronic power switching device such as a Darlington transistor or VMOS power FET. This will be driven fully ON when the micro outputs a logic 1 signal and it will be OFF when the micro output is logic Ø.

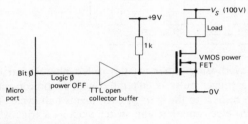

Fig. P13a Interfacing to switch d.c. loads using a power FET

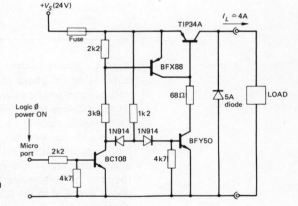

Fig. P13b Interfacing to switch d.c. power using a BJT

2 A more complicated arrangement has to be set up when the power in the load needs to be controlled over a wide range, and the techniques involved depend upon the type of supply being used. For d.c. situations it is best to use a pulse width modulation system (PWM). Suppose the speed of a d.c. motor is to be controlled over the range 60 rev/min to 3000 rev/min (*fig. P14*). This can be achieved by simply varying the d.c. voltage applied to the motor, but a PWM method does it by switching the motor on for a variable time period. For low speed, the motor would be switched to the d.c. supply for a relatively short time in one cycle, whereas for high speed the motor would be switched on for nearly the whole time period in one cycle. The width of the switching waveform and the frequency could be controlled via the program in the microprocessor.

Fig. P14 Pulse width modulation control

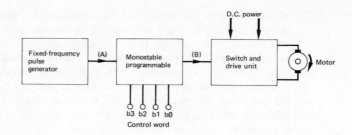

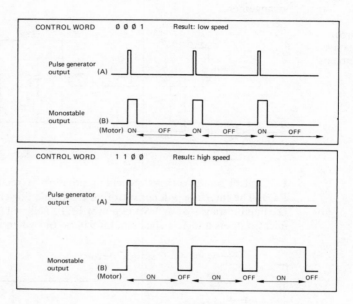

3 A.C. power control is achieved using either what is called phase control or burst firing. In **phase control**, a trigger pulse is generated with its time position variable (set by the micro) with respect to the start of each mains half-cycle. This trigger pulse is used to "fire" an electronic latching switch such as a triac which then connects power to the load. As the mains waveform goes through zero, the latching device switches off and then conducts again at a point in the negative half-cycle when the next trigger pulse is generated. This is more easily seen from a waveform diagram as in *fig. P15*. This shows that the greater the delay between the start of each mains half cycle and the trigger pulse, the smaller will be the power supplied to the load. The delay time can be controlled at the interface by a digital command signal from the microprocessor. The method is particularly useful in lamp dimmers and a.c. motor speed control.

Where a load has a much slower response, heaters being an obvious example, the **burst firing** technique can be used. In this method, the load is connected to the mains supply by the switching device for a set number of whole cycles. (Each cycle in the 50 Hz mains takes 20 msec.) Thus for low power dissipation in the load, the switch may be on for only a few cycles in every hundred (10 in a 100 gives 10%), whereas fifty cycles in every hundred would give half power. One of the advantages of this method compared with phase control is that very little interference (electrical "noise") is generated because the actual time of switching takes place when the mains voltage has just passed through zero. This is shown in *fig. P16*.

● INTERFACE CIRCUITS   ● ZERO CROSSING DETECTOR

Fig. P15 Phase control in
a.c. power circuits

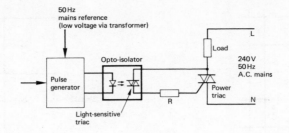

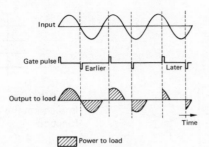

Power to load

Fig. P16 Burst firing

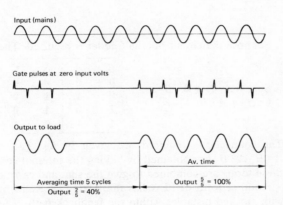

Program Counter (PC)	An essential register within a microprocessor (CPU) that holds the address of the next program memory location. The program counter is initially loaded with the address at which the program starts, and is then automatically incremented after each operation to formulate the next address. ● FETCH-EXECUTE CYCLE ● MICROPROCESSOR
Programmable Logic Array (PLA)	These are integrated circuits which basically consist of an array of uncommitted logic devices. These can be programmed by the user to create a desired logic circuit. The final logic function of the circuit is either user-programmed by electrically blowing fuse links (Field Programmable Logic Array) or set up during the final manufacturing stage by a mask (Mask Programmable Logic Array). The PLA is therefore closely related to the ROM (Read Only Memory) device but in the PLA both the addresses and the stored pattern are determined by the programming. The simplest form of PLA consists of a set of inputs with invertors, a rank of AND gates so that various combinations of the inputs can be ANDed together to give product terms, and then a bank of OR gates to allow selected product terms to be combined into output signals. The general outline of this structure is shown in *fig. P17*.

199

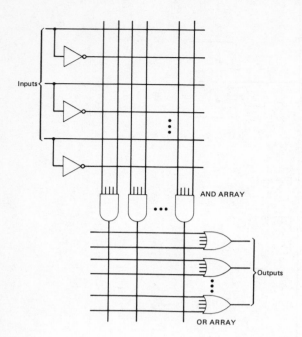

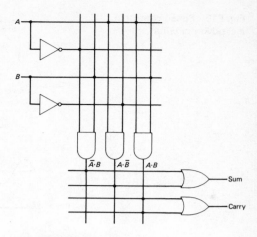

Fig. P18 Use of a PLA to implement the half-adder function

Fig. P17 Architecture of one form of PLA

Suppose the circuit of a half-adder is required. The logic function is

$$Sum = \bar{A} \cdot B + A \cdot \bar{B}$$
$$Carry = A \cdot B$$

B	A	S	C
Ø	Ø	Ø	Ø
Ø	1	1	Ø
1	Ø	1	Ø
1	1	Ø	1

The connections required are given in *fig. P18*. The product terms $A \cdot B$, $\bar{A} \cdot B$, $A \cdot \bar{B}$, are obtained by linking the internal connections as shown and then these terms are combined to give the sum and carry outputs via the OR gates.

Another form of PLA has the AND-OR ROM matrices but is also provided with clocked bistables within the feedback path. This is shown in *fig. P19*. This type of array provides for the implementation of a wide variety of sequential logic functions, for example a 4-bit parallel-in/parallel-out shift register.

Fig. P19 Another form of PLA

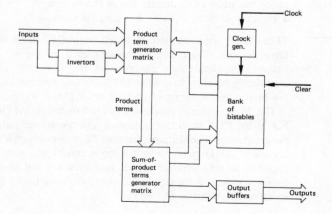

Having decided on the logic function required for a design based on a PLA, the pattern has to be translated into an appropriate fuse model. Computer programs such as PAL Assembler or CUPL (Compiler-based HLL) are available for this purpose. These basically accept an input file of Boolean equations and then assemble the data into a "fuse map" that can then be downloaded via a suitable interface to the PLA programmer.

● UNCOMMITTED LOGIC ARRAY

Programmable Logic Controller

This term is used to describe the range of industrial process controllers which use reprogrammable logic. They provide sequence control for industrial tasks such as conveyor belt movement and automatic assembly. Early types were constructed using relay logic or arrays of logic gates but the more sophisticated systems use a microprocessor and memory. These basically form a microcomputer controller with input/output circuits specifically designed to drive loads such as solenoids, pumps, motors and other actuators. Thus a PLC system is made up of the following units:

Central processing unit (microprocessor)
Memory (RAM and ROM)
Programming panel (with display)
Input/output unit

Most systems are modular with the units as separate plug-in cards or subsystems which can be mounted into a rack. In this way the user is given flexibility and ready expansion (more memory or I/O).

The CPU needs to have only a small data word—1 bit up to 4 bits is common—and a limited instruction set. This means that programming the system for a particular task is relatively simple. Usually an LED or CRT display gives a simulation of the control sequence being set up so that the operator can readily see the program steps required for any new task. Many systems are also provided with EPROM so that, once the program for an industrial process is designed and working, it can be fixed as firmware.

● DEDICATED CONTROLLER

PROM

Acronym for Programmable Read Only Memory. An i.c. memory chip having a fixed program (called firmware) which has been set up by the user. This is normally achieved by blowing fuse links within the memory array using a PROM programmer.

● MEMORIES

Pseudo Instruction

An instruction interpreted and used by the assembler and not incorporated into the object program.

● ASSEMBLER

PUSH/PULL Instruction

Instructions that can be used to save the contents of a register on the stack (using PUSH) which can then be retrieved at a later point in the program (using PULL). The instruction POP is used in some processors for the PULL operation.

● STACK

RAM

Acronym for Random Access Memory. Memory in which any location can be accessed in the same time as any other. The term RAM is now normally reserved to describe Read/Write memory, the type which can have its contents changed rapidly and which is therefore used to hold current program and data. RAM is volatile and will lose its data when power is removed.

● MEMORIES

Real Time

Any computer system that has a program which accepts input data and then uses this data to update its records and produce outputs almost immediately is said to be operating in real time. Examples are control systems of all types where sensors are continually monitoring the output effect so that the program, using the data from the sensors, outputs words to adjust the power drive devices.

● CONTROL SYSTEM

Reduced Instruction Set Computer (RISC)

This is a processor design which has a much simplified instruction set, the objective being to increase the machine's operating speed. The argument behind this approach is that, while the majority of instructions used in a computer program are straightforward data transfer types (LD, ST, MOV), the more complex instructions built into most processors tend to slow down the speed at which simple transfers are executed. By changing the processor design and reducing both the number and complexity of the instructions, higher speed is made possible without loss of computing power.

Register

A number of bistable elements (8, 16, 32, etc.) grouped together and which act as a whole and can be made to carry out certain functions. These might be: shift left, shift right, hold a result, decrement, increment, and so on. A microprocessor will contain a number of registers which are allocated specific functions. These are: Accumulator, Program counter, Index register, Stack pointer, Status register, and Instruction register.

● BISTABLE   ● MICROPROCESSOR

Relative Addressing

An addressing mode used with conditional branch/jump instructions where the destination address (the address the program itself is branching to) is relative to the contents of the program counter.

In assembly language, a Label would be used next to the conditional branch instruction, and in machine code an offset (twos complement form) will be given. This offset is added to the contents of the program counter to formulate the destination address. Since the offset can be negative or positive, both backward and forward branches can be taken.

Example [6800 code] (*fig. R1*)

LABEL	MNEMONIC	OPERAND	ADDRESS	HEX. CODE
	XX	XX	1000	XX XX
LOOP1	INX		1002	08
	XX	XXXX	1003	XX XX XX
	XX	XX	1006	XX XX
	ADD A	$3000	1008	BB 30 00
	BCC	LOOP1	100B	24 F5

Code for branch   Offset
instruction

(XX: other instructions/data/addresses within program.)

In 6800 processors the offset can be calculated from the formula:

$$D = (PC + 2) + R$$

where D = Destination address
PC = Contents of PC at first byte of Branch instruction
R = Offset required (twos complement)

Fig. R1

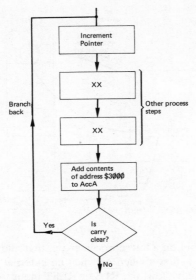

In the example

$$R = D - (PC + 2)$$

$$= 1002 - (100B + 2) = -11$$

−11 in twos complement is $F5 in hex.

● BRANCH INSTRUCTION   ● CONDITIONAL BRANCH/JUMP   ● OFFSET   ● TWOS COMPLEMENT

Relocatable Code

A *relocatable program* is one which can be moved to any part of the memory of a system simply by giving the program a new start address. It follows that, for a program to be relocatable, addresses used within the program code should be relative to the origin of the program and not absolute addresses. The only exception to this could be system port addresses or subroutines located within the system monitor.

A relocatable assembler is normally used in conjunction with a link editor to develop relocatable code. The use of relocatable code for programs allows different sections to be developed separately and then linked together at a later date to make the complete program.

An example of a relocatable program using 6800/6802 assembly language is the following segment which is a subroutine for outputting a message to a VDU:

```
        NAM     SUB1
        ORG     $0000
OUTEE   EQU     $E1D1
START   LDX     #TAB        Set pointer to message
LOOP    LDA A   0,X         Load ASCII code into Acc
        JSR     OUTEE
        INX                 Increment pointer
        CMP A   #$2E        Look for full stop
        BNE     LOOP        Branch back
        RTS
TAB     FCC     /MESSAGE/
        END
```

The origin of this program segment can be changed and the program located anywhere, as required, in the system memory.

● ASSEMBLER

Fig. R2 RESET/RESTART operation

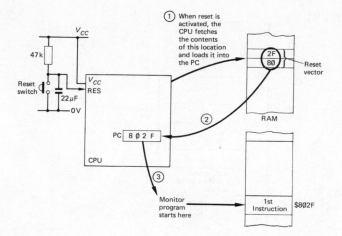

① When reset is activated, the CPU fetches the contents of this location and loads it into the PC

2F
80 — Reset vector

RAM

PC 8 0 2 F

CPU

②

③

Monitor program starts here

1st Instruction $802F

| RESET/ RESTART |

A control input pin on a microprocessor i.c. that allows a system to be initialised when the power is first applied or when an external reset switch is momentarily closed. Usually active low, the $\overline{RES}$ or $\overline{REST}$ input forces the program counter to be loaded with the address held in the RESET vector (*fig. R2*). This address will contain the first instruction of the initialisation and control routine, which in a microcomputer will be the monitor program.

● MONITOR ● VECTORED ADDRESS

RETURN Instruction

Used to terminate a subroutine (Return from Subroutine RTS) and an interrupt service routine (RTI). When a subroutine is called, the return address to the main program is saved on the stack. At the end of the subroutine the instruction RTS causes this address to be pulled off the stack and placed in the program counter.

● CALL INSTRUCTION ● INTERRUPT ● SUBROUTINE

Robotics

A *robot* can be defined as a programmable mechanism designed to move and do work within a defined volume of space. Robotics incorporates simple pick-and-place mechanisms through to complex systems which, in addition to controlled and accurate movement in several axes, are provided with sensors for position, force and vision.

Industrial robots consist of the following main parts (*fig. R3*):

a) The mechanical manipulators
b) Control and drive units
c) A stored and alterable program.

and they can be put into the following categories:

Pick-and-place
Lightweight electric
Heavy duty (hydraulic or pneumatic, with ultra-long reach)
Special purpose

The pick-and-place is a relatively simple, low-cost system which is capable of limited movement between predetermined limits. Its grasping jaws are then used to carry out the repetitive task of loading or stacking items. The system can be reconfigured for other tasks by altering the program.

The other types are developments from this basic concept. A typical lightweight robot arm is illustrated in *fig. R4*. The arm, given five or six independent axes of motion, can be driven to any point within the defined operating space. The independently controlled axes provide great flexibility in positioning. Three axes are used to position the hand and three (usually) to orient the hand. The working space is typically 80 cm radius.

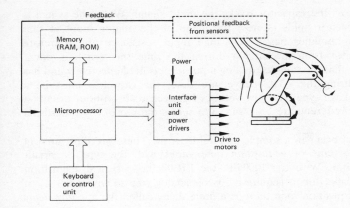

Fig. R3 The basic elements of an industrial robot

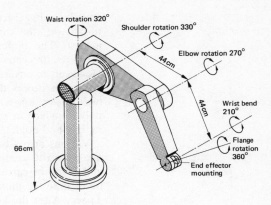

Fig. R4 Typical configuration of a lightweight electric robot

Open loop control can be used, with stepper motors being driven directly from the control interface. A fixed number of pulses will drive the motor through a known angle and fairly precise position of a selected joint is possible. However, much improved accuracy and repeatability can be obtained using a closed loop servo (position controller with feedback) for each joint. Each section then requires a motor drive, a position sensor, velocity feedback for stabilisation, and, possibly, a brake of some kind.

Although the software for any required movement sequence could be developed independently, it is more usual for the robot to be "taught" any new task by a "lead-by-the-nose" method. The sequence of movements is then stored in the program memory by the operator.

● CONTROL SYSTEM   ● SENSOR   ● STEPPER MOTOR

ROM

Acronym for Read Only Memory. A type of memory in which the stored data is fixed and cannot be changed. Used to hold fixed programs and data.

● MEMORIES

Sample-and-Hold

A circuit used to hold an analog signal at a steady value while it is being converted into digital. The analog value is sampled at the start of the conversion and is then held steady until the conversion has been completed.

The basic components of a sample-and-hold circuit are a fast electronic switch, a capacitor and a buffer amplifier (*fig. S1a*). The switch, usually a MOSFET, performs the sampling function. When the control signal is high, the switch closes

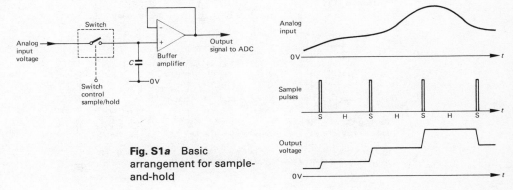

Fig. S1a Basic arrangement for sample-and-hold

205

and the voltage across the capacitor tracks the input signal. When the switch is turned off, the capacitor holds (stores) the value of the analog input at that instant. The buffer amplifier has a very high input resistance and therefore prevents the capacitor from discharging during the time the switch is open. However, to ensure that the sampled analog input level is held effectively and has minimum droop during the ADC conversion time, the capacitor must be a high-quality low-leakage type with low values of dielectric absorption; usually a polypropylene or polystyrene are best. *Fig. S1b* shows the use of a standard i.c. sample-and-hold.

Various errors can occur in a sample-and-hold circuit. These are illustrated in *fig. S2*. The *sample time* or *acquisition time* varies with the type of circuit and value of capacitor. With $C = 1000\,pF$, the LF398 has a typical acquisition time (time for the capacitor to acquire a 10 volt analog step to within 0.1%) of $4\,\mu sec$. After the acquisition time there is a finite delay called the *aperture delay*

Fig. S1*b*   Standard IC sample-and-hold: typical application circuits

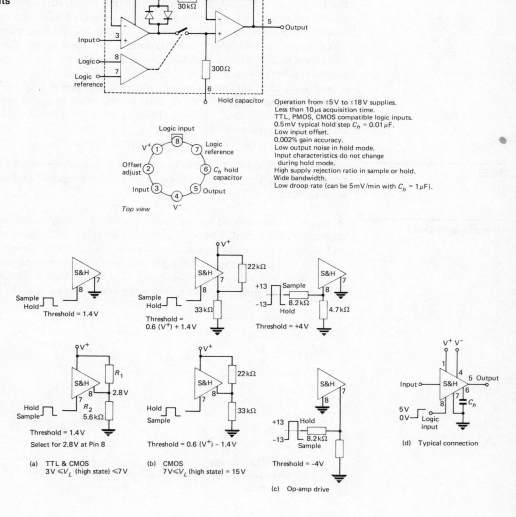

Operation from ±5 V to ±18 V supplies.
Less than 10 μs acquisition time.
TTL, PMOS, CMOS compatible logic inputs.
0.5 mV typical hold step C_h = 0.01 μF.
Low input offset.
0.002% gain accuracy.
Low output noise in hold mode.
Input characteristics do not change during hold mode.
High supply rejection ratio in sample or hold.
Wide bandwidth.
Low droop rate (can be 5 mV/min with C_h = 1 μF).

206

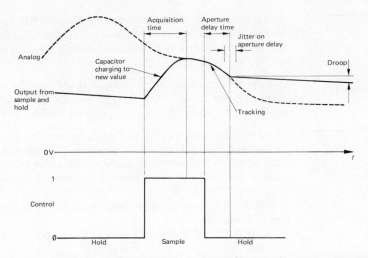

Fig. S2 Errors and timing in a sample-and-hold circuit

time—the time between the hold command to the opening of the switch. This is typically about 100 nsec. Of more concern is the jitter of this delay time, called "aperture jitter". This uncertainty can lead to errors in the digital output. Take the case of a sine wave input:

$$1 \text{ LSB in the digital output} = \frac{2V_p}{2^n}$$

where V_p = peak value of sine wave analog signal
n = number of bits used in the ADC.

$$\therefore \quad 0.5 \text{ LSB} = \frac{V_p}{2^n}$$

Since $v = V_p \sin \omega t$

$$\text{Rate of change of } v = r = \frac{dv}{dt} = \omega V_p \cos \omega t$$

This rate of change r is a maximum when $\cos \omega t = 1$

$$\therefore \quad r = \omega V_p$$

If t_{aj} = timing jitter or uncertainty of t_a, then

$$r t_{aj} < \frac{V_p}{2^n} \quad \text{for errors of less than 0.5 LSB}$$

$$\text{or} \quad t_{aj} < \frac{1}{\omega 2^n}$$

To illustrate this point, suppose a 10-bit ADC is used to sample analog which has a maximum frequency component of 10 kHz.

$$t_{aj} = \frac{1}{2\pi f 2^n} \quad \text{for errors of less than 0.5 LSB}$$

$$\therefore \quad t_{aj} = \frac{1}{2\pi \times 10 \times 10^3 \times 2^{10}} = 15.5 \text{ nsec}$$

If more bits are used in the conversion, the specification on minimum aperture jitter becomes even tighter.

● ANALOG-TO-DIGITAL CONVERTOR ● CONTROL SYSTEM ● GLITCH

207

Schottky TTL	A variant of Transistor Transistor Logic (TTL) which uses non-saturating transistors as the switches. Schottky TTL operates in the same way as standard TTL but has a much lower value of propagation delay time.

● TTL

Scratch Pad Memory   A term used to describe an area of RAM, usually of limited size, used by the main program for the temporary storage of data and results where the data and results are required by the main program for further calculations.

Sensor   In microprocessor-based control systems, sensors are the input transducers used to convert the energy being monitored (temperature, flow-rate, movement, light-level, and so on) into useful electrical signals. The important parameters used in the specifications of sensors are defined as follows.

RANGE   The maximum and minimum values of input quantity over which the sensor is usable.

ACCURACY   The degree to which the output of a sensor is in agreement with the true value.

SENSITIVITY   This refers to the change in output for a unit change in input quantity. Example: a thermocouple may have a sensitivity of 40 μV per °C.

RESOLUTION   The smallest change in the input quantity which will give a measurable output.

REPEATABILITY   The variations or "scatter" in a series of repeated readings.

RESPONSE TIME   This is the time taken for the sensor output to change and settle to a new value following a step-like input change.

STABILITY   The output level from a sensor will drift even when the input is held constant. The drift will be caused by ageing and by environmental changes. Temperature changes in particular will cause most sensors to drift, and the temperature characteristic or temperature coefficient may well be quoted separately.

Temperature sensors

SENSOR	FEATURES	TYPICAL USEFUL TEMPERATURE RANGE
THERMISTOR	Resistance falls with temperature.	−80° to +300°C
THERMOCOUPLE	Voltage output rises with temperature.	0° to +1000°C
PLATINUM RESISTANCE	Resistance rises with temperature.	−50° to +500°C
SEMICONDUCTOR TYPES	Voltage for pn junction falls by 2 mV/°C. Current output rises with temp.	−55° to +150°C

1   A **thermistor**, made of sintered oxides of nickel and manganese, is a device that undergoes a very large change of resistance with temperature. The name is derived from *therm*ally sensitive re*sistor*. Most of the types have a negative temperature coefficient (NTC) but some positive temperature coefficient varieties (PTC) are also available. The material can be formed into rods or small beads, but for sensing purposes the small bead shape is used in order to get the fastest possible response. The bead is then sealed inside a glass envelope or into a stainless steel probe (*fig. S3*).

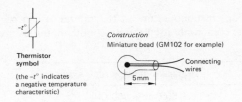

Thermistor
symbol

(the $-t°$ indicates
a negative temperature
characteristic)

Construction
Miniature bead (GM102 for example)

Connecting
wires

5mm

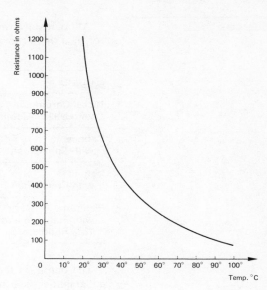

Fig. S3 Thermistor
symbol, construction, and
characteristics

The resistance follows the law:

$$R_2 = R_1 e^{B(1/T_1 - 1/T_2)}$$

where B = characteristic temperature constant (K)
T = bead temperature (K)
R_1 = resistance of thermistor at temperature T_1
R_2 = resistance of thermistor at temperature T_2
e = 2.7183.
For a device such as the GM102, which has a quoted resistance at 25°C of 1 kΩ,
$B = 3000$. Therefore, at +100°C (the maximum temperature for this thermistor is
125°C),

$$R_2 = 1000e^{-2.018} = 133 \ \Omega$$

Fig. S4 Thermocouple

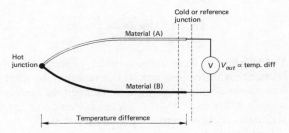

Cold or reference
junction

Material (A)

Hot
junction

V $V_{out} \propto$ temp. diff

Material (B)

Temperature difference

2 A **thermocouple** is a sensor which consists of two junctions of dissimilar
metals. The operation, based on a discovery in 1921 by Seebeck, is that an e.m.f.
will be generated proportional to the temperature difference between these two
junctions (*fig. S4*). One junction is used for measuring temperature while the
other is used as a reference. The reference is normally maintained at a constant
temperature, say 0°C, or in a temperature-controlled enclosure at a value slightly
higher than ambient.

Alternatively, variations in temperature at the reference can be compensated for by a thermistor. The commonly used thermocouple materials are

MATERIALS	WORKING TEMPERATURE RANGE
Nickel Chromium with Nickel Aluminium	−50°C to +400°C
Copper with Constantan	−250°C to +400°C
Iron with Constantan	−200°C to +1200°C
Platinum with Platinum and 13% Rhodium	−50°C to +1750°C

The output of thermocouples is not high—a typical value is 40 μV per °C—so an amplifier is essential to boost the signal before applying it to an ADC. However, thermocouples have the advantage of being linear devices with good accuracy and high stability. A typical circuit using a NICR/NIAL type is shown in *fig. S5*.

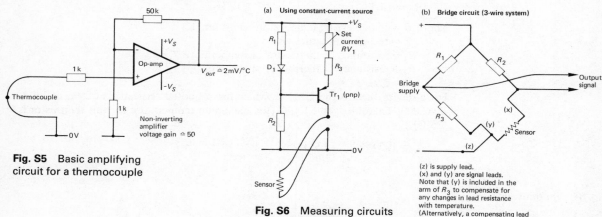

Fig. S5 Basic amplifying circuit for a thermocouple

Fig. S6 Measuring circuits for use with PRTD

(z) is supply lead.
(x) and (y) are signal leads.
Note that (y) is included in the arm of R_3 to compensate for any changes in lead resistance with temperature.
(Alternatively, a compensating lead may be included in series with R_3).

3 Platinum, an inert stable material, exhibits a known and repeatable change of resistance with temperature. It can therefore be used as an accurate temperature sensor over a wide range without the need for function compensation. The sensor is made either using a coil of platinum wire on an insulating former or as a film of platinum deposited onto an alumina substrate.

Typical data is:

Resistance at 0°C	*Temperature coefficient*	*Temperature range*
100 $\Omega \pm 0.1\ \Omega$	+0.385 Ω/°C	−50° to +500°C

Thus over the range 0°C to 100°C, the resistance changes by 38.5 Ω. By passing a small constant current through the sensing film it is then possible to get an output voltage that increases with temperature. Alternatively, a bridge circuit can be used. Typical outputs in either case are about 1 mV/°C so some form of amplifier is essential. Measuring circuits are shown in *fig. S6*.

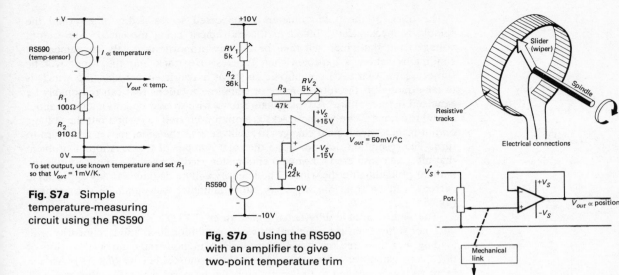

Fig. S7a Simple temperature-measuring circuit using the RS590

+V

RS590 (temp-sensor)

$I \propto$ temperature

$V_{out} \propto$ temp.

R_1 100Ω

R_2 910Ω

0V

To set output, use known temperature and set R_1 so that V_{out} = 1mV/K.

Fig. S7b Using the RS590 with an amplifier to give two-point temperature trim

+10V

RV_1 5k

R_2 36k

R_3 47k

RV_2 5k

$+V_S$ +15V

$-V_S$ -15V

V_{out} = 50mV/°C

R_4 22k

RS590

0V

-10V

Fig. S8 Potentiometer

Slider (wiper)

Spindle

Resistive tracks

Electrical connections

V'_S +

Pot.

$+V_S$

$-V_S$

$V_{out} \propto$ position

Mechanical link

Spindle

Pot.

4   The leakage current of **semiconductor** materials such as silicon increases with temperature. This means that the voltage required to forward bias a pn junction (a diode or the base/emitter junction of a transistor) also falls with temperature. Typically this fall is about 2 mV/°C. This characteristic enables a pn junction to be used as a temperature sensor by supplying it with a constant current and detecting the changes in forward voltage.

Commercial semiconductor temperature sensors such as the RS590 utilise the temperature-dependent characteristics and are devices which produce an output current proportional to absolute temperature. Over the supply voltage range of +14 V to +30 V d.c. the RS590 acts as a high resistance current generator with the value of current being 1 μA per degree Kelvin. The temperature range is from −55°C to 130°C with an accuracy of ±2.0°C.

Very simple circuits to sense temperature can be made by placing a resistor in series with the sensor (*fig. S7a*). This also shows a method for trimming out any small calibration error. A more complicated circuit with a two-point temperature trim is also shown (*fig. S7b*). The circuit is initially adjusted by varying RV_1 to give zero volts output when the sensor is at 0°C. The sensor temperature is then set to +100°C (other suitable known value) and RV_2 is adjusted to give a full-scale output of say +5 V.

Position and Force sensors
Many devices are available for sensing angular position, linear displacement, force and pressure.

1   The resistance **potentiometer** is one of the simplest types of position sensor. In its basic form (*fig. S8*) it consists of a linear resistive track on which a sliding contact (called the wiper) rotates.

211

The track of the potentiometer is connected across a d.c. supply and the spindle is mechanically linked to the movement being measured. The output voltage from the wiper will then be directly proportional to the movement. If continuous action is expected then the resistive track and the wiper will be subjected to wear. All potentiometers have a restricted working life which is usually quoted as the total number of complete rotations that can reasonably be expected before failure. A typical figure for a wire-wound potentiometer is about 50 000 rotations. Wire-wound tracks are often preferred to carbon but the voltage output from a wire-wound changes in small steps as the slider moves from turn to turn. The resolution depends upon the total number of turns. Another problem that must be considered for any potentiometer used in a sensing application is the amount of loading on the wiper. The linearity will be degraded if any appreciable current is taken from the wiper. A buffer amplifier will eliminate this problem (*fig. S8*).

2 The **linear variable differential transformer** (LVDT) is a position sensor that does not suffer from the problems of wear, resolution loss, and nonlinearity with loading. For these reasons it is used extensively in industrial control. It consists of three coils wound on a former inside which is a moveable core (*fig. S9*). An a.c. input voltage is applied to the centre coil (the primary) while the other two coils form the secondary windings. These are connected in series opposition, which means that, when the core is dead centre, the induced e.m.f.s in both secondary windings are equal and therefore cancel out to give zero output voltage.

As the core is moved away from centre, the induced voltage in one secondary winding is greater than in the other and an a.c. output voltage is given. The amplitude of the output voltage is a very linear function of the core displacement. Nonlinearity is typically better than ±0.5% of maximum output. The measuring range of LVDTs can be from 0.1 mm up to 75 mm.

Fig. S9 Linear variable differential transformer

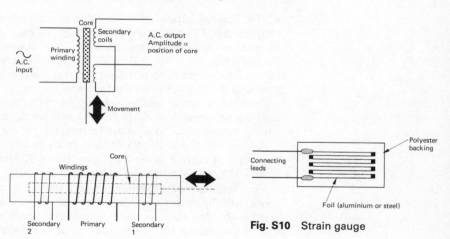

Fig. S10 Strain gauge

3 The measurement of strain, force, load and torque can only be made by the measurement of the relative displacement of points on a surface. To do this a **strain gauge** is used. This basically consists of an etched resistive track or wire on a flexible insulating base (*fig. S10*). The gauge is then bonded (i.e. cemented) to the mechanical member in which the strain is to be measured. The principle of operation depends on the fact that the resistance of an element changes when its dimensions are altered. Therefore, if the member to which the gauge is bonded is stressed, the strain caused can be measured by recording the change in resistance of the gauge. The formula for the resistance of a thin wire or film is

$$R = \rho \frac{l}{a}$$

where ρ is resistivity, l is length, a is cross-sectional area.

A change in resistance due to strain can be expressed as

$$\frac{\Delta R}{R} = \frac{\Delta \rho}{\rho} + \frac{\Delta l}{l} - \frac{\Delta a}{a}$$

where $\frac{\Delta l}{l} = \varepsilon$ is the strain, usually expressed in $\mu m/m$.

The key parameter for a strain gauge is called the *gauge factor K*:

$$K = \frac{\Delta R/R}{\Delta l/l} = \frac{\Delta R/R}{\varepsilon}$$

A typical value for K, which is a dimensionless quantity, is 2. (Semiconductor gauges are much more sensitive, with gauge factors of 100 or more.)

Fig. S11 Strain gauge bridge circuit

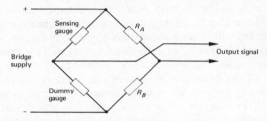

A strain guage is usually placed in a Wheatstone bridge arrangement to give an output voltage proportional to strain. For the circuit of *fig. S11*, the change in bridge output voltage is given by

$$V_o = \frac{R_A R_B}{R_A + R_B} IK\varepsilon$$

where I is the current in the gauge.

● ANALOG-TO-DIGITAL CONVERTOR ● INTERFACE CIRCUITS

Serial Data Format

The typical arrangement for serial transmission is as follows. The signal line is normally high, so the beginning of a character is indicated by a start bit going low. The data bits, seven for ASCII characters, are then sent with the LSB first. A parity bit (D7) using either odd or even parity is added and finally the end of the character is indicated by two stop bits, both high states. (See *fig. S12*.)

● ASCII

Fig. S12 Format used for asynchronous serial data

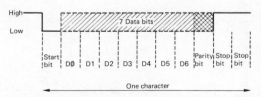

Serial Interface Adaptor

Any interface chip designed to interface between a microprocessor and peripheral devices which receive and send data in serial fashion over one line. Normally the SIA has additional features such as handshake lines and the ability to communicate via a modem. Other names for an SIA are ACIA, UART, and USART.

● ASYNCHRONOUS COMMUNICATIONS INTERFACE ADAPTOR ● UNIVERSAL ASYNCHRONOUS RECEIVER/TRANSMITTER

Fig. S13 Driving a 7-segment common anode display

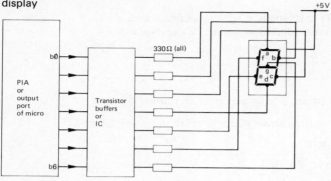

Display	g	f	e	d	c	b	a	Output Code
0	0	1	1	1	1	1	1	$3F
1	0	0	0	0	1	1	0	$06
2	1	0	1	1	0	1	1	$5B
3	1	0	0	1	1	1	1	$4F
4	1	1	0	0	1	1	0	$66
5	1	1	0	1	1	0	1	$6D
6	1	1	1	1	1	0	1	$7D
7	0	0	0	0	1	1	1	$07
8	1	1	1	1	1	1	1	$7F
9	1	1	0	0	1	1	1	$67
A	1	1	1	0	1	1	1	$77
b	1	1	1	1	1	0	0	$7C
C	0	1	1	1	0	0	1	$39
d	1	0	1	1	1	1	0	$5E
E	1	1	1	1	0	0	1	$79
F	1	1	1	0	0	0	1	$71

Seven-segment Display

Seven-segment displays with either common anodes or common cathodes (*fig. S13*) can also be driven via transistor or IC buffers from an 8-bit port. Since each segment will require about 10 mA, the total current with all segments on is in the region of 70 mA, so care must be taken to ensure that the buffer IC is not overloaded. The segments are labelled a, b, c, d, e, f and g and it is possible to get all the hexadecimal numerals and letters displayed. The software, unless an external decoder IC is used, must do the job of producing the correct output code. For the common anode type, the buffer must receive a logic 1 to light a segment. Thus if the numeral 2 is required to be displayed then segments a, b, d, e and g must be on (logic 1 required) and segments c and f off. The output at the port must be $5B.

As shown in the table there is a unique code for each hexadecimal character and these codes can be held in a look-up table in RAM or ROM ready to be outputted as required. The code table is accessed and the code selected by using the number or letter required as an offset for the index register. (See *fig. S14*.)

● LIGHT-EMITTING DIODE

Fig. S14 Flowchart for outputting the code for a 7-segment display

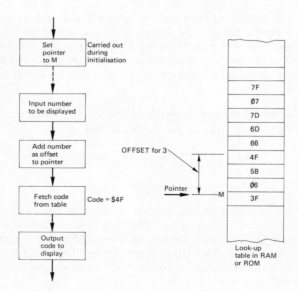

Sign Bit

The most significant bit in the data word in signed binary numbers indicates the sign of that number.

$MSB = \emptyset$ number is positive

$MSB = 1$ number is negative

Signed numbers are usually in twos complement form:

$$+30_{10} = \begin{array}{c}\text{Sign} \\ \text{bit Magnitude} \\ \downarrow\overline{} \\ \emptyset\emptyset\emptyset11110\end{array}$$

and $-30_{10} =$ $1110\emptyset\emptyset1\emptyset$

A flag in the status register within the processor will indicate, after an operation, the state of the MSB. This flag is labelled S (sign) or N (negative).

● TWOS COMPLEMENT

Sink/Source Current

A logic gate output or port output of a microprocessor system can be at either logic $\emptyset$ or logic 1. When in the low state ($\emptyset$), the output will "sink" current, that is take current in. If the output is high, current will be supplied from the circuit, i.e. it will "source" current (*fig. S15*). In many cases more current can be taken by a gate output in the "sink" state than can be sourced, and the specification of the logic used should always be consulted before any interface circuits are designed.

● CMOS   ● INTERFACE CIRCUITS   ● TTL

Fig. S15 Sink/source current

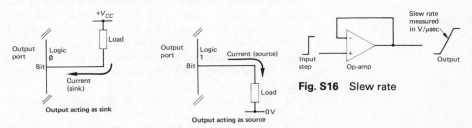

Fig. S16 Slew rate

Slew Rate

A parameter used in op-amp and analog comparator circuits as a measure of the speed with which the output changes in response to a sudden step input (*fig. S16*). Slew rate is measured in volts/μsec and varies depending on the i.c. type from values of about $0.5\,V/\mu$sec for general-purpose op-amps (741) up to $500\,V/\mu$sec for a fast op-amp. The latter will therefore give a 5 V change of state in approximately 10 nsec.

● COMPARATOR   ● OPERATIONAL AMPLIFIER

Source Code (Source Statement)

This is code in which a high-level language or assembly language program is written before it is compiled (for HLL) or assembled into the appropriate machine code for the processor on which the program is to be run.

Source statements in assembly language could be:

```
LABEL    OPERATOR    OPERAND    COMMENT
LOOP     LDA         #$FØ       Load Acc. with FØH
         STA         $32ØC      Store Acc. at address
         INX                    Increment pointer
```

● ASSEMBLER

Stack and Stack Pointer

The *stack* in a computer or microprocessor system is a reserved area in RAM used for temporary storage of data, return addresses and register contents. This stack area is defined by the number loaded into a register called the *stack pointer* (SP).

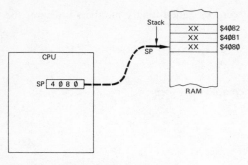

Fig. S17 Defining the stack

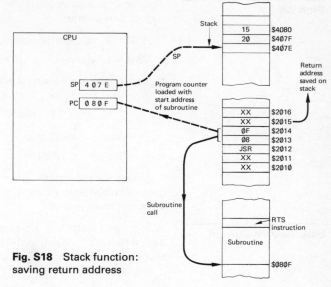

Fig. S18 Stack function: saving return address

Hence the instruction

LDS   #$4080   Load SP Immediate with hex. value 4080

causes the stack to be initially defined at address $4080 (*fig. S17*). Essentially the stack acts as a push-down file with the stack pointer being automatically decremented when data or a return address is pushed onto the stack. The last entry of data to the stack must be the first retrieved and, when this occurs, the stack pointer automatically increments. In this way the SP always points to the next available location in the stack. The stack concept performs three important functions:

1 Saving the return address to the main program when a subroutine is called (*fig. S18*).

2 Saving the contents of some (or all) of the important registers in the processor when an Interrupt Request (IRQ, INT) or Non-Maskable Interrupt (NMI) is actioned. The content of the registers is then restored after the interrupt service routine is completed. The last statement RTI (Return from Interrupt) does this. (*fig. S19*.)

3 Acting as a temporary store using the PUSH and PULL (POP) instructions (*fig. S20*).

Example

PSH   A   Push contents of Reg. A on stack
PSH   B   Push contents of Reg. B on stack
Later instructions, when required:
PUL   B   Restore content to B
PUL   A   Restore content to A
● SUBROUTINE   ● INTERRUPT

Status and Status Register

Status, depending on the type of microprocessor, is taken to mean the content or state of one register or a group of registers at one particular instant.

The *Status Register* (called Condition Code Register in the 6800 series or Flag Register in the 8080 range) contains the flags (carry, parity, zero, sign and overflow) that indicate the state in the processor resulting from the last instruction or operation.

● FLAG AND FLAG REGISTER

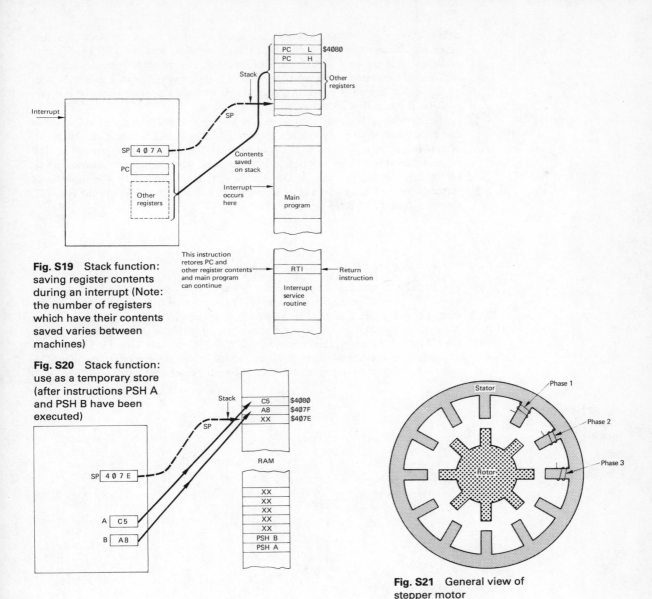

Fig. S19 Stack function: saving register contents during an interrupt (Note: the number of registers which have their contents saved varies between machines)

Fig. S20 Stack function: use as a temporary store (after instructions PSH A and PSH B have been executed)

Fig. S21 General view of stepper motor

Stepper Motor

Stepper motors are ideal for use in a microprocessor system for these motors use what is termed direct digital control for movement and position of the rotor (*fig. S21*). The general principle is that, when a group of pulses of the correct sequence is applied to the stator windings, the rotor will be advanced through a series of steps. The precise angle of each step depends on the design of the particular motor but is typically 1.8°, 2.5°, 3.75°, 7.5°, 15° or 30°. Stepper motors can be used with a digital system in very simple speed or position controllers under open loop conditions with a high degree of precision and accuracy. This follows because the number of pulses sent out by the digital controller can be easily counted.

There are three main versions of stepper motors. The **permanent magnet type** has a permanent magnet rotor with a large number of poles. The stator

217

construction is such that, when pulses are applied to the stator windings, the poles, which have the same number as the rotor poles, reverse. The rotor is then attracted to align itself so that each of its S-poles is mid-way between a pair of N-poles on the stator, and each rotor N-pole is mid-way between a pair of S-poles on the stator. Speed is controlled by the rate of pulses applied to the stator and position is controlled by a fixed number of pulses.

The **variable reluctance** stepper motor requires a multi-phase drive signal to cause the rotor to step. Typically a sequence of four pulses is required. The rotor, of soft iron, has a number of teeth unequal to the number of stator poles. The rotor is forced to change position as it aligns itself with the path of least magnetic reluctance. The step angle, set by the design, is controlled by the number of stator poles and rotor teeth. For example, if a motor has $S_P = 16$ and $R_T = 12$, then the number of steps per revolution is

$$N = \frac{S_P R_T}{S_P - R_T} = 48$$

$\therefore$ Step angle $= 360°/48 = 7.5°$

The variable reluctance stepper motor is capable of operation at high stepping rates. The general principle of its operation can be seen from *fig. S22* for a motor with 8 stator poles and 6 rotor teeth (step angle $= 15°$). When phase 1 of the stator is energised, two of the rotor teeth line up with the stator while the others are 15° out of alignment. Energising phase 2 causes the rotor step 15° to align two of the other teeth and so on. If the stator coils are energised sequentially 1–2–3–4, the rotor will move in 15° steps counter-clockwise.

Fig. S22 Four-phase variable-reluctance stepper motor

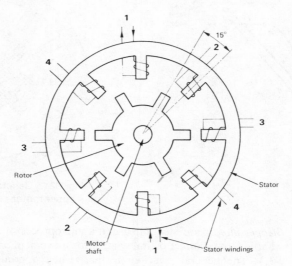

The third type is the **hybrid stepper** motor, which as its name implies combines construction features of both the PM and VR types.

Specialised ICs have been developed for stepper motor drive circuits, one example being the SAA 1027 shown in *fig. S23*. This IC, intended for driving four-phase stepper motors (such as the ID04), consists of a three-input stage, a logic circuit, and an output stage. Each output can supply up to 350 mA of drive and is provided with an internal protection diode.

● CONTROL SYSTEM ● INTERFACE CIRCUITS

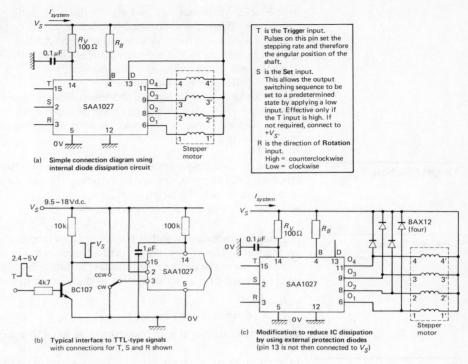

Fig. S23 Using the SAA 1027 to drive a four-phase stepper motor

T is the **Trigger** input.
Pulses on this pin set the stepping rate and therefore the angular position of the shaft.

S is the **Set** input.
This allows the output switching sequence to be set to a predetermined state by applying a low input. Effective only if the T input is high. If not required, connect to $+V_S$.

R is the direction of **Rotation** input.
High = counterclockwise
Low = clockwise

(a) Simple connection diagram using internal diode dissipation circuit

(b) Typical interface to TTL-type signals with connections for T, S and R shown

(c) Modification to reduce IC dissipation by using external protection diodes (pin 13 is not then connected to V_S)

STORE Instruction (ST)

A data transfer instruction that moves the contents of a selected register to memory. A variety of addressing modes are normally available for use with this instruction:

Direct (or Zero page)
Extended (or Absolute) and Indexed

Examples [6502 code]

STA $8Ø   Store Acc. at address $8Ø
               (*zero page addressing*)
STA $Ø25Ø   Store Acc. at address $Ø25Ø
               (*absolute addressing*)

● ADDRESSING MODE   ● INSTRUCTION   ● MOVE INSTRUCTION

Subroutine

This is a relatively small program segment which is likely to be used repeatedly by a main program or programs. The subroutine needs to be written only once and then can be called when required. Typical uses are in input/output routines, time delays, and arithmetic operations (finding the mean value or square root for example).

The advantages of using subroutines are:
1) Program writing is easier and less prone to error.
2) It gives a structure to programs.
3) The overall program is easier to debug.
4) The memory space required for the complete program is reduced.

One disadvantage is that the run-time of a program using subroutines will be longer than one without.

The stack provides an orderly method of calling and returning from a subroutine. When the subroutine is called, e.g.

JSR   AVER   Jump to subroutine called AVER

the return address to the main program is saved on the stack.

At the end of the subroutine the instruction:

RTS   Return from subroutine

causes the processor to retrieve the return address from the stack. This is loaded into the program counter and the main program can continue.

● CALL INSTRUCTION   ● NESTING   ● RETURN INSTRUCTION   ● STACK AND STACK POINTER

Target Machine

Suppose a 6809-based system is being used with cross-assembler software (or cross-compiler) to produce machine code to be run on a Z80-based system. The Z80 system is then the target machine.

● CROSS-ASSEMBLER   ● CROSS-COMPILER

Test and Branch

A group of instructions within the set for a microprocessor that carry out checks on the status flags (carry, sign, overflow, zero, etc., in the flag or status register) and then cause the program to branch if certain conditions are met. The branch is either forward or backward relative to the content of the program counter.

Example
BCS   Branch if carry bit set (C = 1)

● CONDITIONAL BRANCH INSTRUCTION   ● RELATIVE ADDRESSING MODE

Timer

In microprocessor systems there is often a need for accurate timing of events or to produce pulses at fixed time intervals to initiate controlling action. The microprocessor itself, since it is provided with a master clock circuit (crystal controlled normally), can be used with software to produce accurate time delays but in practice this has disadvantages. Valuable system memory space may be used up, programming time will be wasted, and the timing function may be upset by such things as Direct Memory Transfer or Interrupts.

An alternative method which does not tie up the processor is to use *hardware timing devices* (*fig. T1*). These can be:

1 Timers included in an interface adaptor. The 6522 VIA (Versatile Interface Adaptor), a support chip for the 6502, is an example. In addition to parallel and serial ports, the VIA has two 16-bit timers which can be programmed via the processor,

2 Special-purpose timer ICs, such as the 6840, a Programmable Timer Module (PTM) used with the 6800 processor family which has three 16-bit counter/times each of which can be independently programmed using software.

These chips can be connected into a system bus and can be memory mapped. In this way the counters inside the chip can be addressed individually via the processor. Usually the value to which the timer is set is held in a buffer register and therefore only needs to be programmed in once. Timing is set by a reference clock input which causes the counter to count down (decrement) on every clock pulse. At zero count an output signal is generated from the chip which indicates that the required interval is completed. This could be used to interrupt the processor so that it can carry out the necessary control action required at that time. The more timers available in the chip the greater the flexibility of the system.

Timers can also be used as "event counters" by operating the internal counters in a cyclic mode. The number held in the buffer store will be automatically reloaded into the counter when it reaches zero. Then either the number of events

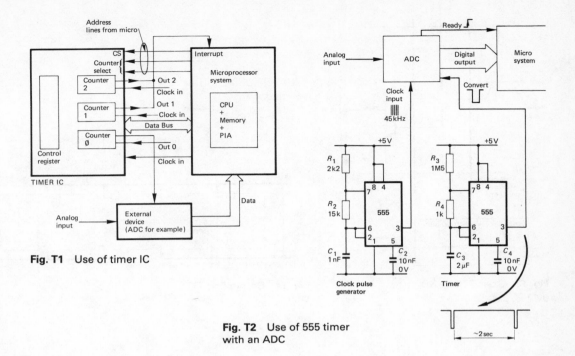

Fig. T1 Use of timer IC

Fig. T2 Use of 555 timer with an ADC

occurring during the time between interrupts can be counted (using software) or the count value reached by the counter itself can be read to determine the time between events.

Other systems may require an accurate Real Time Clock. This unit, usually battery powered or provided with a back-up supply, is an external chip that generates pulses at fixed times such as every second, minute, hour and so on. It will also usually give the date. These are used when it is essential to synchronise the computer or microprocessor control system to real time. Typical examples would be computers used for booking seats for airlines or theatres, or timing for a heating system.

Where external timing which is not highly accurate is required, simple chips such as 555 Timers can be used. *Fig. T2* illustrates the principle where an analog-to-digital convertor is given the convert command from a timer formed using a 555 chip. This chip is used to set the time between samples, set in this case to 2 sec, and the convert command pulse. A second 555 is used to generate the clock pulses to drive the ADC counter. At the end of the conversion time the ADC then signals to the processor that data is available.

● DELAY   ● INTERRUPT

| **Transistor Transistor Logic (TTL)** | A popular and widely used logic family. It combines fast speed with moderate levels of power consumption and reasonable levels of noise margin. The main types are: |

    Standard TTL 74 series
    Schottky TTL 74S
    Low Power Schottky TTL 74LS
    Advanced Low Power Schottky TTL 74ALS

One of the basic circuits is the NAND gate (*fig. T3*) and this will be used to describe the TTL operation.

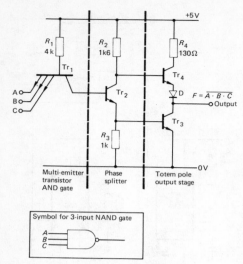

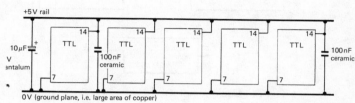

Fig. T3 Basic TTL NAND gate

Fig. T4 Decoupling TTL chips

The inputs are to a multi-emitter transistor Tr_1 which gives the AND function. Tr_2 is a phase splitter and Tr_3 and Tr_4 form an output stage (given the appropriate name of *totem pole*) which has a low output resistance in both logic states.

If all inputs are high, then Tr_1 passes current from its collector to turn on Tr_2. With Tr_2 on, Tr_3 is forced to conduct while Tr_4 is held off. The output is therefore low at logic $\emptyset$.

If any input is taken low, that particular base/emitter junction conducts, diverting current away from Tr_2. Both Tr_2 and Tr_3 turn off, while Tr_4 then conducts taking the output high to logic 1.

The action can be summarised as:

all inputs high (1)   resulting output low ($\emptyset$)
any input(s) low ($\emptyset$)   resulting output high (1)

The design for the circuit inside the IC gives TTL (standard type) the following typical performance figures:

Power consumption   10 mW
Noise margin   1 V
Propagation delay   10 nsec
Fan-out   10

The power supply to TTL should be a reasonably well regulated +5 V with an absolute maximum of 7 V. Any fault in the power supply which puts more than 7 V across a TTL IC will cause damage to the IC. For this reason, TTL power supplies are usually fitted with an overvoltage protection circuit.

As a TTL gate switches there is a brief instant when both output transistors (Tr_3 and Tr_4) conduct, causing a pulse of current to be drawn from the supply. "Spikes" on the supply rail can then be generated and may cause false triggering of other gates. However the problem can be easily overcome by decoupling the +5 V rail to 0 V using a 100 nF ceramic capacitor. In a TTL system several such decoupling capacitors will be wired in across the supply leads at suitable points, usually one capacitor for every four "gate" type TTL ICs (see *fig. T4*).

● CMOS   ● DIGITAL CIRCUIT   ● ECL   ● SCHOTTKY TTL

Tri-State

This is a description used for logic gates which have outputs that can be connected to a common signal line along with the outputs of other similar gates. With most logic (TTL and CMOS), connecting gate outputs together, apart from not producing the required logic result, would probably damage the ICs. When one output was low while others were high, the low would override the other states and an overload current would be passed. If TTL gates are used which are "open-collector" (i.e. no top transistor in the totem pole output stage), then several such gate outputs can be connected together with a common pull-up resistor to give what is called the wired-or facility. But this will restrict the maximum switching speed of the system. **Tri-state logic** overcomes the problem by having *three* possible output conditions:

a) Low state = Logic Ø
b) High state = Logic 1

Fig. T5 Tri-state buffer

c) A high impedance state which effectively open-circuits the output.

Input	Chip select	Output
0	0	High-Z
0	1	Ø
1	0	High-Z
1	1	1

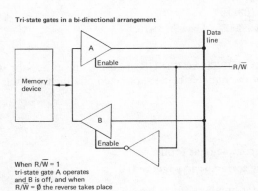

Input — Output
Enable (chip select)

Tri-state gates in a bi-directional arrangement

Memory device

A
Enable

B
Enable

Data line

R/W̄

When R/W̄ = 1 tri-state gate A operates and B is off, and when R/W̄ = Ø the reverse takes place

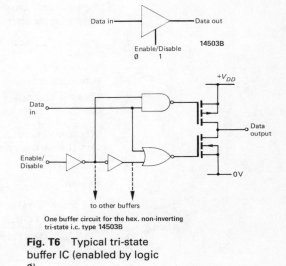

Data in — Data out
14503B
Enable/Disable Ø 1

Data in
Enable/Disable
to other buffers
+V_DD
Data output
0V

One buffer circuit for the hex. non-inverting tri-state i.c. type 14503B

Fig. T6 Typical tri-state buffer IC (enabled by logic Ø)

A tri-state gate has to have an extra input (see *fig. T5*) called the control or enable. This either allows the gate to operate normally to give a logic state output (Ø or 1) or causes the gate output to go into the high impedance state. Several tri-state gates can therefore be used to drive a common line with only one tri-state gate being on at any one time. Gates like these are used extensively in micro systems for bidirectional buses. (*See fig. T6.*)

● BUS ● BUS CONFLICT

Twos Complement

The twos complement form for representing binary numbers is often used in microprocessor arithmetic operations and for expressing offsets used in branch instructions. It is a means of representing signed binary numbers and is used because it automatically produces the correct sign and result for an arithmetic operation.

In twos complement form, as in ordinary signed binary, the MSB is used to indicate the sign (Ø for positive and 1 for negative) and the rest of the bits are used to give the magnitude.

223

Thus (for 8-bit numbers)

$00011010 = +26_{10}$

and $11100110 = -26_{10}$

To obtain the twos complement form for a negative number the rules are:
1. Write down the positive binary equivalent of the number and invert all bits (this gives the ones complement).
2. Add 1 to the LSB of the result of 1. This will give the twos complement form.

Example -12_{10} can be converted as follows:

1. $+12_{10} = 00001100_2$

Invert all bits 11110011

2.   Add 1 1

Twos complement 11110100 Result = -12_{10}

The twos complement form is used in arithmetic since it gives the true additive inverse of a number; this cannot be achieved using the ones complement.

Example $+26 - 26 = 0 = +26 + (-26)$

Using twos $+26$ $00011010 +$
complement -26 11100110
Carry is ignored ⟵―――― 00000000 Answer correct

When an instruction such as SUBTRACT (SUB) is used, the processor will obtain the twos complement of the number being subtracted and then add this to the other number.

Example $26_{10} - 12_{10}$

$+26_{10} = 00011010$ Add
$-12_{10} = 11110100$ (Twos complement form)
$+14_{10}$ 00001110 Answer correct (carry ignored)

The range of twos complement numbers (for 8 bits) is:

For *negative numbers*

from $-1_{10} = 11111111_2 = FF_{16}$
to $-128_{10} = 10000000_2 = 80_{16}$

For *positive numbers*

from $+0_{10} = 00000000_2 = 00_{16}$
to $+127_{10} = 01111111_2 = 7F_{16}$

The twos complement form is used in branch instructions to give the offset required. Suppose a branch-back of 60 places (from the offset position) is required. The offset is given in twos complement form. Therefore

$+60 = 00111100_2$
$-60 = 11000100_2$ in twos complement form
$\quad = C4_{16}$

The branch instruction would be written [6502] as:

MNEMONIC   MACHINE CODE

BMI   LABEL   3Ø   C4

                      code   offset

                      for

                      BMI

● BINARY AND BINARY CODED DECIMAL   ● BRANCH INSTRUCTION
● OFFSET   ● SIGN BIT

UART

Abbreviation for ● UNIVERSAL ASYNCHRONOUS RECEIVER/TRANSMITTER.

Uncommitted Logic Array (ULA)

This is a type of integrated circuit used for custom designed microelectronic chips. In its basic form it consists of arrays of unconnected logic gates, resistors, transistors and interface functions. The ULA slices are processed without any interconnections between the various gates and devices and the final metal connection pattern, to create a working microchip, is made to the customer's specification. This could be for a special interface/interrupt controller or complex address decoder for use in microprocessor systems, or perhaps a specialised A-to-D convertor. The aluminium connection pattern, which is just one mask process step, is the only part of the ULA which is unique to a particular application. The method gives an excellent cost effective solution for medium to

Fig. U1 Basic ULA cell

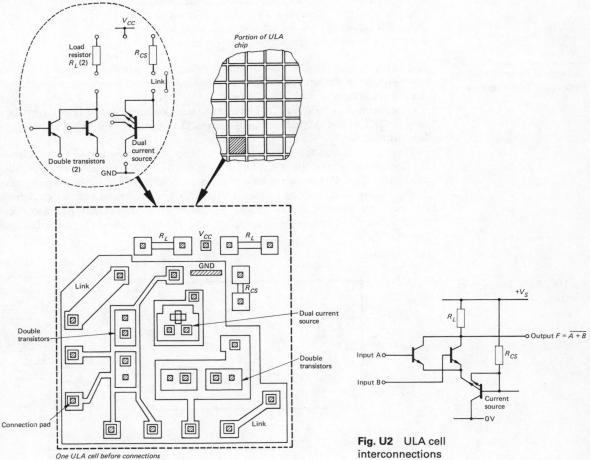

One ULA cell before connections

Fig. U2 ULA cell interconnections

Output $F = \overline{A + B}$

225

complex circuits and allows a mix of linear and digital functions on the same chip.

ULA designs typically use a non-saturating current switching logic, or current mode logic (CML) which gives a good speed-power product. A basic cell (*fig. U1*) consists of dual two-input NOR gates (*fig. U2* gives the interconnections required). This NOR element of 2 inputs can be extended to give more inputs by common connection of transistor collectors, and the gates created can then be used to give bistables (six cells for a D type), shift registers, counters and so on. A wide range of resistor values is usually included, and the array of gates is often supplemented with special-function interface elements. These allow the chip to accept input data from mechanical switches or from other logic, and also to provide output signals to drive logic, relays, LEDs, and triac.

By using certain ULAs it is possible to achieve total system integration (all functions inside one chip). These ULAs include linear and digital gate functions which can be connected internally to give oscillators, reference sources and linear amplifiers in addition to the required logic.

(*ULA is a Ferranti tradename and uses bipolar technology.*)
- PROGRAMMABLE LOGIC ARRAY

Unconditional Branch/Jump

A branch or jump instruction that will be executed by the microprocessor irrespective of any flag conditions. Such instructions are useful in terminating programs, e.g.

| JMP | MON | Jump to the address of the monitor |
| BRA | OUT | Branch always to the address of OUT |

Extended (absolute) and/or relative addressing modes are used.
- BRANCH INSTRUCTION - CONDITIONAL BRANCH

Universal Asynchronous Receiver/Transmitter

A UART is the standard serial interface adaptor used as a support chip in microprocessor systems for the task of interfacing devices which receive and send data in serial format (one bit at a time).

Other names include: ACIA (Asynchronous Communications Interface Adaptor); DART (Dual Asynchronous Receiver/Transmitter); and SIA (Serial Interface Adaptor).

These devices are programmable by software and are provided with facilities for handshake, parity checking, and format control of the serial word. Basically, the UART (*fig. U3*), which is either assigned an address within the memory map of the system or is located in the isolated I/O area, converts parallel data from the microprocessor to serial for the peripheral (transmit output). It also takes serial data in and converts this to parallel for use by the microprocessor (receive input).

Fig. U3 Basic principle of UART

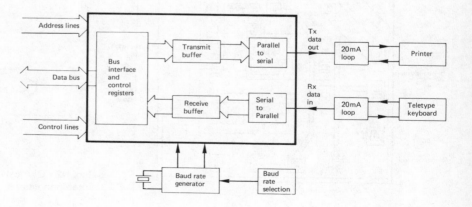

Asynchronous transmission of data is used for relatively low-speed links (up to 9600 baud) and is a system that deals with each character separately. The bits are sent at a fixed rate but character rate can vary. Between characters the signal line is kept high. The start of a character is indicated by the "start" pulse (the signal line going low); next the bits for the word are sent with the LSB first (7 bits for ASCII); following this, the parity bit (if required) is sent; and last of all, one or more stop bits (high). Synchronisation between the transmitter and receiver is achieved by the start pulse (low for one-bit period). For high-speed transmission of blocks of data, this asynchronous mode is inefficient simply because of the extra start and stop bits necessary.

Synchronous transmission using a USART (Universal Synchronous or Asynchronous Receiver/Transmitter), which does not require these extra start and stop bits, is achieved by a synch. character sent at the start of a block of data. The characters are sent in a continuous stream and the end of the block transmission is indicated by a stop signal.

A good example of a commonly used UART chip is the 6402 (and the 6402–1). This CMOS device can be linked in with most microprocessors and can be programmed to give:

Word length   5 to 8 bits
Stop bits   1, $1\frac{1}{2}$ or 2 bits
Parity   none, odd or even

An external baud rate (clock) generator is required (d.c. to 1 MHz for the 6402) which gives a maximum baud rate of 62.5 K baud. The pinout with definition of pins is shown in *fig. U4* together with the block diagram. In a microprocessor or system, the data inputs TBR1 to TBR8 would be paralleled up with RBR1 to RBR8 and connected to the data bus.

Fig. U4*a*   Pinout for the 6402 UART

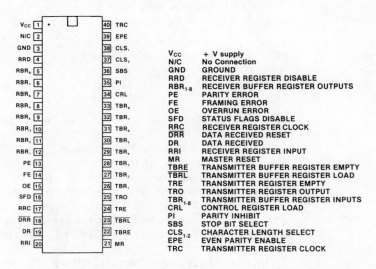

Using the CRL (control register load) input, taken high to load, the character length selection can be made using CLS1 and CLS2.

CLS2	CLS1	RESULTING CHARACTER LENGTH
Ø	Ø	5 bits
Ø	1	6 bits
1	Ø	7 bits
1	1	8 bits

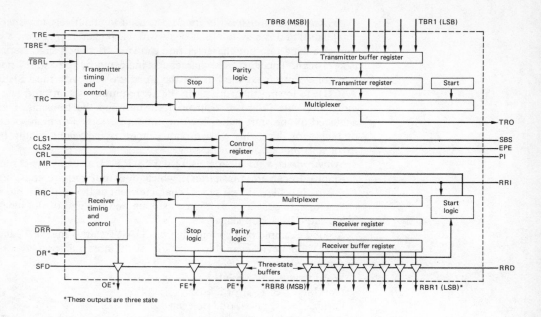

TBR8 (MSB)   TBR1 (LSB)

*These outputs are three state

Fig. U4b Block diagram of
the 6402

Parity can be set using the following:

P1   High level inhibits parity generation
EPE   High level = even parity ⎱ P1 low
          Low level = odd parity ⎰

Stop bit selection is made using SBS but the number of bits used also depends upon the length of the character previously selected:

SBS	CHARACTER LENGTH (bits) 5	6, 7 or 8	
Ø	1	1 ⎫ Stop bits
1	1½	2 ⎭ selected

Transmit Operation Data is loaded from the bus into the transmit buffer by a logic Ø on TBRL. When TBRL returns high, TBRE goes low indicating that the transmit buffer is not empty. If the transmit register TR is also empty (TRE status high), the data with the added start, parity and stop bits, as previously selected during initialisation, is then sent out at a rate set by the generator.

Receiver Operation The serial data from a peripheral is clocked into the receive register (RR). When no data is being received, this line must be left high. A low level on the DRR clears the DR line and then, during the first stop bit, the data is transferred to the receive buffer (RBR). This can then be taken by the microprocessor.

The state of the status flags FE, OE and PE can be interrogated using the status flags disable input (SFD).

FE   going high indicates a framing error
      i.e. the first stop bit is invalid
OE   going high indicates an overrun error
PE   going high indicates a parity error.

A simple LED indicator can be used for error indication.

● ASYNCHRONOUS COMMUNICATIONS INTERFACE ADAPTOR (ACIA) ● SERIAL DATA FORMAT ● UNIVERSAL SYNCHRONOUS/ASYNCHRONOUS RECEIVER/ TRANSMITTER (USART)

Universal Synchronous/ Asynchronous Receiver/ Transmitter (USART)

A serial interface adaptor that can be programmed to act in either asynchronous or synchronous mode.

The *asynchronous mode* gives operation as described in the section on UARTs.

Synchronous operation in serial links allows a continuous stream of data to be transmitted and received without the need for start and stop bits to define each character. Three bits in every 11 bits are saved per character when this mode is compared to asynchronous operation, and in this way more rapid data transfer is possible. Blocks of data can be transmitted/received with only one or two extra synch. bytes required to define the block. When power is first applied, the USARTS (TX and RX) will be initialised and synch. characters will be sent. The receiver searches for a match to the synch. character with which it has been programmed and, as soon as the transmitter and receiver are synchronised, data can be transferred. Control lines will indicate this state.

Fig. U5*a* Pin definitions for the 8251 USART

Pin Name	Pin Function
D7-DØ	Data bus (8 bits)
C/D̄	Control or data is to be written or read
R̄D̄	Read data command
W̄R̄	Write data or control command
C̄S̄	Chip select
CLK	Clock pulse (TTL)
RESET	Reset
T̄x̄C̄	Transmitter clock
TxD	Transmitter data
R̄x̄C̄	Receiver clock
RxD	Receiver data
RxRDY	Receiver ready (has character for CPU)
TxRDY	Transmitter ready (ready for char. from CPU)
D̄S̄R̄	Data set ready
D̄T̄R̄	Data terminal ready
SYNDET/BD	Sync. detect/break detect
R̄T̄S̄	Request to send data
C̄T̄S̄	Clear to send data
TxEMPTY	Transmitter empty
V_{CC}	+5V supply
GND	Ground

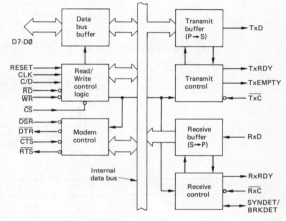

Fig. U5*b* Block diagram of the 8251

The Intel 8251A USART is taken as an example (see *fig. U5*). This chip can be memory mapped using its chip select input ($\overline{CS}$ active low), and a register select input (C/D̄) gives access to the internal registers. C/D̄, connected to the AØ address line of the system, selects either the control/status registers or the transmit/receive data registers. The $\overline{RD}$ and $\overline{WR}$ input signals are used in register selection as follows:

C/D̄	W̄R̄	R̄D̄	Register selected in USART
Ø	Ø	1	Transmit data buffer
Ø	1	Ø	Receive data buffer
1	Ø	1	Control register
1	1	Ø	Status byte register

Initialising is carried out by writing two control words into the control register. The first is called the MODE word (see format in *fig. U6*).

Bits Ø and 1, both low, specify that the USART is to be set up for synchronous operation.

For asynchronous mode, bits 2 to 7 specify character length, parity and the number of stop bits.

Fig. U6 Formats of 8251 words

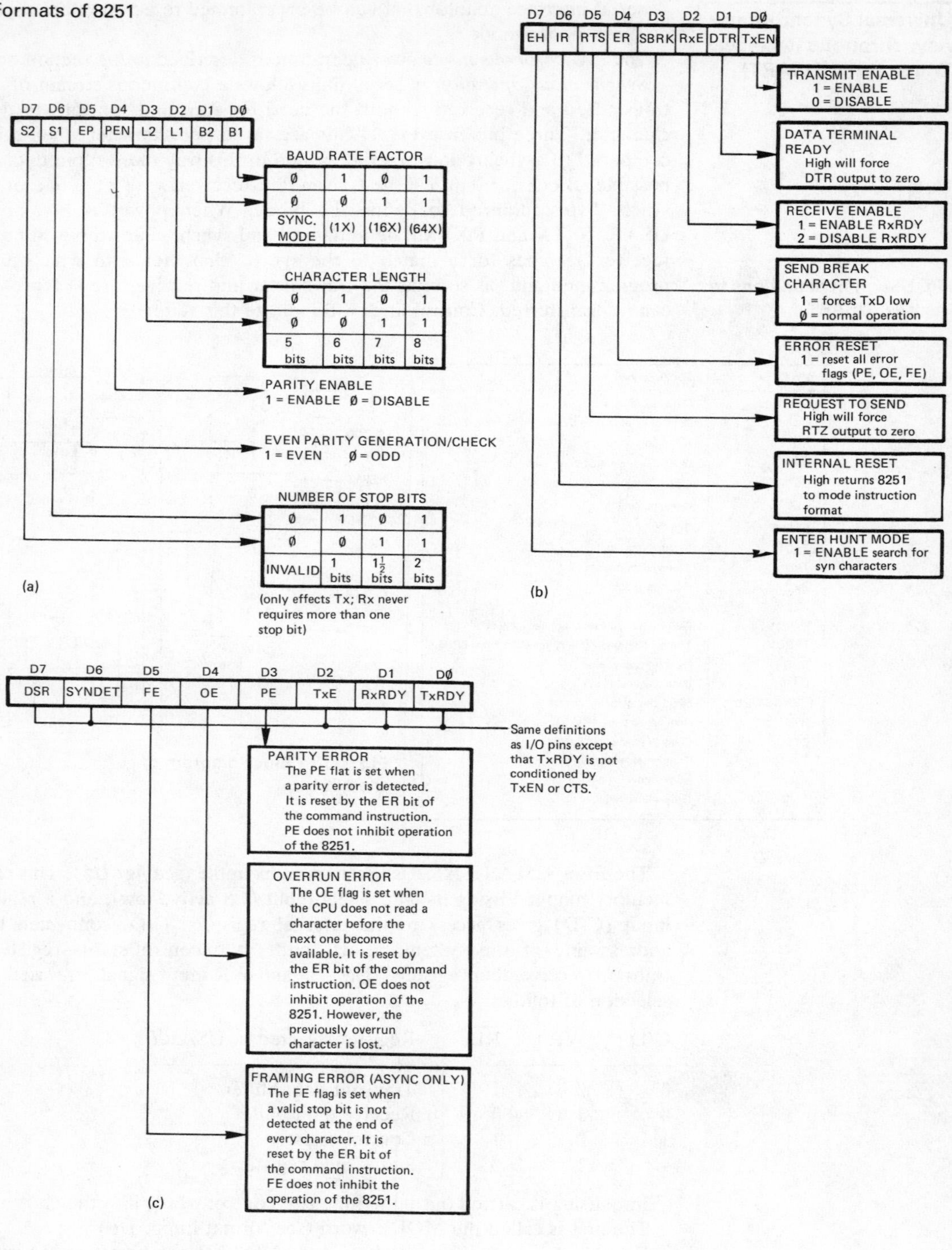

(a)

D7 D6 D5 D4 D3 D2 D1 D0

| S2 | S1 | EP | PEN | L2 | L1 | B2 | B1 |

BAUD RATE FACTOR

Ø	1	Ø	1
Ø	Ø	1	1
SYNC. MODE	(1X)	(16X)	(64X)

CHARACTER LENGTH

Ø	1	Ø	1
Ø	Ø	1	1
5 bits	6 bits	7 bits	8 bits

PARITY ENABLE
1 = ENABLE Ø = DISABLE

EVEN PARITY GENERATION/CHECK
1 = EVEN Ø = ODD

NUMBER OF STOP BITS

Ø	1	Ø	1
Ø	Ø	1	1
INVALID	1 bits	1½ bits	2 bits

(only effects Tx; Rx never requires more than one stop bit)

(b)

D7 D6 D5 D4 D3 D2 D1 D0

| EH | IR | RTS | ER | SBRK | RxE | DTR | TxEN |

TRANSMIT ENABLE
1 = ENABLE
0 = DISABLE

DATA TERMINAL READY
High will force DTR output to zero

RECEIVE ENABLE
1 = ENABLE RxRDY
2 = DISABLE RxRDY

SEND BREAK CHARACTER
1 = forces TxD low
Ø = normal operation

ERROR RESET
1 = reset all error flags (PE, OE, FE)

REQUEST TO SEND
High will force RTZ output to zero

INTERNAL RESET
High returns 8251 to mode instruction format

ENTER HUNT MODE
1 = ENABLE search for syn characters

(c)

D7 D6 D5 D4 D3 D2 D1 D0

| DSR | SYNDET | FE | OE | PE | TxE | RxRDY | TxRDY |

Same definitions as I/O pins except that TxRDY is not conditioned by TxEN or CTS.

PARITY ERROR
The PE flat is set when a parity error is detected. It is reset by the ER bit of the command instruction. PE does not inhibit operation of the 8251.

OVERRUN ERROR
The OE flag is set when the CPU does not read a character before the next one becomes available. It is reset by the ER bit of the command instruction. OE does not inhibit operation of the 8251. However, the previously overrun character is lost.

FRAMING ERROR (ASYNC ONLY)
The FE flag is set when a valid stop bit is not detected at the end of every character. It is reset by the ER bit of the command instruction. FE does not inhibit the operation of the 8251.

230

For synchronous mode, bits 2 to 5 specify character length and parity and bits 6 and 7 set up synch. operation.

For example, suppose $9C is loaded as the mode word. This gives:

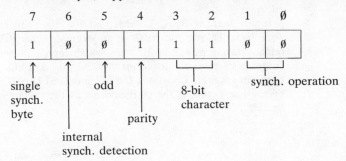

Following the mode byte, one or two synch. bytes are set up within the USART. These synch. bytes are sent at the start of transmission of a block of data and also when no data is being sent. The receiver USART removes these synch. characters before the data is taken by the peripheral or microprocessor.

Since the USART is memory mapped, the data buffers can be read from or written to, via a register in the microprocessor, when the USART status register indicates that the buffers are available.

● ASYNCHRONOUS COMMUNICATIONS INTERFACE ADAPTOR ● UNIVERSAL ASYNCHRONOUS RECEIVER/TRANSMITTER

Unpack

A term used to describe the process of separating out the upper 4 bits and the lower 4 bits of a packed BCD word. Suppose the accumulator holds the packed BCD word 93:

$93_{10} =$

| 1 | 0 | 0 | 1 | 0 | 0 | 1 | 1 | BCD |

The upper 4 bits can be masked off using the AND instruction, i.e.

AND A #$0F
Result in Acc

| 0 | 0 | 0 | 0 | 0 | 0 | 1 | 1 |

and the lower 4 bits (the unpacked BCD) stored at a memory location, i.e.

STA A $1000

The upper 4 bits (assumed to be reloaded) can be unpacked by shifting the contents of the accumulator 4 places right.

● BINARY AND BINARY CODED DECIMAL

Unsigned Binary

The most basic and most common form of number representation for microprocessors. All numbers are positive and the binary word is simply the binary weighted equivalent of the decimal value.

The weightings for an 8-bit word (one byte) are:

$$2^7 \quad 2^6 \quad 2^5 \quad 2^4 \quad 2^3 \quad 2^2 \quad 2^1 \quad 2^0$$

MSB   LSB

Thus:

$$33_{10} = 00100001 = 21_{16}$$

● BINARY NUMBERS ● TWOS COMPLEMENT

Vectors are necessary in microprocessors to give start addresses for particular routines, for example an interrupt service routine or restart routine. The vector acts as an address pointer, with the address given being called the *vectored address*.

Inputs such as $\overline{\text{RESET}}$, $\overline{\text{NMI}}$ and $\overline{\text{IRQ}}$ to a microprocessor require vectored addresses. Taking the 6502 as an example, the $\overline{\text{RESET}}$ line when pulled low (either during power up or by a switch input) causes the processor to fetch the contents of memory locations $FFFC and $FFFD and to load them into the program counter. Locations $FFFC and $FFFD contain the vectored address (set by the user), that is the start address of the restart routine for the system. (See *fig. V1*.)

Fig. V1 Use of the RESET vector in the 6502

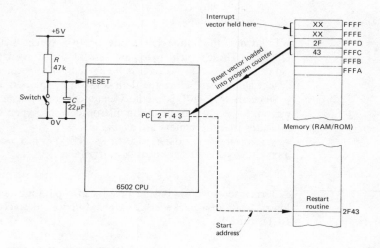

Fig. V2 Mode 2 interrupt to the Z80 showing how the interrupt vector is generated

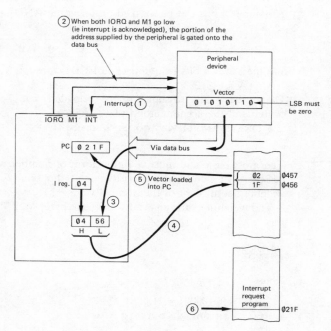

Both 6800 and 6502 processors fetch the interrupt service routine vectored address from a high memory location ($FFF8 and $FFF9 for the 6800; $FFFE and $FFFF for the 6502), whereas processors such as the Z80 can obtain the vectored address for an interrupt (INT) from both the peripheral causing the interrupt and an internal register. The peripheral places an 8-bit address on the data bus and this is used by the Z80 as the low-order byte for an address containing the interrupt vector. The high-order byte for this address is held in the interrupt page register (I register). (See *fig. V2*.)

● INTERRUPT ● MICROPROCESSOR ● RESET/RESTART

Virtual Address and Virtual Memory

A *virtual memory* is provided in certain operating systems of relatively large computers and allows the programmer to specify addresses for a program without regard to the actual physical locations of the memory. The machine translates *virtual addresses*, those used by the programmer, into absolute addresses using backing stores if required to give extra memory space.

● ABSOLUTE ADDRESS

Volatile

This refers to any memory that loses its stored data when the d.c. power or refresh clock source is removed. Read/Write memory (RAM) is volatile and, if retention of data or program is essential in the event of power failure, some form of back-up power source must be provided. *Fig. V3* illustrates one simple method of providing battery back-up for a RAM (CMOS type). When the d.c. power is applied, D_1 is forward biased and D_2 reverse biased with the battery isolated. If the power supply fails, D_2 becomes forward biased and D_1 reverse biased. The battery then supplies power to the CMOS RAM preventing loss of data until the normal power supply is reconnected.

● MEMORIES

Fig. V3 Battery back-up for RAM

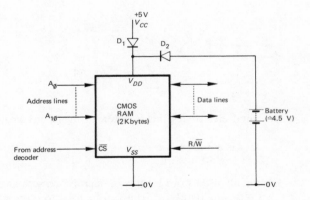

V-Flag

Another name for the overflow flag, a flag provided in a microprocessor that indicates when a carry or borrow into the MSB of a result occurs. For 8-bit machines this is a carry or borrow into bit 7. This flag is used in checking twos complement results and can be used for sign correction. It goes high when a twos complement result is out of range under the following conditions:

a) When two large positive numbers are added.
b) When two large negative numbers are added.
c) When a large negative number is subtracted from a large positive number.
d) When a large positive number is subtracted from a large negative number.

In twos complement notation, the MSB gives the sign of the number (∅ for positive, 1 for negative) and bits ∅ to 6 are used for the magnitude. This restricts any result to a maximum of:

$$+127_{10} = 01111111_2 \quad (7F_{16})$$
$$\text{and} \quad -128_{10} = 10000000_2 \quad (80_{16})$$

Suppose the twos complement numbers +97 and +42 are to be added together.

$$+97_{10} = 01100001_2 \, +$$
$$+42_{10} = 00101010_2$$
$$\underline{+139_{10}} \quad \underline{10001011} \quad \text{Result incorrect}$$

carry into V-flag

V $\boxed{1}$

Here the result contains a carry from bit 6 to 7 making the result incorrect both in magnitude and sign. The V-flag goes high and can be tested to check for incorrect result.

● OVERFLOW ● TWOS COMPLEMENT

Wired Logic

This refers to the use of gates with open collector or open drain outputs that have their outputs hardwired together to produce some required logic function. Typically in microprocessor applications, hardwired logical-OR is required for the interrupt request input. Each peripheral device has an open drain output and these can be connected all together with one external common pull-up resistor. Any one peripheral taking the line low ($\overline{\text{IRQ}}$) then causes an interrupt.

Fig. W1 shows how two open collector TTL gates can be used to give the hardwired exclusive-OR function.

● OPEN COLLECTOR ● INTERRUPT

Fig. W1 Wired logic using open collector NAND gates to give the exclusive-OR function

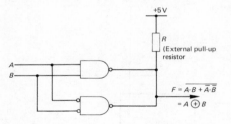

$$F = \overline{A \cdot B} + \overline{\overline{A} \cdot B}$$
$$= A \oplus B$$

Word

In digital electronics this is taken to mean any grouping of binary digits (*bits*). Thus:

$\quad$ 011 is a 3-bit word
10111 is a 5-bit word

Commonly used word lengths in microprocessors are:

8 bits (one byte)	This can be used to represent decimal numbers from 0 to 255.
16 bits (two bytes)	This can be used to represent decimal numbers from 0 to 65 535

In microprocessor systems a word may be an instruction, an address or data.

● BINARY AND BINARY CODED DECIMAL ● SIGN BIT

Zero Crossing Detector

An electronic circuit used in a.c. power control that produces a short duration pulse or edge every time an a.c. input signal passes through zero. This pulse or edge can be used to trigger a power device such as a triac which then switches mains power to a load with the minimum generated interference. The simplest arrangement shown in *fig. Z1* is an op-amp with one input (−) tied to zero volts as a reference and the other (+) connected to the a.c. signal. Note that a limiting resistor and diodes may be necessary if the amplitude of the a.c. signal exceeds a

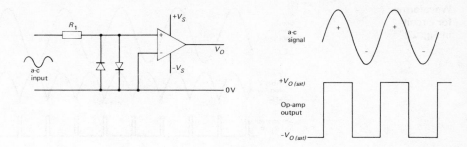

few volts. As the a.c. passes through zero going positive, the op-amp output switches high to positive saturation and remains at this value until the a.c. signal passes through zero going negative. At this point the op-amp output switches low to negative saturation. A square wave is therefore produced at the op-amp output with the edges timed to occur at the a.c. zero crossing points. An op-amp with fast slew rate is necessary to reduce timing errors to a minimum.

The second circuit (*fig. Z2*) shows how the output from a microprocessor system port can be synchronised to zero crossing signals derived from the a.c. mains. A step-down transformer with 6.3 V a.c. output has its secondary voltage rectified by the bridge circuit (D_1 to D_4) and the approximate 9 V amplitude rectified signal is applied to a transistor switch (Tr_1). Tr_1 switches out of conduction for the brief period when the a.c. signal is crossing zero, producing a positive pulse to one input of the NAND gate. If the micro port is high (output = 1), the LED in the opto-isolator conducts, which then causes the main triac to fire and apply power to the load. The triac will only switch on and off when the mains voltage is near zero volts and in this way radiated interference is reduced to a low value.

This type of circuit can be used in *burst cycle* control for controlling power to a.c. loads such as heaters, and for on/off switching of lamps and motors.

As shown in the diagram several outputs from the port can be synchronised with the same zero crossing signals to allow switching and control of many a.c. power devices.

● CONTROL SYSTEM ● POWER CONTROL

Fig. Z2 Use of zero crossing detector to switch a.c. power

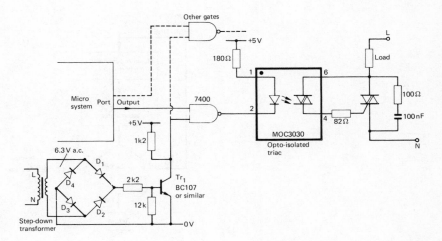

Waveforms for circuit in Fig. Z2

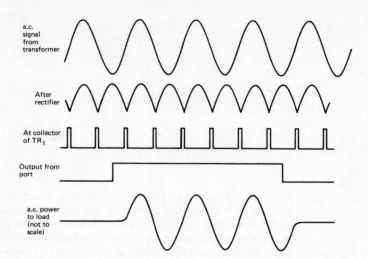

a.c. signal from transformer

After rectifier

At collector of TR₁

Output from port

a.c. power to load (not to scale)

Fig. Z3 Use of zero flag

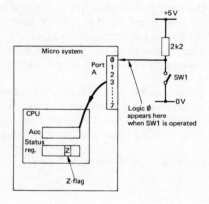

Micro system

Port A

0
1
2
3
...
7

+5V

2k2

SW1

0V

Logic Ø appears here when SW1 is operated

CPU

Acc

Status reg.

Z

Z-flag

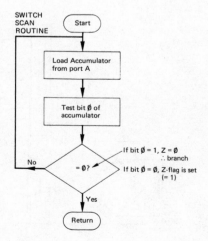

SWITCH SCAN ROUTINE

Start

Load Accumulator from port A

Test bit Ø of accumulator

= Ø?

No

Yes

If bit Ø = 1, Z = Ø ∴ branch

If bit Ø = Ø, Z-flag is set (= 1)

Return

Zero Flag (Z)

A status flag in a microprocessor which is used to indicate when the result of an operation is zero. Typical instructions that set or clear the Z-flag include:

COMPARE   AND   OR   BIT   SUBTRACT

Following the execution of one of these instructions, the state of the Z-flag can be tested using a conditional branch as shown in the next program segment (*fig. Z3*).

```
LOOP   LDA A   PORT    Get switch input
       BIT A   #$01    Test LSB
       BNE     LOOP    Branch if not zero
       RTS
```

If the result of the bit test is zero (LSB = Ø), then the Z-flag will be set and the branch not taken. This only occurs when the switch has been operated.

● BRANCH INSTRUCTION   ● FLAG AND FLAG REGISTER

Zero Page and Zero Page Addressing

In a microcomputer or microprocessor system, the addresses from $ØØØØ to $ØØFF inclusive, which are located at the base of the memory, are said to be on *zero page*.

Since any location on zero page can be specified without the need to write the leading zeros contained in the high byte, instructions to write or read from this page need only be two bytes long. This saves program space.

Examples [6502]

STA $8Ø   Store Accumulator at address $ØØ8Ø
LDA $ØA   Load Accumulator from address $ØØØA

In the 6502 this mode of addressing is called zero page.

● ADDRESSING   ● DIRECT ADDRESSING   ● MEMORY MAP   ● PAGE

Assembly Language Programs

The next few pages contain some basic and short program examples. These are intended both as an introduction to assembly language and programming and as an aid for further understanding of microprocessor operation. A different instruction or addressing mode is illustrated with each example.

All the programs are written in 6809 mnemonics and have been developed on a Concept 09 system using the Flex disc editor/assembler. Each program finishes with an instruction that returns control to the assembler (JMP WARMS) but a return from subroutine (RTS), software interrupt (SWI) or jump to monitor (JMP MON) could also be used. Once the structure and technique have been appreciated, the programs can be rewritten for other processors such as the Z80, 6502 or 8085.

Program 1
Exchanging the data in two memory locations.
This program illustrates the use of the accumulators and simple transfer instructions.

```
 2                       ******************************************
 3                       *Program that exchanges the contents of
 4                       *  two memory locations.
 5                       ******************************************
 6                       * EQUATES
 7              0080      MEM1     EQU      $0080
 8              4000      MEM2     EQU      $4000
 9              CD03      WARMS    EQU      $CD03
10                       *
11                       *
12                       *PROGRAM
13      0100                      ORG      $0100
14      0100 96      80   START   LDA      MEM1       get first value
15      0102 F6      4000         LDB      MEM2       get second value
16      0105 B7      4000         STA      MEM2       exchange
17      0108 D7      80           STB      MEM1
18      010A 7E      CD03         JMP      WARMS      return to flex
19      010D                END

 0 ERROR(S) DETECTED
```

Program 2
Finding the sign of a number.

An introduction to conditional branch instructions. Note that a negative number will have the MSB set to 1 (numbers from $FF to $8Ø) and that the N flag will be set if the number loaded into an accumulator is negative.

```
 2                         ******************************************
 3                         * Program to determine the sign of a
 4                         * hex number.The number to be tested
 5                         * is held at address $1000.If the
 6                         * number is +ve address $1001 is cleared,
 7                         * if it is -ve address $1001 is loaded
 8                         * with $FF.
 9                         ******************************************
10                         *
11                         *      EQUATES
12             1001        FLAG    EQU     $1001
13             1000        LOC     EQU     $1000
14             CDØ3        WARMS   EQU     $CDØ3
15                         *
16                         *
17                         *      PROGRAM
18   0200                         ORG     $0200
19   0200 7F   1001        START   CLR     FLAG       clear flag address
20   0203 B6   1000                LDA     LOC        get hex number
21   0206 2B   Ø3                  BMI     NEG        is it -ve?
22   0208 7C   1001                INC     FLAG       add 1 to flag address
23   020B 7A   1001        NEG     DEC     FLAG       take 1 from flag address
24   020E 7E   CDØ3                JMP     WARMS      return to flex
25                                 END
```

Ø ERROR(S) DETECTED

Program 3
Searching a block of data for a particular character.
This shows the use of an index register as a pointer and the indexed mode of addressing.

```
 2                              ****************************************
 3                              * Program that searches a block of memory
 4                              * from $1000 to $10FF for the character Y.
 5                              * The address at which Y is found is stored
 6                              * at $1100 and $1101.If Y is not found both
 7                              * $1100 and $1101 are cleared.
 8                              ****************************************
 9                              *
10                              *
11                              *     EQUATES
12                  CD03        WARMS  EQU    $CD03
13                              *
14                              *
15                              *     PROGRAM
16    0300                             ORG    $0300
17    0300 7F   1100            START  CLR    $1100
18    0303 7F   1101                   CLR    $1101        clear result addresses
19    0306 8E   1000                   LDX    #$1000       set pointer to block
20    0309 A6   84              SEARCH LDA    0,X          get data byte
21    030B 81   59                     CMPA   #'Y          is it Y?
22    030D 27   09                     BEQ    HOLD
23    030F 30   01                     LEAX   +1,X         increment pointer
24    0311 8C   1100                   CPX    #$1100       end of block?
25    0314 26   F3                     BNE    SEARCH
26    0316 20   03                     BRA    OUT
27    0318 BF   1100            HOLD   STX    $1100        store address
28    031B 7E   CD03            OUT    JMP    WARMS        return to flex
29    031E                             END
```

Ø ERROR(S) DETECTED

Program 4

Conversion of a hexadecimal number into its equivalent ASCII.

An introduction to code conversion techniques, showing the use of the logical shift instruction and masking using logical AND. Also illustrating the use of a subroutine which in this case converts the lower few bits held in accumulator A into the ASCII value. A useful routine when it is required to output hex values to the screen.

```
  2                          ********************************************
  3                          * Program to convert a hex number at
  4                          * address $0600 into its ASCII equivalent
  5                          * The ASCII equivalent of the upper 4 bits
  6                          * will be stored in $0601 and the lower
  7                          * 4 bits in $0602.
  8                          ********************************************
  9                          *
 10                          *
 11                          *     EQUATES
 12            0601          RESULT  EQU    $0601
 13            0600          HEXLOC  EQU    $0600
 14            CD03          WARMS   EQU    $CD03
 15                          *
 16                          *
 17                          *     PROGRAM
 18    0400                          ORG    $0400
 19    0400 B6   0600        START   LDA    HEXLOC     get hex byte
 20    0403 44                        LSRA
 21    0404 44                        LSRA
 22    0405 44                        LSRA
 23    0406 44                        LSRA            get high nibble
 24   >0407 BD   041B                 JSR    CONV
 25    040A B7   0601                 STA    RESULT     put ASCII code in memory
 26    040D B6   0600                 LDA    HEXLOC     get hex byte
 27    0410 84   0F                   ANDA   #$0F       get low nibble
 28   >0412 BD   041B                 JSR    CONV
 29    0415 B7   0602                 STA    RESULT+1   put ASCII code in memory
 30    0418 7E   CD03                 JMP    WARMS      return to flex
 31                          *
 32                          *
 33                          *     SUBROUTINE
 34    041B 81   0A          CONV    CMPA   #$0A       is it a letter
 35    041D 25   02                  BLO    ADJ        if so adjust it
 36    041F 8B   07                  ADDA   #$07
 37    0421 8B   30          ADJ     ADDA   #$30       adjust to ASCII
 38    0423 39                        RTS
 39    0424                          END
```

0 ERROR(S) DETECTED

Program 5
An exchange of two blocks of memory.
This illustrates the use of the two index registers and the auto indexed mode of addressing.

```
2                             *********************************************
3                             * Program to exchange the contents of two
4                             * 1K blocks of memory.
5                             *********************************************
6                             *
7                             *
8                             *         EQUATES
9              1000    BLOCK1   EQU     $1000
10             5000    BLOCK2   EQU     $5000
11             1400    BLKTOP   EQU     $1400
12             CD03    WARMS    EQU     $CD03
13                             *
14                             *
15                             *
16                             *         PROGRAM
17    0500                             ORG     $0500
18    0500 8E    1000    START   LDX     #BLOCK1    set 1st pointer
19    0503 108E 5000            LDY     #BLOCK2
20    0507 A6    84     NEXT    LDA     0,X        get byte from block1
21    0509 E6    A4             LDB     0,Y        get byte from block 2
22    050B A7    A0             STA     0,Y+       swop and increment
23    050D E7    80             STB     0,X+
24    050F 8C    1400           CPX     #BLKTOP    end of transfer?
25    0512 26    F3             BNE     NEXT
26    0514 7E    CD03           JMP     WARMS      return to flex
27    0517                      END

0 ERROR(S) DETECTED
```

Program 6
Setting a series of memory locations so that a table is formed with ascending hexadecimal values. An illustration of the use of a counter and indexed addressing.

```
 2                              ****************************************
 3                              * Program to set  a series of locations
 4                              * with increasing hexadecimal values.
 5                              * Locations from $0080 to be loaded
 6                              * with $00 up to $50.
 7                              ****************************************
 8                              *
 9                              *
10                              *     EQUATES
11             0800      TAB      EQU     $0800
12             CD03      WARMS    EQU     $CD03
13                              *
14                              *
15                              *     PROGRAM
16    0600                        ORG     $0600
17    0600 4F        START  CLRA              clear counter
18    0601 8E   0800         LDX     #TAB     set pointer
19    0604 A7   80      LOOP   STA     0,X+     store and increment
20    0606 4C               INCA             add 1 to counter
21    0607 81   51          CMPA    #$51     last value?
22    0609 26   F9          BNE     LOOP


23    060B 7E   CD03               JMP     WARMS    return to flex
24    060E                 END

Ø ERROR(S) DETECTED
```

Program 7

Data acquisition from an ADC.

A program that shows:

  a) PIA initialisation.
  b) The use of the control line CA2 in the "follow" mode.
  c) Masking of the F and I interrupts.
  d) The use of dummy instructions to create short delays (the start conversion pulse is set to 10 microseconds).
  e) A time delay subroutine which is used to set both the 150 microsecond wait for conversion complete and with a multiplier (line 42) to make the 2 second delay between samples.